PRAISE FOR *PLACE ENVY*

"*Place Envy* is an engrossing and provocative book. Lowenthal is a vivid narrator of his journeys as a young gay man, sharing his travels by car, bus, plane, Amish buggy, and cruise ship from Brookline to Buchau and Scotland to Salvador, Brazil. Throughout, he never hesitates to approach the third rail—and then grasp it. Beautifully written and crafted, the story reaches back generations as it explores the tortuous interplay between where you are and who you are." —Will Schwalbe, author of *The End of Your Life Book Club*

"The question 'Where am I?' sometimes asks for a kind of orientation that no GPS can provide. So it is for Michael Lowenthal—a gay Jew from a family of Holocaust refugees—in this brilliantly written and, in the end, deeply moving account of a years-long passage from inner homelessness to home at last." —Jack Miles, coauthor of *A Friendship in Twilight: Lockdown Conversations on Death and Life*

PRAISE FOR MICHAEL LOWENTHAL

"Lowenthal is a sensitive chronicler of the tensions that animate a life." —Brandon Taylor, *The New York Times Book Review*

"Michael Lowenthal . . . [has] won raves for smart, unsettling books with complicated characters and deep emotional resonance." —Eugenia Williamson, *The Boston Globe*

"Fine writers, at least according to one school of thought, should be disturbers of the peace of mind. They should set sail, that is, to our most turbulent cultural waters and challenge, rather than affirm, our most comfortable pieties. . . . [I]t's easy to suspect that Michael Lowenthal wholeheartedly embraces this philosophy." —Andrew Furman, *Miami Herald*

"[Lowenthal's] particular talent . . . is exploring gray areas with wisdom and confidence." —Mark Athitakis, *The Washington Post*

"Lowenthal uses luminous language that often imbues ordinary gestures and events with deeper meaning." —Linda Barrett Osborne, *The New York Times Book Review*

"[Lowenthal] has an uncanny eye for detail and the ability to shore up an entire relationship or the unobvious mood in a room with an economy of exacting, carefully chosen words." —*The Bay Area Reporter*

PLACE ENVY

MACHETE

Joy Castro and Rachel Cochran, Series Editors

Place Envy

Essays in Search of Orientation

Michael Lowenthal

MAD CREEK BOOKS, AN IMPRINT OF
THE OHIO STATE UNIVERSITY PRESS
COLUMBUS

Library of Congress Cataloging-in-Publication Data available online at https://catalog.loc.gov
LCCN: 2025041915

Cover design by adam bohannon
Text design by Juliet Williams and Stuart Rodriguez
Type set in Sabon LT Pro

For Bennett, my best place

Also by Michael Lowenthal

Contents

I

A Good Place
(Part 1)

But to live in the world at all is to be committed to some kind of a journey.

If you are ready to go and cannot, either because you are not free or because you have no one to travel with— or if you have arbitrarily set a date for your departure and dare not go until that day arrives, you still have no cause for concern. Without knowing it, you have actually started. On a turning earth, in a mechanically revolving universe, there is no place to stand still.

—William Maxwell, *The Folded Leaf*

Out of Nowhere

THE EMAIL CAME from my father's eighty-two-year-old half sister. "Please send me 'Saying Kaddish for Peter,'" read the subject line, followed by just her address and "Thanks. Chaninah."

By this point, in 2014, I'd had no contact with Chaninah for seven years; we had only ever met three times. What unsettled me even more than her curtness was her request for an essay I'd published two decades earlier, in my twenties. The titular Peter was her brother, who'd died in 1945 at Bergen-Belsen, but my piece had disregarded her and her real loss, focusing on my fantasies of Peter. I had long since stopped fretting that she might find the essay, but now she'd finally gotten wind of it.

Peter was, or would have been, my half uncle, but I had learned of his existence only at fourteen, when my father's father died and I read his obituary: "Rabbi Lowenthal and his wife, Suzanne (Moos), fled to New York in July 1939, escaping the Nazi purge of the Jews. However, a son, Peter, from an earlier marriage, was a victim of the Holocaust."

I was staggered. Who was this uncle who'd turned up out of nowhere? A forebear who, just as he appeared, also perished.

I ached to learn about him, but also—self-involved teenager that I was—to learn what he might show me about myself. I had often felt like an alien in my own family, unconvinced that I deserved our name. I latched on to Peter as a possible connection, dreaming of the links we might share. (I'd seen twins on TV shows, separated as infants and, years later, reunited.) Like me, he would be moony, into folk songs and hiking alone. Like me, he would wonder how he fit in.

I was dying to ask someone about him, but who?

I'd met Chaninah a few years earlier, when she came to Passover at my grandparents' place, in Brookline, Massachusetts. She'd struck me as a sanded-down version of Papa Eric—that was what we called my grandfather—her old-world accent a touch less gruff, her stare as hard but with a little give. I'd thought it odd that although we both lived in Maryland (her home, in Annapolis, less than an hour from mine), we were meeting hundreds of miles away. Was she, too, a misfit, undeserving?

I didn't see her again until Papa Eric's funeral. I know she attended—she was his daughter, after all—but I can't summon an image of her there. In truth, I have few memories from that day, so jarred was I by the loss compounded by an awful adolescent embarrassment. My face, as it did often then, had swollen with hives; my eyes bulged like oozing goiters. Mortified, I tried to hide behind mirrored sunglasses. Through my fog of shame, I couldn't see that the flashy lenses only drew attention to my face, or that in the synagogue they would seem profane. (Did my dad try to talk me out of wearing them? Did anyone?)

By the time I read the obituary, days later, and learned about my grandfather's first son, Chaninah was gone again, her place in the family largely notional—which was why, I suppose, I didn't register that she had probably grown up with Peter. And why, even as my curiosity surged, I didn't think to ask her about him.

Instead, I turned to my father. I had no idea when he himself had learned of Peter, who must have died before my dad was five. Dad was mostly a distant presence, emotionally and geographically. A scholar of Latin America, he was always dashing off to Buenos Aires or Bogotá, and when he found the time to talk with me and my sister, the topic was rarely personal. (More likely—Reagan's Cuba policy.) Our parents had split up when I was eleven, and he'd soon moved to California.

Did I even manage to ask directly about Peter? Long-distance calls were pricey then; I was always aware of a meter ticking. (Then again, that was how I often felt with Dad, even when we talked face to face—as though I were burning through a precious resource: his patience.) Probably I said something about the obit's shocking facts, and he allowed a scant, brick-wall reply, like "Yes, it's sad."

The person who would be able to tell me the most, I figured, was my father's mother, Nana Susi, but I couldn't imagine daring to ask her, especially not while she was mourning her husband of half a century. Like Papa Eric, she spoke in a striking German accent that had always both enthralled and alarmed me: I'd understood, long before I understood why, that it marked a fissure in her life. In America, despite the accent, she shunned her native language, at pains to squelch anything from Before.

I knew that her father, Franz Moos, had died at Theresienstadt, the so-called model concentration camp. She often gazed at a photo of him—a genially fat, bald man in a suit—but never mentioned his manner of death, or why she and Papa Eric had escaped Germany but he hadn't. (Her mother, Ida, had died of a heart attack, weeks before the Nazis began deporting Jews from their town.) I also knew that she, like my grandfather, had had a previous marriage in Germany, and a son from that marriage: Uncle Henry. Henry, who was from England, had visited just once. Young as I was, I'd been more intent on his

British accent than on wondering why he'd grown up
without his mother, in a land
where she had never lived.

As little as I understood
of Nana Susi's life, I sensed
these were the shadows that
tinged her days with darkness, and I knew the past was
better left unprobed. Peter
was a riddle I would have to
solve without her.

There was a photo of
him, too, in my grandpar-
ents' apartment. I'd seen it on
Papa Eric's desk—a small head shot, black and white, framed
in dark-green imitation leather—but only now, after reading the
obituary, did I identify the subject. Peter, smart in a jacket and
tie, with a high sweep of hair, must have been in his mid- or
late teens when it was taken—just older than I was at the time.
He has small ears and a strong nose, soulful eyes behind wire-
rimmed glasses. He gazes to the side, his full lips on the verge of
a smile, as if withholding a self-delighting thought.

How handsome he was, movie-star-ish but also somehow
accessible, and—there's no other way to say this—I grew a
crush on him. I'm tempted to claim it was a spiritual and not
a sexual crush, a longing for a male mentor to give me what
my father mostly couldn't. Peter, in my fantasies, could be that
masculine guardian, the special guy to whom I'd tell my secrets.

Yes, but.

My biggest secret, gaining force as puberty roared through
me, was my growing attraction to other boys. And so my crush
on Peter was erotic, of course it was. The incest-taboo aspect

of these stirrings didn't trouble me, considering that my feelings were wholly theoretical. The worse taboo, it seemed to me, was lusting after a Holocaust victim.

I shared these thoughts with no one. I'd become an expert at keeping the truth from breaking out—until it would, in the form of my hives. Only I recognized their meaning: punishment for my unspeakable cravings.

THERE WAS ONE other family member with whom I did talk about Peter. My cousin Andy—the son of my father's sister, Judy.

Born eleven days apart, the only male first cousins in our family, Andy and I had always been close, and as we approached adulthood, we spoke often of our responsibility to carry on our grandparents' traditions. He wondered about Peter, too, and we would daydream about going to Germany together, to learn about our in-the-shadows uncle.

But then, in college, our paths parted.

I came out as gay, and Andy—who, like me, had grown up only moderately observant in his Judaism—took a dogleg to Orthodoxy. By our early twenties, he was at a yeshiva in the Jewish enclave of Monsey, New York: a move that, to our temperate family, was almost as alienating as my gay activism.

At first, this didn't thwart our friendship. We bonded about having been cold-shouldered by the family: I for abandoning one version of tradition, Andy for too closely clasping another. Our ancestors had stood up for their principles, we agreed, and each of us, in his way, was honoring that history.

Eventually, though, Andy grew dogmatic. In long handwritten letters, he argued that a Jew who didn't keep the commandments, although he might fool himself into feeling fulfilled, was "estranged from his most fundamental identity." Citing a rabbi's warnings against "an overemphasis on the physical dimension of one's personality," he bemoaned the corrosion of traditional family values.

I knew he was bashing what he called my "gay lifestyle." It grieved me that our sense of shared responsibility had curdled into rivalry. The message was clear: he was the rightful heir to our traditions—including whatever Peter represented.

I refused to yield to Andy's premise: that being gay and being a good Jew must be opposed; that you could not be loyal to yourself—your own desires—and also to a family, a faith. At gay rights protests, I wore a shirt with the recently invented ACT UP logo: SILENCE = DEATH beneath an upturned pink triangle. The triangle, of course, had marked gay men in Hitler's camps, just as Jews had suffered the yellow star; prisoners who were gay *and* Jewish wore overlapping triangles—one pink, one yellow—forming a Star of David.

At this stage—the early '90s; I was twenty-four—I was bent on becoming a published writer. The image of the doubled triangles inspired a new short story:

A Holocaust survivor is visited by her grandson. She invites him to synagogue, but he cagily declines. She suspects he's come to town for the gay pride parade, but he has never revealed his sexuality. His visit triggers memories of 1930s Berlin, when the man she hoped to marry—I gave him Peter's lips, his high sweep of hair—is caught in a Nazi raid of an underground gay club. At the story's climax, the grandmother breaks the Sabbath by hailing a cab downtown. She spies her grandson dancing in the street to "Hava Nagila," arm in arm with a gay Jewish group. She calls out, but he doesn't hear. The parade passes on.

The story, if schematic, was full of youthful passion; a couple of leading journals almost took it. Their rejections offered the same critique: the contemporary action sparkled but the scenes in Germany failed to come alive.

To salvage the story, I needed texture, a keener sense of Berlin back then. I needed—wasn't it obvious?—to talk with Nana Susi. To ask her, at long last, about her life Before. And Peter's.

But how could I be honest about the reasons for my asking? Like the fictional grandson, I had never come out to her. I had promised my family I wouldn't.

THE PROMISE had come about in relation to my college graduation.

During my senior year at Dartmouth—in late 1989—I had learned I would be named class valedictorian, meaning I'd give a speech at commencement. I knew I'd want to grab the chance, in front of eight thousand people, to rouse some rabble. On campus, I'd been militant: organizing sit-ins, helping to start a queer newspaper called *In Your Face*. But I was still closeted to my father and his side of the family.

Dad and I were mutually bewildered more than antagonistic. When I was sixteen, he'd hired me to build a deck at his house in Santa Monica. (He is notoriously unhandy; I have never seen him hold a hammer.) The deck turned out fine, and he was full of praise. But he'd been out of town when I built it, and I never got to use the deck; by my next visit, he had sold the house. It felt like a clumsy metaphor.

By now, we'd lapsed into a kind of remote politeness— and it was mostly politeness that prompted my coming out. Although I felt little rush to show him my new self, it seemed rude to keep him in the dark, and I wouldn't dream of blindsiding him with my speech.

I wrote him a letter, talking about my activism and my boyfriend, Chris. For a week, then two, then four, I heard nothing. Finally, on Day 39, he called (I marked my calendar), to wish me happy holidays—just that. I was more discomfited than I let myself admit. My dad had often rankled me, but if he pulled away for good and wasn't there to knock against, what cliff's edge might I stumble over?

A month before commencement, I got another call: Aunt Judy told me she'd heard the news. "Why would you do this to your grandmother," she said, "after all she's been through?" (She sounded rattled. This was just when Andy was "coming out" as Orthodox.) Aunt Judy issued an ultimatum: if I insisted on "advertising" my gayness in the speech, she would keep Nana Susi away.

Academic success was no small matter in my family. My father, and his father, and his father before him, had each earned a PhD. I could hardly imagine barring Nana Susi from cheering me on. But neither could I imagine giving a watered-down speech.

The conversation left me fuming, but also secretly relieved. I had grappled with worries not dissimilar from Aunt Judy's. Why burden my grandmother with yet one more upheaval?

My aunt and I came to terms: I would stick with my speech, Nana Susi would stay at home, and nobody would tell her I was gay. (I don't recall our lame excuse—something about her stamina, the ceremony's length.)

On the big day, Dad and I were amiable, if skittish, as if meeting for the very first time. But when I found him after the speech, he beamed. He and my mother had run into his college classmate Barney Frank, famous as the first congressman to come out voluntarily as gay. Barney had started to gush about the speaker, and Dad had exulted, "That's my son!" That night, on his red-eye home, he would write a loving letter, calling me "a fine man, and already an inspiration."

The speech made a bigger splash than I could have envisioned. A piece in the next day's *New York Times* featured my coming out, and I received heaps of mail—mostly fan, some hate. It was heady and gratifying to feel my words had made a difference, but also not a little discordant. My "fans" claimed my honesty had inspired them; what if they knew of my coward's bargain, the lies I hid behind with Nana Susi?

THREE YEARS LATER, writing my story—my fantasy of a nana and her gay grandson—I was resigned to my deal with Aunt Judy. As a result, I'd avoided visits with Nana Susi. I longed to see her, and lived in New Hampshire, an easy drive to Brookline, but went only once or twice a year. Our visits left me hollowed out: the conversation we weren't having would blare so loudly in my head that I could hardly hear the one we were having.

But now, when the story's rejections spotlighted my ignorance of the past, I tugged my thoughts into a new alignment. Even if I couldn't tell her the truth about my life, why should I not learn the truth of hers? At eighty-six, she was increasingly frail; time was short.

I still figured she was my best bet to learn about Peter, even though he hadn't been her son. And Peter was my best bet—I felt this with atavistic instinct—to pick the lock of my doubts about belonging.

I drove to Brookline, tape recorder in hand. After my grandfather's death, Nana Susi had moved to what I dubbed the "Hebrew high-rise," an apartment complex filled on every floor with aged Jews. Year by year, the residents grew feebler, pushing walkers, many of them with Nazi-tattooed arms. The place's sterility made me miss my grandparents' old apartment, with its smells of stewed meat and cigars, but Nana Susi greeted me with all her usual warmth.

She'd always been petite, but age had shrunk her to less than five feet tall; her finishing-school posture now seemed brittle. She stalled me with her typical treats, mandelbrot and Dr. Brown's soda. At last, she let me start the recorder.

Listening to the tape now provokes conflicting feelings. Just the sound of her voice—the only recording I have of it—bathes me in primal comfort. But her speech is halting, split apart by sighs, and I can hear how desperately she wanted not to talk. Also plainly audible: her slipping mental faculties. Mixed-up names, easy words misplaced. To hear how hard I pressured her anyway drenches me with shame, but I was sure this was my last chance.

I started with softballs about her girlhood in Buchau, a small town in the German state of Baden-Württemberg, hoping she might make me feel that I could claim it too. I'd always suffered from what I called, with a nod to Freud, "place envy." Chevy Chase, the blandly well-off DC suburb where I was raised, was a town where people lived but almost no one came from; we'd moved there for my dad's job, after living, for the same reason, in Princeton, New Jersey, and Lima, Peru—in none of these places had anyone in my family lived before. I envied folks who spoke with potent local twangs, who summered at family homesteads, who sported clan tartans. Above all, I yearned to be from somewhere.

I did manage to pry from Nana Susi some vibrant details, such as the tale of her first remembered sin and punishment, when she and a neighbor snuck into a church and "played Catholic." But when I asked about the friends and family she'd grown up with, her answers devolved into a mantra—"They were all very good people. They were good, that's all"—a wall erected around a lost world.

Later, when I asked what Berlin was like in the '20s (she'd moved there at nineteen, with her first husband), she said, "I don't remember things. I don't *want* to remember things." And then again, when I asked about the young Papa Eric, her voice rose: "I don't want to remember!"

Soon after, when she returned to a version of her mantra—"I know everyone was good . . . and I was lucky"—I sensed an opening, and asked, "What made you lucky?"

"That I met Papa," she said, "and that he fell in love with me."

She almost trilled the words, and in my mind I heard my grandparents singing psalms in harmony, at the end of every Seder meal. I could see them shining across the table at each other, sharing something passionately private.

". . . that he fell in love with me," Nana Susi was saying, "even though we were both still . . . connected."

Connected.

I had never heard her come this close to a confession: that when they fell in love, they were both married to other people. I knew no further details, but that fact alone suggested a drama. Going against culture and law, they had given in to what their own hearts demanded.

Wasn't that what I had done in coming out as gay? Shouldn't she understand that, maybe even applaud it? I can remember leaning forward, wanting to grab her mottled hands and spill what I'd been hiding.

I tried to draw out details of their illicit affair, but Nana Susi cackled a "No!" that cut off further questions. I asked instead about life in Berlin under the Nazis. She and Papa Eric had stayed until 1939; how had they finally known when to go?

Nana Susi bunkered herself behind a neutral pronoun: "One had to leave. If one had waited longer, one would have been taken." They managed, she said, to get a rare non-quota visa, reserved for clergy. Of course they had to go, even if it meant leaving behind other loved ones, including children. She went to see her parents—sensing it would be the last time—and Papa Eric went separately, because "he wanted to say goodbye to . . . was it Chaninah and Peter?"

There it was: the name I had waited so long to hear.

The question mark in her voice should have served as a warning, but I couldn't resist pressing on: "Did you know Peter? Can you tell me anything about him?"

Was he as soft as he looks in his picture? Did he, too, chafe against our family? Would he have loved me?

"No," she said, "I don't know anything about him. I didn't know him."

I asked if Papa Eric, because of his divorce, had forfeited the chance to raise Peter.

On the tape, Nana Susi doesn't answer for ten seconds. "I don't remember," she says at last, then stops for another ten seconds that feels like fifty. "I mean," she goes on, "Peter died in"—five grueling seconds of more silence. Finally she whispers, "a concentration camp."

A slew of questions clobbered me. All of them intrusive, insufficient.

Another harrowing emptiness, and then she cries, "Oh, please! I don't want to think about these things anymore! I want to be grateful for what is good in everyone, and I want to be forgiven for anything I did that wasn't right."

ALTHOUGH I had failed to breach her wall of reticence, our talk did lead to a breakthrough. As I was leaving, she gave me a tape of Papa Eric recounting his memories. (Why had she never mentioned this tape? Had anyone heard it before me? Had Andy?)

I was stunned that Papa Eric had gone in for such a project; there had always hovered about him, along with cigar smoke, a daunting cloud of reserve. The date on the tape indicated he'd made it after his eighty-second birthday, by which point he knew that his cancer was metastasizing; he died less than three months later.

At home, with a dreadful thrill about what I might hear—hoping for a portrait of Uncle Peter—I snapped the tape into my stereo.

"The first job as a rabbi of my late father was in Tarnowitz," Papa Eric starts, with the formality that had often made me feel frivolous around him. "In 1903, my father accepted the position at the Orthodox Neue Dammtor Synagogue, in Hamburg . . ."

I could hardly pay attention to the words, so spellbound was I by his voice—his rusty, ratchety voice, like a dredge hauling muck from the deep—hitting me for the first time in a decade. I'd always been riveted by the forbidding rolled r's of his accent, which made him sound prophetic even when his meaning was harmless or tender (like his praise for Nana Susi, after every holiday: "Thank you, Suzanne, for a marvelous meal"). Hearing him now, I could picture his Leninesque goatee and the black yarmulke perched atop his pate: a landing pad, or so my boyhood self had thought, for messages sent by God.

The shuffling of pages caught my ear as Papa Eric began a story about his first best friend, Erich Posen. I realized he was reading from a written document.

He and Erich, as college students, had hiked from Munich to Italy. "But in Gossensass," he says, "high in the Italian mountains, [Erich] tumbled and fell and died. I had to wait for his relative to bring his remains to Berlin."

I had only ever heard this story's barest outline. How much more might my grandfather reveal, reciting from written recollections? "Waiting for him," says Papa Eric, "it was the first time that I ate treyf"—unkosher food—"which the mountain police gave me." Then, without so much as a pause: "My relation with my former wife, Ilse Marienthal, was the result of the death of Erich Posen, whose girlfriend she had been."

Ilse: this was Peter's mother. I turned up the volume.

Papa Eric says he felt obliged to marry Ilse, out of loyalty to Erich, but that he never loved her. "To be honest," he says, "I was still a virgin and wanted to sleep with a woman. Ilse was eager to comply. My poor father officiated on May 2, 1923."

What was Peter's mother like? What was her family background? Nothing about this from Papa Eric. He had rushed on to "the crazy time of inflation," when he emigrated to Palestine, intending to establish a printing business: "I took along a suitcase filled completely with fountain pens, which I sold slowly to live on." He mentions his departure date, the storms during the passage; he notes the population of Tel Aviv and the titles of British officials at a Hannukah celebration . . .

So what? looped so loudly through my thoughts—*so what? so what?*—that I nearly missed his next statement: "In January 1924, my wife arrived with her sister and brother, giving birth to our son, Peter, born in Tel Aviv on February 17."

Peter! The name I had never heard him say.

"There were just a few people for the circumcision," he goes on, "so that the physician, Dr. Hillenthal, went to the porch and a minyan was soon established for the *bris milah*. On April 9, 1924, we returned to Berlin with our son, who died in Bergen-Belsen concentration camp on March 13, 1945."

Wait, could that be all? A son's whole life, shrunk to those few lines?

"We lived with our son-in-laws," Papa Eric continued.

I hit Pause. Son-in-laws? That wasn't even grammatical. Also, they *had* no son-in-law.

Then it struck me: "our in-laws," he must have meant

to say, but his gaze had snagged on the script's previous line ("with our son") and he messed up. A simple slip—or maybe something more. In naming the calamity he so rarely acknowledged, had Papa Eric fractured his composure? Subconsciously, did he long to speak about his son?

"I forgot to mention," he hurries on, "that I also shipped three Hebrew typewriters from Berlin to Palestine," and he's off again, this time on a jag about his move into the mother-of-pearl market: buttons, necklaces, Catholic rosaries.

I listened with a growing sense of letdown. I wanted to be forgiving: Who was I to judge a man who'd lost his country, his son? Still, his choices baffled me. Why bother to write and record his deathbed memories, only just to magnify the trivial? It was as though he'd stared at himself through a telescope's wrong end.

The banalities of his business life took up five more minutes. I was starting to tune out when he came to the death of his father, the rabbi of Berlin's Kaiserstrasse synagogue, one of the largest Orthodox congregations in Germany. "I loved my father very much," he says, "and I knew his deep sorrow that I had alienated myself from Jewish tradition."

Alienated shot a painful shiver down my spine. What had been said between them, I wondered—and what else had been swallowed—about the fact that a rabbi's son was hawking rosaries?

Papa Eric describes the shiva, the dignitaries who came to pay respects. "On about the fourth day," he says, "our son, Peter, led me to the study."

There he was again. I'd given up too soon.

The shiva had taken place in July 1928; Peter would have been four years old. I tried to conjure a younger version of the handsome teen in the photo.

"On the huge table," Papa Eric says, Peter "had spread

opened books from the bookshelves and told me, 'Study them!' That was like a voice from heaven. At that moment, I decided to become a rabbi myself."

I was amazed, not least because Papa Eric, despite his rabbinical career, was as unspiritual as anyone I've known. A man of logic and scholarship, emitting not a whiff of the transcendental. I had never heard him mention heaven.

Even more astounding was the image of young Peter as a precocious oracle: support for my fantasy of him as a guardian angel. (Then again, the anecdote might strike Andy differently: as affirmation of his own conversion to observance. And of his claim to Peter's legacy.)

If Peter, at only four, had changed Papa Eric's course so sagely, surely the tape would lay bare more evidence of his magic. I listened as Papa Eric talked about the Sukkot holiday in 1938, when he persuaded a Nazi official to let him build a ritual sukkah, because his own "führer"—Almighty God—commanded its construction, only to have the sukkah smashed the next day by police; and about Kristallnacht, three weeks later, after which Papa Eric hid in the home of neighbors (one deaf, one sick, so the Gestapo were less likely to raid them).

The details gripped me—I'd never heard him talk about the Nazis—but as his story's tension mounted, so did my awareness of Peter's absence. My uncle would have been fourteen (exactly the age I was when I'd learned of his existence). Who was taking care of him? Was he in hiding too?

Papa Eric relates that with the help of an aunt in Switzerland, he was invited to teach Hebrew school in Zurich. But after a few months there, sensing war's approach, he and my grandmother chose to flee farther, to America. Vouched for by the chancellor of the Jewish Theological Seminary, they obtained their special clergy visa. "I forgot which charitable organization gave the money for our passage," he says, "on the beautiful *Île de France.*" Before boarding the ship, though, he flew to Amsterdam, to say farewell to Peter and Chaninah.

Amsterdam? Why were his children there? A boy now fifteen, a girl of only seven and a half. Had Papa Eric bucked them up with hopes of reuniting soon? Had Peter offered any last oracular advice?

Papa Eric doesn't say. "Then I embarked for England," he moves on.

He describes his rabbinical posting in America, the births of my father and Aunt Judy, but then, as abruptly as it started, his story stops. Forty-six minutes of memories, and only those precious few mentions of Peter.

PRECIOUS FEW MENTIONS of Peter, yes, but of Chaninah, only one—in fact, just her name. No account of her birth or precocious prophecies; no sign of what she meant to her father.

I'm ashamed to say I considered none of this when I wrote to her, in the fall of 1993, and told her about Papa Eric's tape. He had left so much unsaid. Would she be open to answering some questions?

To make it more of a fair exchange, I offered a sketch of my life, making sure to mention "my partner, Chris." (When I'd agreed to Aunt Judy's demand that I stay closeted, neither of us had thought to include Chaninah in the deal.) I often went to Maryland to see my mother, I noted; hopefully, the next time I was there, I'd see her too.

I worried about my forwardness, revealing I was gay. I knew little about Chaninah other than that she was a professor at St. John's College. On one hand, college teachers tended to be enlightened. On the other, St. John's was known for Western-canon conservatism. What if she was some kind of cultural reactionary?

I was thrilled when she wrote back. Her terse card said nothing about my gayness. Without addressing my request, she asked for a copy of the tape.

Although her answer's brevity suggested wariness, I decided to forge ahead. Along with the tape, I sent a letter. The last thing I wanted was to cause further pain, I said, but she was my last potential source of knowledge. My questions ranged from the logistical (post-divorce, how often did Papa Eric see her?) to the profound (what kind of a father was he?).

Finally, I confessed my eagerness to know about Peter. "I'm not sure I can explain this," I told her, "but as soon as I learned about him, I felt a connection. I'm not at all mystical, but I had a visceral sense that Peter and I would have shared something deep." Trying not to sound like a love-smitten schoolboy, I asked about his education, his hobbies, his ambitions, saving for last a carefully neutral question: "Did he have any romances that you were aware of?"

My teenage crush on Peter had evolved into a fantasy that he, too, might have been gay. Why had this notion taken such hold of me? He had died at twenty-one, likely before much sexual exploration. *That's* what I should have focused on: the tragedy of a life cut short. But Peter's death—all his sadly unfulfilled potential—made him a perfect screen to project my wishes onto. I wanted a kindred predecessor, to prove that I was not alone. My gayness had been deemed unfit for family conversation; Andy had said it doomed me to estrangement. But maybe, if the dead could talk, Peter would assure me I did belong.

Chaninah's reply didn't mention Peter's romantic life. In fact, she answered none of my questions. All she sent was a list of Papa Eric's siblings, noting, "I am not in touch with any."

Below her list, she added, "Come visit us? Chaninah."

I HAD every intention of taking her up on the offer, but weeks passed, then months. I didn't call.

How could I have gone from barraging curiosity to what must have struck her as aloofness? The barrage itself provides part of the answer: after having peppered her for so much information and getting so guarded a response, I felt self-conscious, even stung. I fled to the safer ground of avoidance.

True enough. But not the whole story.

I'd seen a call for submissions for an anthology about gay men and religion. Wouldn't Peter, my angel, make for good material? To write an essay, however, I would want more facts. Probably that was why I'd approached Chaninah when I did: not immediately after hearing Papa Eric's tape, but months later, when I hatched my essay. (Maybe Chaninah was guarded, it occurs to me now, because she sensed my literary gold-digging; I had told her I worried about swamping her with questions, "the answers to which could easily fill a book.") At first, when she had kept mum about Peter, I had felt not only self-conscious but frustrated: the anthology deadline loomed; how would I write my essay? But then it hit me: my dearth of facts could be the essay's feature, not a bug. To write about filling up my family's silence with fantasy, maybe it was better *not* to know Chaninah's stories.

I finished the essay without consulting her or anyone else. I wrote of Papa Eric's tape and how its brief scene of Peter made him seem more mythical than real. But Peter, I argued, was less about reality than possibility: the possibility of a rosary salesman transforming into a rabbi, of a gay teenager having someone to turn to. Maybe this was all too convenient, I allowed: a lonely kid's wish-fulfillment dream. "But in synagogue," I wrote, "when we recited the Mourner's Kaddish, I always said it for [Peter]. I would see him sitting on the edge of the bimah, dangling his legs awkwardly as if embarrassed that I would call his name."

THIS WAS the piece I sent Chaninah, in 2014, when she requested "Saying Kaddish for Peter."

In the decades between, we'd been in touch sporadically, always polite but awkward. Typical was a note from her that rushed to its conclusion: "I continue w. my regular routine of teaching, writing, cooking, cleaning, gardening. Chaninah."

Now she told me she'd been googling her grandfather, but what she had found when she typed *Rabbi Lowenthal* was a link to my essay's first page. The internet refused to "cough up" the rest of the piece.

Maybe just as well, I responded; I had written it ages ago, when I was young and knew nothing of Peter. What I didn't say—but which, when I thought of her learning it, turned my guts to stone—was that she was missing from the essay. I'd referenced her just once, not even by name, calling her only "a daughter" from my grandfather's first marriage. *Daughter* was the second-to-last word on page one, but when she read further, she would find I'd reenacted Papa Eric's failure: erasing her from our family's story.

WHEN "SAYING KADDISH" had been published, a week before my twenty-sixth birthday, I was elated. The book it appeared in was a HarperCollins hardcover featuring contributors I revered. But my celebration was stained by grief. I could never show the piece to my most hoped-for reader. The problem was no longer my being in the closet; the problem was, two months earlier, Nana Susi had died.

If she hadn't, how would I have handled the publication? Probably as I'd handled my graduation speech: by saying nothing and hoping for the best, caught between believing that the best was for her never to hear the truth or for her somehow to find out.

Andy had come home for the funeral. When the rabbi, enacting the symbolic rending of garments, had snipped the black ribbons pinned to our clothes, Andy, in performative piety, slashed his suit's lapel. All day long, we hovered within arm's length of each other but shared not a single private word.

He had now spent three years at yeshiva; his mind was terminally hardened. Weeks before, he'd sent a final letter: "It's impossible for me to have a friendship with someone whose lifestyle I find repugnant." Going on about the "grave value-clash which divides us," he rejected my suggestion, from a previous letter, that I visit him at the yeshiva, then added, "This is *pure* estrangement."

When we buried Nana Susi, the rabbi, using her Hebrew name, said, "May Shoshana go to her place in peace." Then each family member tossed dirt onto the casket—just a bit, with the back side of a shovel, to show reluctance—but most of the grave still needed to be filled. Andy and I each grabbed a shovel. To other mourners, maybe it looked like cousinly communion as he and I raced to close the hole.

I couldn't know his mind—and, since we no longer speak, I can't ask about it—but it's not a stretch to guess that with every toss of dirt, he was having the very same thought I was: *I'm* her grandson, *I'm* her grandson, *I* am.

SOON AFTER, when we divided Nana Susi's belongings, I claimed only a few items: a stylish glass-topped coffee table, a cheap but useful blanket. And—slipping it into my bag when no one looked—the photograph of Peter in its green fake-leather frame.

My dad took hardly anything (books, a couple paintings), but we did ship a box of his parents' papers to California. Months later, on my next visit, I dug in.

The trip came at a tricky time for me. I was on a book tour, promoting a collection called *Friends and Lovers: Gay Men Write About the Families They Create*—a project I'd inherited from a mentor who'd recently died of AIDS. Its premise was that gay men, so often denied the bonds of blood family, invent our own versions of lineage and kinship. I'd contributed one of the essays, focusing on my boyfriend Chris's older brother John, whom I affectionately called "my brother-out-law." John, also gay, had taken me under his wing. I wrote of how my family tree had always struck me as withered—in each next generation, fewer children born; branches stunted by the Holocaust—and how, in that context, being gay had seemed like one more blight. But then, in John, I had gained a brother: a green sprig of homosexual growth.

But Chris and I, a month before the book came out, had broken up—a slow collapse quickened by my falling for someone else. John had called me, just before I flew west for the tour, and reamed me out: "Treat my brother like shit, and you think we're still *family?*"

Plus, in California, I would face my father. I'd been wanting to talk with him about our family tensions, to make the case that I, not Andy, was showing true "family values." My case would be strengthened by my love for Chris, I'd hoped—a steady "normal" relationship that helped Dad get comfortable with my gayness. But now I'd blown that up. Rationally, I knew my split with Chris was only that: the failure of our own relationship. But it felt like the failure of a bigger cause, my plea for recognition.

What a phony! Shilling a book about transcending blood family, but still so invested in proving I deserved a place in my own.

It was with this mindset that I sat at my dad's dining table to start sifting through the box of papers.

One of my first finds was a sizable family tree: Nana Susi's Buchau forebears, going back for eight generations. (Not so withered, after all.) Below that, documents in German: Nana Susi's parents' Nazi passports, stamped with big red *J*'s for *Jude*; a typed instruction sheet from August 1942, listing my great-grandfather's *Transportnummer* as 125.

A Red Cross cable to Nana Susi, from days before that deportation, was boldly signed "*Vater.*" (Even I, with no German, knew the word meant *father.*) This was my first glimpse of my great-grandfather's handwriting, whose loops reminded me of his bald dome in Nana Susi's photo.

To handle these private records—never shared, as far as I knew, with anyone—filled me with a voyeur's guilt but also with the wrenching variety of nostalgia you can feel for a past you weren't part of. My tangled feelings were heightened by my ignorance of German. The records were our family's most intimate inheritance, and I couldn't even understand them.

But then, farther down, a manuscript in English: Nana Susi's girlhood memories. She described her neighbors, her Jewish one-room school, World War I soldiers in her town. The details were compelling but what really mesmerized me was her voice—blunt and gutsy—resounding from a time before she'd faltered. "My sister was crazy about my nose," she wrote, "and she liked to touch it. I sold that privilege to her for things I wanted, like . . . for not telling when I had scratched her in a fight till blood came out of her arm."

The sharpness of the prose was even more remarkable because, as I learned in reading the next section (the narrative skipped ahead to America), Nana Susi had immigrated, at thirty-two years old, knowing hardly a word of English. Still, she had refused to speak German, even to Papa Eric, living largely in silence until she learned her new country's language—first by listening to the radio and then, after my father was born, by playing records of childhood rhymes and singing along to him.

The chronicle jump-cut back to Germany. In 1933, her first marriage having failed, she had returned with her son Henry to her parents' home in Buchau. Ashamed of her divorce—and of her affair with Papa Eric—she had hidden the news from her parents until it was irreversible, and only then discovered how adverse were the terms she'd accepted. Her ex had agreed to give her custody of Henry, but then, on the pretense of "visiting" with the five-year-old, took him away and, later, stole him off to England. There was nothing Nana Susi could do.

Noting that she was recording these thoughts on Holocaust Remembrance Day—also the anniversary of her own father's death—she confessed to survivor's guilt, holding herself responsible for ruining her parents' life and honor: "How can I blame it solely on the evils of Nazism, if I know that had I been in possession of my usual judgment and sound instinct . . . I could have convinced my parents to take the necessary steps which would lead to their rescue? But I was enmeshed in my own guilty secrets."

For so long, her silences had pained me. Finally hearing the facts behind them only sharpened that pain, even as those facts cinched our bond: like me, Nana Susi had doubted what she deserved. No wonder she had cried to me, "I don't want to remember!"

But here, on the page, she *was* remembering—writing next of Papa Eric, her life's "only passion." In 1936, he'd finally secured a divorce from Ilse and was able to marry Nana Susi. "After our marriage," she wrote, "his son Peter lived with us for some months until after his bar mitzvah, in 1937, for which his father prepared him."

Peter? He had lived with them? She had told me she didn't know anything about him!

I could not believe she'd meant to lie. Maybe her self-defending mind, knowing how Peter died, had buried deep the memory of his life.

Then I came to the next lines, and I understood that burial differently:

"Since the boy was intelligent but couldn't carry a tune, the strain was great for both [him and his father]. One Shabbat, after a trying session with Peter, my husband hit me for no reason at all. Then, and for so many years after, I was afraid to lose his love. How ignorant I was, I never really had it, he was incapable of loving."

I read the lines again, every inch of my skin tight with shock. Shock not only because of the heartbreaking emotion but also because Nana Susi—cautious, yielding Nana Susi— had let herself set it down in writing.

The memoir came to a hasty end—Kristallnacht to emigration in two paragraphs—and I got up to pace around my father's dining room. What exactly did I hope to inherit from this family? Self-blame? Emotional suppression?

That was when my dad came home. Poking his head into the room, he spied the spread of documents, and asked breezily, "Finding anything good?"

This was what I'd wanted, wasn't it—for us to talk? But I was shaken by what I'd read. If Dad and I discussed his parents' marriage, what might that lead to? Would he ask for details of Chris's and my breakup? Would he deem *me* "incapable of loving"?

I shrugged. "Define 'good,'" I said.

"I just thought that maybe you were . . . I don't know," he said.

A different version of me, a more courageous version, receded in my mind like a stranger in a rearview, shrinking as a car speeds away.

"Okay, well," Dad said tightly. "Dinner in a bit?"

"Yeah, sure," I said. "Sounds fine."

He walked off, leaving me both deflated and relieved. Needling through my thoughts came the phrase *runs in the family.* Runs—as if, whatever it is, it wants to get out fast.

THE NEXT MORNING, before departing, I went through the box again, choosing items to xerox and bring home. Plucking out my grandmother's memoir, I saw papers I'd missed the day before.

Among them was a birth certificate for Peter Achmed Yehuda Loewenthal. Achmed? Yehuda? Those were news to me. I was startled by the name's ecumenicism: the German of Peter, the Arabic of Achmed, the Hebrew of Yehuda. Startled and then, the more I thought, saddened. When Peter was born, only six years after the Great War's end, Papa Eric must have named him dreaming of peaceful coexistence. But Peter's surname was still spelled the German way, of course—*L-o-e* instead of our *L-o*—because, unlike his emigrant parents, who would later Americanize it, he had not survived the next war.

Under the birth certificate sat a three-page stapled document. Hard to read, a copy of a copy. At the top, a dateline: *Tröbitz, 11 Mai 1945.* That was only three days after V-E Day, I knew, the day when the war in Europe ended.

Lieber Erich, the text began. *Dear Eric*—a personal letter to my grandfather?

And then, in the first line, a name that all but poked up from the page: Peter. *Peter in Bergen-Belsen,* it said, a German phrase that spoke for itself. Also, a date: 13 März 45. Hadn't Papa Eric said that Peter had died on March 13?

Beyond this, the letter was impenetrable to me, a thicket of faded words in a language I didn't speak. Except for just one word, in nearly every paragraph. *Peter. Peter, Peter, Peter.*

At the letter's end was a blurry signature—but whose? Someone who, at the war's finish, knew of Peter's fate and needed to inform Papa Eric.

Holding the pages, my hands shook, just as I imagined my grandfather's had trembled when he found this letter in his mailbox—the mailbox of a sturdy triple-decker on Pleasant Street, in the town of Leominster, Massachusetts, where, by 1945, he was a popular rabbi, father of two young American children. Did he rip the envelope, rushing toward its news, or slit the paper gingerly, as if keeping the letter intact could safeguard the loved ones it brought word of?

My sorrow as I thought of Papa Eric reading the message competed with a crudely selfish feeling of expectancy. At long last, was I approaching Peter?

SOON AFTER, a stroke of serendipity: my German friend Stefan called, saying he would come to Boston, where I now lived, the following month. Could he maybe crash on my couch awhile?

Of course, I said . . . but for a price. Could he translate a German letter I was dying to read?

CONSIDERING how long I'd been in the dark, I was prepared to wait for his translation, but my imagination was less patient. All the recent family strife had me gunning to write my first novel, and every step closer I got to Peter's truth, the more my uncle interfered with my fiction.

Like many first-time novelists, I was in a bind: inspired by the stories I knew but also stymied by that very knowledge. My struggle with Andy dramatized the issues that compelled me—family, faith, and sexuality; the competition to claim a legacy—but as a plot ("a cousin gives the silent treatment"), it stank.

My first improvement: making the characters not cousins but twin brothers. One gay, one religious—proxies for me and Andy, as well as for my own conflicting selves.

Better, yes. But still static.

I put the pious brother at a yeshiva in Israel, where the parents send his twin: a kind of rescue mission. Maybe in hashing out a fictional rapprochement, I could trigger a real one with Andy. But the plot still needed a twist, a catalyst for healing.

This was where my notions about Peter kept intruding.

Staring at his photo, I dreamed up the saga of a boy lost in Germany: Josef, the firstborn child of the family Rosenbaum, whose patriarch, Papa Isaac—a stern, rule-bound rabbi—outwardly resembled Papa Eric. In 1941, the family goes into hiding in the attic of an Aryan clan, the Schmitts. Josef, seventeen, befriends the Schmitts' son, and soon they spend hours outside the attic. His sister, Ingrid, guesses they've joined the resistance.

Then one day: a crash, and Josef bursts inside. Chased by the Gestapo? No, by Papa Isaac, who caught him in the bathtub with the Schmitt boy. Papa Isaac kicks him out, recites the Mourner's Kaddish. Josef will be easy prey now for lethal Nazis, but to his father, he's already dead.

The family flees to America and has another son—a son who, in time, fathers his own boys: the twin-brother heroes of my novel.

Josef is never spoken of again.

Or not until his sister, Ingrid, shows up, decades later. Angry at her father, she has lived in self-imposed exile. But now, as the twins' fight threatens to split the family, she appears—a long-lost aunt, not unlike Chaninah—and shares Josef's story and its message. Everyone suffers, she warns, when just one way of life is kosher; all will survive only when all are welcome.

Which of the brothers resembles Josef? Who deserves the birthright? Both, of course: they're identical twins.

WRITING FICTION based on real people warped my recollections: the made-up versions started to dislodge the ones I'd known. Once, after a day of drafting a tricky chapter, I called my sister to see if she recalled a certain incident, when Papa Isaac asked us kids to—

"Wait," she said. "You mean Papa *Eric?*"

"That's what I said," I mumbled, hoping she might overlook the lapse.

Which is to suggest my frame of mind when Stefan arrived, and I gave him the letter about Peter.

He placed it on Nana Susi's glass-topped coffee table. The work would take time, he said; I should go do something. But couldn't he tell me, at least, who had written the letter?

He scanned the pages, squinting, as if the old text glared. "A mother," he said, sounding anguished. "The mother of Peter and Chaninah."

"Ilse," I said. "My grandfather's first wife." I had considered Ilse as the possible letter writer. But how would she have known, so soon after the war, the details about Peter's death?

"The dateline says 'Tröbitz,'" he said. "I don't know this place."

I had done some research, so I knew. Tröbitz had been the

destination of an infamous "Lost Train"—the last of three
Nazi transports sent from Bergen-Belsen in the chaotic closing
weeks of the war. Hoping to hide their crimes from advanc-
ing British troops, the Nazis had loaded thousands of inmates
onto the trains, intending them to reach Theresienstadt, where
gas chambers were hastily being built. But the final transport,
rerouted by Allied bombing, never reached its destination.
Instead, it zigzagged around eastern Germany, until finally,
after a depleting two-week trip—six hundred passengers died
along the way—the train was liberated by Soviet troops in a
village called Tröbitz. There, two thousand surviving Jews were
put up in a makeshift camp, in huts formerly used by forced
laborers.

Now I tried to imagine Ilse writing her letter in one of those
huts. Where did she sit—on a mattress, laid on a muddy floor?
Were pen and paper offered by a kind Soviet soldier, or did
they come from someone brutish, who badgered her for favors
in return?

There I went again, spinning up a story. Soon, I wouldn't
have to; I would have the facts.

It took Stefan an hour to finish the translation. He gave it to
me, cradled in his palms like something sacramental. My pulse
pinched the sides of my throat. I read.

"Dear Eric: on March 13, 1945, at 8:20 p.m., Peter died of
hunger in Bergen-Belsen. Me and the other caretakers had long
been too weak to bed him comfortably."

This was how she'd known the details: by some diabolical
and equally merciful twist of fortune, Ilse had been there, at
Peter's side.

"And what had we not done," she adds, "to spare him this
fate."

Thus begins her chronicle of the years leading to Peter's
death.

In July 1942, he had gone into hiding in the attic of some Dutch citizens ("small-minded, but good people, in their way"). After three months, he was relieved when his mother and sister joined him. They made the best of the tiny space, studying languages and teaching "school" for Chaninah. But neighbors got suspicious of the household's large consumption of potatoes. Peter determined it was time to go.

Next, they found asylum at the home of two other friends. "They especially loved Peter," Ilse writes. "With his wonderfully warm and yet distant demeanor, he understood how to win people over."

Reading this line, I lost my breath. Not that it revealed anything exceptional—a mother convinced of her own offspring's charms—but I had been granted my first view of Peter as a person someone loved.

In February, they celebrated his nineteenth birthday "in good hope." But soon, the house was searched. They survived in a hideaway in the wall but knew that they must go.

"Now begins our wandering in earnest," Ilse writes. While she and Chaninah took refuge in their former maid's home, Peter posed as an Aryan student and joined the Dutch resistance, working with a Quaker network to care for fugitive Jews. Maria, a fellow resistance fighter, took him in "as a son," but she was actually spying for the Nazis.

Peter was arrested, then managed to escape. He hid in some heather, but the Gestapo caught him again. Taken to Utrecht, he suffered "gruesome torture."

Ilse was present for none of this; she'd heard it from a witness. She herself had also been caught doing resistance work. The Nazis sent her first to Westerbork, then to Bergen-Belsen. She must have feared she would never see her children again.

But on October 1, 1944, at 5:00 a.m., came a scene Ilse describes like so: "I don't recognize the man who suddenly stands at the dark three-tiered bunk bed, and I ask him to return later. The young man leaves without a word and sends Trude Rosenthal to me, to prepare me for my luck."

Incredibly, the young man was Peter.

"That was a joy indeed, as you can imagine!" Ilse writes. "The great miracle happened. It ran through the camp like a light of hope. Many who thought their loved ones lost became brave again. The whole life in hell had a purpose."

But Ilse's joy was undercut when Peter told her everything he'd been through, the story she was now left to share with Papa Eric.

After Peter's purported mentor was outed as a Nazi spy, a committee of "Dutch patriots" had killed her. The Nazis retaliated with a "huge revenge trial," which sent two hundred resistance fighters—including Peter—to the Haaren prison in Brabant. "Peter was in solitary confinement, with Nazi interrogations, visits from spies, confrontations. He didn't talk about it often," Ilse says, "just mentioned once how, after an interrogation, his shirt was in shreds."

One by one, his codefendants were taken out and shot. For two months, Peter waited to meet that same demise. He and the five inmates with whom he shared a cell had little food until, at last, Red Cross packages came. But "he could only savor them for a short while, for his asthma got so bad that the commander took pity on him and transferred him to the hospital."

At the hospital, Peter was given medicine and clothes. The commander, considering him an "escape king," warned him against a getaway. Peter heeded, and for eight months, he thrived, making friends with fellow patients, with whom he staged Christmas and New Year's plays. But then, writes Ilse, camp officials "remembered that Peter was a Jew and sent him to Westerbork."

There, he caught pneumonia. Friends saw to it that when other prisoners were transported to Poland, he was "forgotten" and instead, in August 1944, transferred to Theresienstadt. He formed a "very fond friendship" with a Czech boy named Egon, whom he'd met on a mountain excursion with Papa Eric.

At the end of September, Theresienstadt's population was winnowed. Men between twelve and fifty-five were sent to Auschwitz, where almost all would be killed. But once again, Peter was exempted. The Nazis deemed some prisoners as "exchange Jews," whom they hoped to trade for Germans interned by the Allies. Peter, born in Palestine, was placed in this "privileged" category. Instead of to Auschwitz, he was put on a train to Bergen-Belsen (a camp designed for "holding" inmates, not for outright murder), where, on October 1, in the predawn dark, after nineteen months of separation, he brought hope to his mother Ilse's barracks.

Hope was precious, for Bergen-Belsen was "a terrible camp," writes Ilse. "We were not gassed, but people who knew called it the worst camp, considering food, work, living quarters, and treatment." Luckily, she got Peter into the camp hospital, saving him from the senseless beatings and fourteen-hour workdays.

"For fifteen and a half months," she writes, "fate still loaned me Peter." They spent time talking of the future. Peter hoped to avoid Holland—the climate was bad for his lungs—but still, they aimed to hurry there, to pay back their benefactors and, most important, to find Chaninah.

Beyond that, Peter planned to put himself through school—"He wanted to be independent so badly!"—and to get a job working with people. "We fantasized: social worker, hotel manager, or diplomat." Peter had briefly managed a hospital hall in Bergen-Belsen, and, said Ilse, "showed an amazing talent for dealing with people: respectful, energetic, loving, and warm. The much older male nurses accepted the young lad as the leader."

Ilse, who'd been taking care of children in the camp, switched to a nursing position, to spend more time with Peter. The battle-hardened man, she writes, "became my boy again." But though she had spared him from beatings and forced labor, she could not keep away the hunger.

I had come to the letter's unavoidable conclusion.

"For weeks," Ilse writes,

we had only a little beets with water, almost no bread. When I was finally supposed to get extra rations, after my repeated requests to the Germans, it was too late. [Peter] still delighted at the prospect, for he didn't know. "You act as if I'm seriously ill," he told me two days before his passing. The heart didn't want to go on anymore, breathing was so difficult. We couldn't wash him anymore in his two-tiered bunk bed. Every drop of hot liquid he was longing for had to be fought for; we burned our beds. The end came quickly—he didn't suffer anymore and didn't recognize me. He passed, and looked beautiful, very peaceful with his pure closed boy face.

God grant that I'll find Chaninah safe and sound. She is owed a lot.

Please give this letter to all who loved Peter.

I set down the pages, and Stefan, seeing my tears, hugged me tight.

He asked if I knew the concept of *Vergangenheitsbewälti-gung*—a word coined after the war, for the struggle to cope with the past. "In Germany, every schoolkid reads these testimonies. We all go to visit the camps too. It's awful, yes, but also—can

I say this?—inspiring. You read a letter like this and think: *we have to make it never happen again.*"

Sure, I felt that. All of that. I did.

But what I couldn't express—and couldn't, for a long time, sort out in my mind—was a melee of more private feelings: satisfaction and disappointment, gratitude and loss.

I was pleased to have things in common with Peter, like asthma. And, although our activism could hardly be compared—fighting campus homophobia was a far cry from resisting the Gestapo—couldn't I think we shared a passion for social justice? He was more of a role model than I could ever have hoped for. But Ilse's letter, in bringing me finally the facts of Peter's life, had also blotted out my mythical version of him, the angel who'd watched over me since I was fourteen. It was like falling in love with a face in a reflecting pool and then touching it and watching the face dissolve.

Now I was embarrassed by my adolescent fantasies, and also by how narcissistically I had read the letter, fingers crossed for a self-affirming subtext. (The "very fond friendship" with the Czech boy in Westerbork: Had it gone beyond "just" a friendship?) All these thoughts felt dreadful and profane.

In "Saying Kaddish," I'd said that Peter was about possibility, not reality. But he had been a real man, of course. A man whose starved body, with its pure closed boy face, had weighed in his grieving mother's arms.

Ilse wanted her letter shown to "all who loved Peter"— a group I wanted to say included me. But did I love the real Peter? Or did I mostly love my own ideas?

AFTER STEFAN LEFT, I went back to my novel. Or tried to. I felt my new knowledge of Peter should transform Josef's story, and studied Ilse's letter for facts to use, but every time I tried to put them into a scene of my own, sentence after sentence arrived stillborn.

Finally, I came to uncomfortable conclusions: Peter was a hero but not my novel's hero. My character's trauma need not resemble the real story.

I wrestled with the ethics of trumping up a tragedy, as if history weren't horrible enough. But the truth—it's difficult to say this on the record; I've typed and deleted a dozen versions—is that Peter's death was all too ordinary. There were millions of victims like him—sons adored by parents—but my novel needed the barb of a more contentious trauma.

Feeling new license, I composed chapter after chapter. Although I strayed from Peter's story, he was still the novel's guiding spirit. The day I wrote the final line, I typed a dedication:

To the memory of my grandparents
Eric I. Lowenthal and Suzanne S. Lowenthal,
and also Peter Achmed Yehuda Loewenthal

WHEN MY NOVEL came out, in 1998, I waited for my relatives' reactions. Exploiting our family history had left me ill at ease, but so had taking liberties with the facts. Which would they consider worse: the scenes I'd had the gall to steal or those I'd had the gall to fabricate?

But I was also hopeful that the book would break something open among us. Recently, my dad and I had been getting along fine. He'd been nothing but cordial with Scott, my new boyfriend, helping to set the tone for Aunt Judy, who now— eight years after her ultimatum—lovingly included Scott and me at holidays. In fact, we showed up more than Andy, her own son, who skipped Passover because her kitchen wasn't "kosher enough." And yet, in the years since Andy had rejected me, neither my dad nor Aunt Judy had censured his behavior. So, despite their warm embrace, I had not managed to fully slough off my resentment. Now that Dad would read my book—my answer of sorts to Andy—might he clearly take my side? Or, at least, recognize my heartache?

"Mazel tov," he said when he called. "The novel's wonderful. But"—he sounded tentative—"can we talk about something?"

This was tough for him, I guessed—talking about my pain. "Sure, go ahead," I told him.

"The dedication," he said. "I've never known Peter's middle names. How do you?"

That was what mattered? My having gained some knowledge that he lacked? "His birth certificate's right there in your parents' papers," I said. "Which you'd know if you showed the slightest interest."

My harshness hissed across the line, catching us both off guard.

"I *am* interested," he said almost shyly.

Was he picturing, as I was, the moment in his dining room, when he had asked what I found in the family papers and I just shrugged?

I wanted to retract my words: too mean and, worse, dishonest. The truth was, at every chance I'd had to share our history, I had kept everything to myself. Peter's names. Even Ilse's letter.

At the time, I'm not sure this lapse was even conscious, but now I can see it as callow retaliation for Dad's failure to talk about our past. With the facile judgment of generational distance, I had found him guilty of injuring me with silence—scarcely thinking of how his parents' silences had first injured *him*.

On the phone, we didn't speak. I was thinking of how to make amends.

Dad broke the ice. "Another thing I wanted to say: your metaphors. You use so many! They're great, but shouldn't you have saved some for your next book?"

I assured him I still had plenty left.

He and Aunt Judy never did grill me about the novel's truth. Maybe they sensed that if they sought the facts behind my Josef story, they might also have to ponder the basis of other scenes, like the one when the twin brothers masturbate together. No one dared to ask if that had happened with me and Andy; no one asked me much of anything—a surface-level relief that sank in gradually as a setback.

THE OTHER PERSON whose response I had braced for was Chaninah. We had tumbled out of touch, only trading occasional holiday cards. Whenever I pictured my novel through her eyes, I got flustered. The dedication to Peter, for example: I had meant to pay respect, but maybe she'd see presumption. Plus, what would she make of Peter's stand-in being gay? Even if, as a general matter, she accepted gayness, might she not still be unnerved?

Then there was the character of Aunt Ingrid. My hope was that Chaninah, if she ever read the book, would see herself in Ingrid and recognize my stab at reparations. But what if she saw my effort only as salt rubbed into a wound?

I thought about mailing her a copy but never did.

IT WAS almost a decade before we spoke again. In 2007, I was at a bookstore in Washington, DC, promoting my third novel, *Charity Girl*, when I spotted her in the crowd. In the almost quarter century since I'd last seen her, age had only sharpened her resemblance to my grandfather. Bright, impatient eyes above a blunt and mannish nose; a tight, somehow insinuating mouth.

Sitting at the book-signing table after the reading, I looked up, and there she was, next. She said her name, and I said, "Yes, of course. What a surprise!" Which would be weirder: to stay seated or to stand with the table between us?

"I drove up from Annapolis," she told me. "Just for this." She peered professorially through her wire-rimmed glasses, and I felt like an unprepared freshman.

During the reading, I'd presented a chapter of my novel, as well as an essay about the process of writing it. *Charity Girl* explores America's jailing of its own women in detention camps, during World War I, to curb the spread of venereal disease. In my essay, I talked about my frustration at the unlikelihood of interviewing survivors—they'd have been more than a hundred years old—but how I'd eventually decided that lacking witnesses needn't scuttle my project. Novels, I contended, were exercises in empathy, and I could write these women's stories because I could *imagine* them.

From the lectern, my premise had sounded plausibly high-minded. But now, with Chaninah's stare fixing me in place, my words echoed sourly in my mind. Here was a woman who'd borne her own indelible wartime trauma, whose story I had imagined—had skewed—for my own fiction, when all this time I could have learned her truth.

The line of book buyers stretched behind her, emanating restlessness.

Chaninah said, "Feel free to visit. Any time. We'll talk."

"Yes," I told her. "I would really like that."

Gesturing to the line, she said, "You must attend to your fans."

I stood up to hug her—had we ever touched?—but the table of books got in the way.

IT WAS seven years later when she asked for a copy of "Saying Kaddish for Peter." I'd still never visited, stuck in guilt for avoiding her, for privileging Peter's story over hers.

As nervous as I was when I mailed her the manuscript, sending it was unexpectedly freeing. No more fretting about when or whether she'd find the essay; no more queasy, in-the-closet feeling. Was I finally ready to go see her?

Only, of course, if she responded favorably.

I waited a month. A second month. A third. I didn't want to infer her displeasure, but it was hard not to.

Finally, after five months, an email with an all-caps subject line: "A NOTE THAT I THOUGHT MIGHT TICKLE YOU."

Tickle me. Had my essay, after all, delighted her?

But her email didn't mention my writing. It consisted only of the following: "I have no particular reason for sending this to you, but felt there would be no harm in it. Chaninah." Attached was a document—six pages, single-spaced, entitled "A Lifetime of Addresses." It seemed to be a memoir, in the form of a record of everywhere she'd lived.

"I am told that I was born in Berlin, Germany, in 1931," she begins, "but the children's home/orphanage where I remember living was in Cologne. Next came the Jewish orphanage for girls in Amsterdam."

The word *orphanage* stopped me. Both her parents had been alive; why would they have given Chaninah up?

On Papa Eric's tape, it now came back to me, he describes a heated struggle to get Ilse's consent for a divorce. (By then, he and Nana Susi were passionately "connected.") Had Chaninah become a pawn in the proceedings? Had Papa Eric the adulterer been denied custody? What if he wanted Chaninah, but Nana Susi refused? What if *he* had refused his own daughter?

I thought of Ilse's postwar prayer to find Chaninah: *She is owed a lot.*

Chaninah's next entry is "the apartment at 84 Olympia Square, Amsterdam South, where," she writes, "I lived with my mother and brother and grandmother, from, I believe, 1936 until 1941."

1936 was when her parents, at last, divorced. Ilse must have been granted custody.

"During the German occupation of the Netherlands," Chaninah continues, "I resided at many different addresses— in a suburb of Amsterdam, near the Verkade factory; on one of the old Amsterdam canals, where a former charwoman of my family rented a room to my mother for me to stay in; in the town of Wormerveer, where a wealthy childless couple put me up."

All of this before she'd turned twelve.

After living in yet a different place, arranged by a "committee lady" aiding imperiled Jews, she moved to Utrecht. "It was necessary to take the train, which was of course risky," she notes. "My committee lady brought 'leg brown,' a dye which young women used to disguise the fact that they lacked silk stockings. . . . The committee lady daubed my face and ankles and wrists with enough leg brown for my complexion to become quite dark. That way my Jewish coloring could be overlaid with something vaguely Indonesian. Bear in mind that blond really did prevail in pre–World War II Holland."

She describes her life in Utrecht, with the Mook family, at Distelstraat 7. Pretending she was Sonja, "a little orphan girl whose parents had been killed in the bombardment of Rotterdam," she helped care for the Mooks' seven children until the war was over.

Assuming her family was lost forever, she planned to stay with the Mooks. But Ilse, liberated from Bergen-Belsen, managed to find her. (An old schoolmate of Chaninah's encountered her in Utrecht and told his parents, who shared the news with Ilse.) The two returned to Amsterdam, living first at the home of a Communist couple, and then in a "cheerful garret" with neither a kitchen nor bathroom.

Then came immigration to America, "via Golders Green, London, where," Chaninah writes, "I had an uncle, Ludwig, who was the older brother of my father."

In America, she catalogues multiple locations in New York City and then a sequence of homes along the arc of her career: a "broom closet–sized room" in New Haven, where she studied philosophy at Yale and met her husband, Henry (a fellow Holocaust refugee); a graduate dorm room at Bryn Mawr; a railroad-flat apartment near Penn State. Then back to New York, where she attended library school and soon gave birth to twin girls. Manhattan was followed by Bedford-Stuy, and then a row house in Forest Hills.

Eventually, her job at St. John's brought her to Annapolis—to an apartment, then a rented house, and finally a home they bought. Her husband, upon moving in, said, "Next time to Heaven." To which Chaninah adds, in her final line, "The other place was not in the running!"

The memoir floored me. Despite her ample grounds for bitterness and grief, her prose blazed with droll resiliency. I couldn't help but wonder, though: What was she up to in sending it to me? Why had she said nothing in answer to my essay, and then, after five months, sent this?

Unless the memoir *was* her answer.

Reading it again, I focused on what she'd left out. Only once does she mention Papa Eric—not by name or with any emotion, but just to explain her link to Uncle Ludwig. Neither does she name Peter, saying only that she lived with her "brother" in Amsterdam.

Of course, at only six pages, the memoir had not aimed for

completeness. Still, in choosing to omit all that she had, and also now in choosing to share the work with me, Chaninah sent an unmistakable message.

This is my story, she was saying.

Also: this is *my* story.

I SENT Chaninah's memoir to my father and Aunt Judy.

My father called it "amazing," and praised my connection with Chaninah, saying he was sorry not to have one. This was new, this show of remorse. As was the context he provided. When he and Judy, as children, had first met Chaninah, their parents introduced her as a cousin. Now and then over the years she reappeared, never letting on that their father was also her father. Then, at Dad's bar mitzvah, Chaninah—this decade-older "cousin" he scarcely knew—embraced him with over-whelming intensity; mystified, he'd pulled away and never, to his great regret, tried to bridge the gap.

I found these facts astonishing, but even more surprising was the frankness of his telling. What else might he share with me if sharing became our norm?

Aunt Judy emailed, saying that the memoir had upset her: "I didn't know her mother was in the camp. I didn't know Chaninah was in an orphanage."

I was shocked she knew so little. But then I pictured Ilse's letter, in a box in my closet—the translation I had never shown to her or Dad. I asked Aunt Judy if she'd read it, certain she'd answer "no."

"I was never told about it nor saw it," she confirmed. Then, to further explain her ignorance of Chaninah: "No doubt she had a really, really difficult life, but one day she called me to invite me to Annapolis, and I was about to make plans to go, and she said, 'I'll want to tell you about your father. He was really not a nice person.' I didn't go. I didn't want to subject myself to that."

I SYMPATHIZED with Aunt Judy's self-protectiveness, but I was ready to hear whatever Chaninah had to say. I wrote her in thanks for the memoir, pledging to visit soon.

Half an hour later, she wrote back: "For the sake of my children . . . and because I liked what I saw of you, I wanted you & me not to be on an unfriendly footing. But I have an advanced state of lung cancer and emphysema (Hospice of the Chesapeake has been taking care of me). So it is unlikely that you & I shall see each other."

She signed her note: "Ciao. Chaninah."

FOR TWO DAYS, I wrestled with a response. Scared that now I would never learn the truths she held (how could I have squandered so many chances?), I was burning to ask for more but doubted if I should. I had been self-serving with Chaninah all along, and now even my sadness felt selfish.

Finally I decided to apologize—for myself and the family. We were now, all of us, resolved to face the past. My dad had started musing about a family trip to Germany, to see all the places we were from.

During the time it took to decide I should say this, Chaninah sent three emails, all blank. Was she trying to tell me one more thing?

Nothing, then, for six weeks, when one of her daughters Facebooked me. Early that morning, Chaninah had died, at home.

II

Dislocations and Relocations

Once when my father was studying a handful of dirt, I asked him if he had ever been lost. "No," he answered, "but there's been a few times when I didn't know where anything else was."

—Scott Russell Sanders, *Staying Put*

Ligature

"NERVOUS?" Stefan asked when we crossed the line into Lancaster County.

"Yuh," I said, too tense to form words.

"If it helps," he offered, "I could tell you I'm nervous too."

"You?" I said. "Why?" I had never known footloose Stefan to fret on anything. Plus, whatever his fears, they couldn't match mine. In the place where we were headed, he was well-beloved; for me, this was another leap (I'd made a big one, weeks before) into the unknown.

Stefan tugged his beard. Behind his John Lennon glasses, his eyes seemed to measure something. "The thing is . . . it's complicated," he said.

We were still just getting to know each other. The previous year, we had worked at affiliated summer camps in Vermont, and I'd esteemed him largely from afar, awed by his unorthodox mystique. Most of us counselors were college kids, but Stefan was over thirty. He was German and, it was rumored, had overstayed his visa by a decade. Five years back, he had answered a Lancaster County Amish farmer's ad; the man needed an extra hand, and Stefan, who'd trained in agriculture in Germany, had always wanted to farm with horses. He'd worked there for more than a year, living with the Amish like a brother. Afterward, he had driven a horse-drawn covered wagon up to New Hampshire, more than four hundred miles. He seemed at once a hippie throwback and a visitor from a more enlightened future.

And now he was driving me to Peach Bottom, Pennsylvania, to meet his Amish surrogate family, the Beilers, having arranged for me to live there during a leave from college. I had gotten in touch with him that winter about the prospect, and we had spent the past three months building our new friendship. (Stefan had joined our summer camps' year-round maintenance crew, and I was a sophomore at Dartmouth, forty miles away.) Over those months, I had come to crave his admiration. Although I fancied myself a maverick—my favorite T-shirt said QUESTION AUTHORITY—I was always searching about for men to emulate.

But living among the Amish, when I had first imagined it, had had little to do with Stefan, other than hoping he would give me entrée.

At Dartmouth, I'd declared as a major in religion. Despite my Jewish upbringing, I had never felt the spark of faith, which left me both envious and suspicious of the devout, eager to study why they staked their lives on beliefs beyond my reach. That was my go-to explanation when classmates asked, "The Amish? *Why?*"

In truth, though, I sensed already that I would not be writing any study of the Amish. What drew me to them was more personal but also more perplexing, because I strained to fully understand my own reasons, related to my other recent terrifying leap.

Stefan's balky station wagon wasn't hauling much: my backpack, holding all I'd brought for these two months (including a tin pennywhistle I knew would not be welcome); his small duffel, with only one week's clothes. The wagon's way-back was empty, for now; in Peach Bottom, Stefan would fill it with wheels of Amish cheese, to sell for a nice markup back in Vermont. Sniffing at us between the front seats was his mutt, Harold, named after the death-obsessed teen in *Harold and Maude,* his favorite movie. Stefan had named him thus, I gathered, because he himself so identified with Maude, a puckish, lustful-for-life nonconformist. He was fond of quoting her: "Reach out! Take a chance! Get hurt even. But play as well as you can."

A Turkey Hill milk truck buzzed past on our left.

"Part of what makes me nervous," he said, "is what it'll be like, now that they've sold the cows."

When he had lived with the Beilers, they'd been dairy farmers, but they'd decided to sell their herd, in order for Elam, the father, to concentrate on training horses. Days from now, they would host a liquidation sale. Stefan had a copy of the flyer: "McCormick Deering Corn Binder . . . 8 Set of Heavy Harness . . . Approximately 30 Ton Ear Corn." One of my first tasks would be to help out with the auction.

Stefan went on, "They're even selling Bess and Bell!"—his favorite team of Belgians. "Elam might be making a big mistake, but there's no going back. Anyway, you know what they say: 'Feces occur.'"

I forced a laugh, but my guts were in free fall. *No going back.*

Harold snuffled against my neck, as if sensing I needed reassurance. "Hard to believe it's all really happening," I said, "and not just an April Fool's joke."

It was, in fact, the first day of April 1988.

"You'll be fine," said Stefan, squeezing my knee. "The work is hard—the *life* is hard—but you'll get used to it."

The likelihood of hard work wasn't what daunted me. I'd volunteered on farms before, a day here, a week there, and once, in Costa Rica, for two months. Neither was I concerned about living without electric power; I was used to roughing it on weeklong backwoods hikes.

What worried me, but also somehow lured me to the Amish, had to do with their doctrine of absolute conformity, their infamous shunning of transgressors. Most eighteen-year-olds, I supposed, would shrink at such constraints, but for me, the threat of shunning—losing your whole community—bore down with sudden urgency. Three weeks earlier, at Dartmouth, I'd attended my first meeting of the gay students' group. It had felt essential to jump across that brink, but what might I have cut myself off from?

So far, I'd come out to just a few folks at school. I had told no one in my family—and not Stefan. I had no idea how tolerant he might be (weren't some hippies notoriously homophobic?). But even if Stefan himself might accept my gayness, I was sure that if he knew, he would never let me near the Beilers.

MY PATH to that disjunction had started the previous fall. A student named Allen had sought me out, shortly after I'd led his Freshman Trip. The trips were Dartmouth's orientation ritual, five days of bonding in the wilderness. Allen apparently saw me as a paragon of the school's woodsy, masculine ideal. That was why, he said, he'd chosen me to talk with: because I fit in at Dartmouth but also seemed broad-minded. At which point he tearfully confessed that he was gay. How would he survive at a college so conservative?

Instinctively, I responded as his trip leader: boosterish, skilled at catching curveballs. I was impressed he'd come to me, I said—that took courage!

Hearing the word *courage* from my own mouth made me cringe. Because, of course, I had shown so little of it myself. "You . . ." I started to say. "You should maybe know . . ."

Why was it so hard to say *I*?

At last, I managed: "You should know that I think I'm gay too."

The world has changed so much by now, even I'm surprised to think how little I knew back then. Aside from the one high-school classmate I'd had sex with, I was not aware of having met anyone gay. I had watched *The Zoo Story,* the Edward Albee play in which a suicidal loner spells the word *homosexual*; otherwise, I hadn't seen gayness on stage or screen. I hadn't read a gay magazine. And although I'd grown up next to Washington, DC, and sometimes went downtown to Dupont Circle, where my mother worked, I had no clue that it was DC's "gayborhood."

Was I especially sheltered? I don't think so. In mainstream America then, gay life was barely visible behind its shroud of shame.

That shroudedness had made me terrified to come out, even—especially—to those who loved me most. Chief among them my mother, always my closest ally, all the more so since my parents' divorce. She was progressive politically but still shaped by her stuffy, genteel upbringing. I was barred from her kitchen table unless I wore a shirt; the word *suck* (as in "that sucks") was outlawed. By her own admission, Mom was too judgmental. What if she spurned me as I had seen her, for any number of reasons, do to others?

But now I had come out to Allen: a start.

That first day, flustered, we just kissed; soon, though, we were fooling around. I lived that year with three friends in the basement of a UCC church, and, as a caretaker, I had all the keys. After hours, making sure my roommates didn't see, I would lead Allen to the organ loft. Every time, panic nearly made me turn around. But then, when our lonely bodies met: such relief!

All the same, because we hid it, sex with Allen exacerbated my growing sense of blockage. My gayness felt like a molten truth that needed to erupt; I could picture it blasting out, forming a new landscape, but how much of my old world would burn?

I was also struggling then to plan my coming leave term. At Dartmouth we were required to be on campus during our sophomore summer and to go on leave some other season. I had decided to take off the spring but couldn't settle on what to do.

At first, I got stuck on ideas involving baseball: Intern for a team's front office? Apprentice to a sportswriter? Decent enough ideas—I was a big baseball fan—but now I see them as evidence of defensive magical thinking: as if by clinging to a macho boyhood passion, I could thwart the rise of my queer feelings.

That October, fortuitously, Ted Turner gave a talk on campus. I was drawn not because of his topic—nuclear-arms control—but because he owned the Atlanta Braves. Afterward, when he and his entourage left the auditorium, I tagged along. "Mr. Turner," I called. "Mr. Turner!" He stumped on with practiced inattention. "Please," I shouted. "I would love to work for you. For the Braves?" I was breathless, fighting to sound steady. "Give me a chance. Please, sir. I'd do anything, honestly. I would even . . . I'd even be a batboy."

Turner stopped, setting off a pileup of aides behind him, and whirled at me, his gaze whittled down to pure contempt. "Aren't you," he drawled, "a little bit too old to be a *batboy*?"

What stung was that he was right, I was no longer a boy, but I still felt impossibly far away from being a man—or even simply being my own self. How could I be, when my whole life was built atop a secret? I slunk back to the church basement, despondent.

We lived there rent-free but with certain obligations: changing the roadside letter board to tout each week's sermon, hosting monthly student socials. This entailed wheeling in a TV and a VCR, and watching films as we ate Ben and Jerry's.

Not long after my run-in with Ted Turner, we screened *Witness.* The film involved the Amish, I knew, and they were on my radar because of Stefan's history. Also, we'd discussed them in one of my religion courses: sects and cults, the tug of true believing.

In *Witness,* an Amish boy observes a cop's murder. Soon the detective working the case is shot by the murderer, and he hides at the boy's family's farm. It seems the perfect refuge, but when the detective and the boy's mother, Rachel, fall for each other, attraction poses an existential risk. If Rachel acts on her urges, she'll be banned.

At the movie's climax—a classic thriller shootout—my roommates leaned in, tracking every twist. I was riveted, too, but less by the gunfight than by Rachel's dilemma: How could you reach for self-fulfillment if it required losing the very world that gave you meaning? What if you yearned for both liberation and belonging?

I was struck by a conviction as firm as it was inchoate: I was meant to spend my leave term living with the Amish.

I didn't know if the real-life Amish grappled with issues like Rachel's or like mine. If so, I doubted they'd confide in an outsider. But I was guided only by a feeling: being near them would help me somehow home in on a truth about myself.

A KNOCK. Or had I dreamt it? My eyes opened to unfamiliar darkness.

"Stefan," came a voice. "Stefan, get up."

The previous evening, when we'd arrived, I had been so overwhelmed that I could scarcely notice anything. Stefan and I had gone straight to bed.

Now, beside me on the narrow mattress, he stirred, pawing at me as though I were the disturbance. The swaybacked bed, all night long, had spilled us toward each other.

Another knock, and the door opened. A flashlight's beam caught my watch. 4:15 a.m.

"Grandfather died," said Elam. "I have to tell the relatives."

He meant his wife Beulah's grandfather, who, we'd learned the night before, was sick in a back room of the farmhouse. There had been no mention that his death might come so soon! I wanted Stefan to tell me what to do, how to act, but he leapt up and pulled on his pants, and Elam whisked him away.

Soon they drove off in Stefan's station wagon, and I was left to shadow the Beiler children through morning chores. The kids—there were seven—ranged from one year old to twelve. All but Sadie, the second oldest, were boys.

We shuffled to the barn by the light of kerosene lanterns. Despite the predawn chill, the kids all went barefoot. While Sadie set to milking the cow (the Beilers had kept just one), the boys fed the other livestock. I couldn't gauge their frame of mind. Would no one speak of the death?

Even Jakie, the five-year-old—hair as blond as piles of magic straw in fairy tales—was put to work, herding the pushy chickens. "Hoot, hoot!" he babbled at me, and I searched the rafters for an owl. "No," said Christy, the oldest boy, pointing to his boater; Jakie was saying *hat* in Pennsylvania Dutch. "He says it's funny you don't even know the word for hat."

No, I didn't know that. Or anything else, it seemed—at least, nothing in common with these kids. Unnerving, but not all in a bad way. Wasn't this part of what I'd wanted? A chance to test the edges of exclusion.

"Hey, should we check for rats in the corn crib?" asked Christy. Tiny for twelve, with a beakish nose and blue precocious eyes, he had a baby-hawk look of watchfulness-in-training.

Leading me outside—the sky now streaked with light—he added, apropos of nothing, "So, your wife. Will she be coming too?"

I laughed a little too hard. "Who says I have a wife?"

"Your beard," he said. "Doesn't it mean you're married?"

"Certainly not," I told him.

"Oh. For us, it does."

I had grown the beard in hopes of "looking Amish," but it was only amplifying questions I had hoped to mute for now—about my manhood, the lonely future I feared. Amish guys, at my age, were ready to start families; was I ready even to start living as myself?

Christy grabbed a pitchfork and marched around the crib, his homemade pants hitched high by suspenders. Then he lunged—"Ha!"—and stabbed a squirming rat.

"But I thought you were pacifists," I said.

"For rats?" Christy shrugged. "Nah, they eat the corn." Then, brightly: "Maybe later we could hunt some groundhogs! Dad pays a dime for every one we shoot. A quarter if we kill them with a rock."

As if summoned, Elam returned in the station wagon with Stefan (another misconception slain: the Amish don't own cars but can ride in them, except on Sundays). He shooed us all into the house for breakfast.

The house's main space was a multipurpose room: kitchen and eating area, living room, Beulah's sewing station. A wooden hutch displayed a German Bible. The walls were bare, except for three or four feedstore calendars with photos of agricultural landscapes—permissible for their functional value, as opposed to art for art's sake. The floor's cheap linoleum gleamed improbably clean. On every window, dark-green shades were pulled to precisely the same height.

At the table, when Elam bowed his head, everyone followed. After a long thirty seconds of silence, he cleared his throat, prompting the kids to lift their heads and grab at once for food: bread and honey, potted meat and peaches.

Would it be worse to mention the death or to fail to mention it? Into the quiet, I offered, "Sorry about Grandfather."

Elam nodded. "We'll bury him the day after tomorrow."

Amos, at ten, was the third oldest but biggest of the siblings. He had a soft appeal, a chummy salesman's affect. "Mike," he said, "are *your* grandfathers living?"

"Amos!" Beulah chided. "That's personal."

I explained that my mom's father had died when I was Amos's age, but I had known my dad's father better; he had died just four years ago. "And guess what," I said. "He was German. I bet you could've talked in Dutch and he'd have understood you."

"Just like Stefan!" Amos crowed, earning a wink and a "*Jawohl*" from Stefan.

The thought hadn't crossed my mind, maybe because I had never heard Stefan speak German. How could I ever match his bond with the Beilers?

"If he was German," said Sadie, "why'd *you* end up as just American?"

I hesitated. What might her parents not want her to learn? To stall further, I poured myself a frothing cup of milk, the milk Sadie herself had collected, and downed nearly all of it in a gulp. Milk repulsed me—I had shunned it since I was a toddler—but it was what the Beilers all were drinking.

"Well, you see," I told her, "the countries in Europe were fighting. And Jews—do you know what Jews are? people of the Jewish faith?—Jews couldn't live safely in Germany anymore. The lucky ones moved away and got to start new lives."

"Religious persecution," said Elam, stroking his foot-long beard. "Just like our own people, back in the 1600s. Right, kids? Remember *Martyrs Mirror*?"

I grinned (should I grin at the thought of persecution?), hopeful we might bond, after all.

"Chewish . . ." said Beulah, Elam's wife, her accent thicker than his. She was squat at five feet tall, her round face unflinching. I had watched her stumping about the house—she had a clubfoot—looking at once perky and impatient. "Chewish," she tried again, nibbling the exotic. "You'ns are still waiting for the Messiah to come the *first* time, not?"

I laughed, but her mouth went hard; she was serious. "Sorry, no, you're right," I said. "That's exactly the difference. But," I added, "we're also similar, especially the Jews we call Hasidim. The men have beards and wear black coats. The Sabbath is strict, like yours—no work, no riding in a car—except ours is Saturday, not Sunday."

A surge of mirth around the table: the Beilers had never heard such a thing.

My lungs puffed—I'd charmed them!—but instantly deflated with misgivings. *We,* I'd said of Jewish people. *Ours.* Lately, though, I'd wondered if I still fit in my own tribe.

My worries weren't about religious practice. My grandparents had kept the Sabbath, but they had made peace with my not being observant. No, the trouble was more elemental. My nana Susi, having lost her father in the Holocaust, cherished nothing more than our family's endurance. If she found out I was gay, would she feel betrayed? Would my family keep a place for me?

The Beiler kids continued to buzz, tickled by this strange creature, a Jew. They sat by age, the youngest near their parents at the table's head, the oldest at the foot (where I sat next to Christy). Looking at the boys with identically bowl-cut bangs, and Sadie in her aproned dress, a miniature of her mother's, I felt sure they never doubted the order.

Order was the meaning of *Ordnung,* the unwritten code that every Amish church member agreed to. Stefan had explained this, when I had asked how the Beilers could let outsiders in: Didn't that break some central Amish rule? (In addition to Stefan, the Beilers had hosted two other men, making me their fourth non-Amish guest in some ten years.)

"There *are* no central rules," Stefan had told me. "Every district makes its own guidelines." Beyond that, the *Ordnung* was not akin to a rule book—more like a musical key to live in. The Amish heard their whole lives resounding in that key, attuned to notes that didn't harmonize.

"Elam's neighbors' ears must be clanging, then," I'd said.

Stefan smiled. "They think Elam's an odd duck—and he is! But he would never invite us if his bishop told him no."

At breakfast, the topic of grandfathers having run its course, Elam launched into a yarn that let me glimpse his odd-duck gift of charm. The story was about him and a fat English fellow (the Amish call all outsiders "English") to whom he'd sold a walk-behind plow.

"How he fit in his little Honda, it wonders me," said Elam, puffing his cheeks to mimic the guy's girth. "Fifty bucks for the plow, I say. He says forty would suit him better. Fine! 'Milly will be so glad,' he says. Milly is his wife. 'Paint the handles her favorite red. Plant the gizmo right on our front lawn.' 'Wait a minute,' I tell him. 'I thought you would *use* the plow. An ornament? Now I'm charging ninety!'"

Elam, with a flick of the tongue, popped his dentures out—I almost bit my own tongue in shock—then flipped them back into place. (Still in his early thirties, he suffered vague ailments, for which, Stefan had told me, he had sought out drastic cures, including having all his teeth yanked.)

Elam went on, "The fellow hollers, 'Ninety?' and makes to punch me. I'm about to tell him I'm just joshing, when he says,

'That's not right! Ninety? For my Milly's birthday? No, sir—
make it a *hundred*.'

"'Friend,' I say"—Elam thrust his meaty hand at Beulah,
who shook it, complicit in the spoof—"'Friend,' I say, 'you've
got yourself a deal!'"

Elam whiplashed Beulah's arm. All of us cracked up.

"Mom," said Sadie, "will you ask Dad for a hundred-dollar
present?"

Beulah beamed. "Another gift? He gave me all of *you*."

THAT AFTERNOON, I said to Stefan, "The Beilers seem so
happy!"

He looked puzzled. "Why would they not be happy?"

We were hiking with Harold to the Beilers' telephone, a mile
and a quarter up the road; Stefan had to call one of his cheese
customers. I had thought the Amish forbade all telephones, but
Stefan said that what they opposed was how phones, if used
too much, disrupted face-to-face connections. Exceptions were
made for *inconvenient* phones. The Beilers shared theirs with
four other families; it sat in a shanty behind a muddy pond.

"Who can be happy repressing themselves just to fit in?" I
said.

I was thinking of my religion professor's lecture about how
religion shares a root—*lig*, to tie or link—with words like *obli-
gation, allegiance,* even *ligature*; religions were the fasteners
of duty and belief that bound us to a community. He hadn't
mentioned that *ligature* has contradictory meanings: a filament
to stitch a wound; a weapon of strangulation.

"Just because the Amish reject *our* way of life," said Stefan,
"why do you think they're not true to themselves?"

"Living without so much," I said. "Doesn't it take . . .
coercion?"

Stefan snapped, "You think they only stay because they're brainwashed?"

Spooked by his tone, Harold scuttled off into a hayfield.

I was spooked too; I knew I'd overstepped. Months ago, when I'd asked Stefan if I could meet the Beilers, he had said, "I can't bring just anyone there, you know." That was when I'd resolved to keep buried my biggest truth. But now I'd fucked up anyway. Stefan had never used this tone—it brought the raw milk back into my throat, thick and sour.

We had reached the phone hut. Stefan ducked in, and I stood wondering how to walk things back. But when he came out, before I could talk, he jabbed a finger at me.

"The Amish are not brainwashed. They question lots of things. Take this phone: they ask, *Is the good worth the harm?* Maybe," he added, "some of *us* should question how we live, instead of going along to get along."

Heading home, silence like a barbed wire between us, I was stung but not quite surprised. Stefan's comment was on the nose—so much so that if this were fiction, I'd have made it more oblique—but back then, I was always bracing for people to see right through me.

I was so wrapped up in my own fears of exposure, I didn't think to wonder what his comment might say about him. Leaving Germany, staying on illegally in America, becoming like a brother to the Beilers: this had all struck me as adventurous. But why might Stefan hanker for a family not his own? Was he less an adventurer than an exile?

Even if I'd had those thoughts, I would not have voiced them, because halfway back to the farm, something in my gut went loose, and I was bent on making it home before I shat myself.

I did make it, and locked myself in the bathroom. Only just

enough time to blast the water in the sink, hoping to obscure the coming boom.

THE MORNING of the funeral, the Beilers piled into a single carriage. Somber in their Sunday best—black felt hats, not straw—they said they'd be back by noon.

After they left, I shut myself in the bathroom yet again. The diarrhea, I knew, came from drinking milk, but it felt like a metaphor for my not fitting in, not living up to Stefan's standards. With each spatter, I felt further and further removed from everything I knew.

Or maybe this is truer: I felt removed from all the ways I normally strived to make myself known. At Dartmouth, I was an ace student, a prize-winning writer, a hike leader, a trumpeter in the jazz band. In Peach Bottom, those competencies meant nothing. The Amish attended one-room schools, only through eighth grade. Jazz was not a sound they knew; playing musical instruments was proscribed. They aspired not to stand out but to blend in.

When I emerged from the bathroom, a sullen Stefan awaited. We had hardly spoken since our flare-up. Now he told me, "Elam said to give you a riding lesson. Try to get you better with the horses."

The horses: another of my shortcomings. I had tried to copy the Beilers—feeding the horses, currycombing their flanks—but every time a mare so much as flicked its tail, I jumped. Also, their dander got to me. I was a red-eyed, runny-nosed mess.

In the barn, Stefan helped me onto Peggy, a towering, dapple-gray Percheron, then hoisted himself onto her partner, Patsy. We plodded bareback into the pasture ("Saddles keep you separate," Stefan said. "You have to *feel*"). My knees vised Peggy's girth: a sea of muscle, inscrutable and alarming.

"Loosen up," said Stefan crossly.

"What if she starts to gallop, though?"

"The more you freak out, the faster she'll take off."

Fighting instinct, I unclenched. Peggy shivered, and I was sure she'd buck me. Then she shook her head with a fashion model's swagger and trotted nonchalantly ahead. I slipped back to her haunches but managed to catch myself. I was smiling.

I hoped Stefan had seen my triumph. But no, his face was tilted to the clouds.

The night before, in bed (Stefan slept with his back to me), I'd considered my need for his approval. I had a bad habit of falling for my straight friends. But Stefan wasn't my type—too much bigger and older—and I'd been glad for a friendship that wasn't warped by unrequited pining. Why, then, was his sanction so important? Maybe to prove (more to myself, really, than to him) that I could step away from convention and end up being fine.

Now Stefan was smiling too. Had he noticed my riding, after all? When I asked, he got more aloof. He was thinking, he said, about his next big trip: a cross-country covered-wagon journey to the Pacific.

I sat taller on Peggy, proving my proficiency. "Need an accomplice? I could maybe take another leave."

Stefan purred into Patsy's ear; the horse began to turn. "Almost noon," he said. "We should head back in."

Off he galloped, kicking a cloud of grit into my eyes.

AUCTION DAY, a week since Stefan's and my arrival, would be his last full day in Peach Bottom. He would leave the next morning, and I still hadn't mended things between us.

All day, rain lashed the farm. Amish women in dripping bonnets peddled soup and pastries. The auctioneer—part opera singer, part relentless woodpecker—versified the names of farm equipment: cultipacker, stalk chopper, twenty-eight-blade disc harrow. A very pregnant goat appeared; "Buy her before she pops," a farmer shouted, "or I bet they charge double!"

I was a gopher for Elam, fetching hames and harnesses. Stefan also dashed about, grooming every horse for its big moment.

When all the lots were sold—Bess and Bell, the feed corn, the overbulging goat—the auctioneer said, "Leftover food: profits for Melvin Lapp." Lapp was an Amish neighbor paralyzed in a buggy crash. The bids were crazy: twenty bucks for a Mason jar of chow-chow, thirty for a stale whoopie pie.

Then, just as fast, it was over. The auctioneer disassembled his portable PA system. Neighbors and strangers vanished into the rain.

The Beilers stood in their sodden driveway, their faces as hazy as the sky.

"Well?" said Elam. "I guess let's go inside."

No one moved, including him.

Christy called, "You heard Dad!" and led the family in. Beulah, dragging her clubfoot, went last.

When I followed, Stefan said to wait. I suspected he wanted to give the family some space. A kindness.

We headed to the now cowless dairy. I had never known this farm before its transformation, but I could feel a quaver of uncertainty and change. Not unlike the wobble within myself.

Stefan said, "You need to know: I'm driving home right now."

"Now?" I said. How would we have the chance to patch things up?

"I think it's best for both of us," he said.

All of a sudden, I understood. Stefan had been vetting me; I'd failed. He would tell me to pack my bag and get in the car to go.

"This is so hard," he said. He toed a stanchion pipe.

My shame was heightened by panic about logistics. My spot in the Dartmouth church apartment had been taken, and I'd been counting on free room and board at the Beilers'. How would I afford somewhere else?

Stefan said, "I promised myself I'd say this before I left. You're a great guy, Mike. You know how much I like you. But"—he gulped for air. "But I really . . . really, I think I love you."

I was so bowled over that I blurted, "Love you too. You're the best!" I could hear how badly I'd missed the mark.

Behind his smudged glasses, Stefan's eyes were liquid beads. "Being with you this week. Sleeping in that bed. Touching but not touching," he said. "It's torture."

Relief is what I should have felt. Gladness. Solidarity. To learn my friend, my hero, was also gay.

What I felt was body-seizing dread.

"Probably you're disgusted," Stefan said. "I'd understand." A tear fell and glistened in his beard. "But I had to tell you, Mike. Because I'd like to be with you. The wagon trip—that could be amazing, if you came. But not if . . . not like this. No."

"Wow," I said. It came out more like *whoa*.

I was mentally clicking through a slideshow of the week before. His nervousness on the drive down, his outburst at the phone. He must have feared repelling me just as much as I had feared alienating him.

I could kill that fear right now. Heal us both with a few honest words.

When I'd come out to Allen, we had sealed our bond with

body heat. But if I came out to Stefan, wouldn't I also have to confess I didn't love him *that way*? The truths tugged in different directions, cinching like a snare.

"Don't assume," I finally said, "that what you said disgusts me. Don't assume that this will come between us."

"Okay," he said. He sounded doubtful.

I had yearned to hash things out, but now I couldn't bear to talk. Why had Stefan's confession left me feeling more alone? Plus, I couldn't shake the thought that if I told him I was gay, he would worry I'd out myself somehow to the Beilers—and then, by implication or accident, out *him*.

"They'll be wondering," I said. I pointed to the farmhouse. "Can we maybe talk when you come back?"

He was planning another trip a couple weeks from now.

"Well, but." He stopped himself, seemed to reconsider. He wiped his beard of tears. "Guess you're right."

"Good," I said. "It'll be much better to talk later!" My words sounded hucksterish. I didn't like the person who had said them.

I reached out to hug him, but our shoulders clunked. We both flinched away.

AFTER COMING OUT to Allen, I'm not sure how soon I'd have told anyone else, if not for a certain hockey game.

January 1988. Ten weeks before I moved to Peach Bottom.

I had returned to school from winter break at my mother's. In Mom's eyes, whatever I did or said was "just the *best*." If I stuttered a joke in a middling Cockney accent, she would say, "You're *such* a brilliant mimic." False, I thought. All of it! She didn't really know me. Whenever I'd tried to tell her, though, my lips had felt sutured.

Back on campus—a Friday night—I was glad for the

distraction of a Dartmouth hockey match. A chance to think of nothing much. Certainly not of gayness.

Not until the jerk behind me taunted the other team: "Number eight is a faggot! Your boyfriend hates you, homo!"

Not uncommon at a hockey game. But now it felt more personal. I couldn't take it.

I wrote to the college newspaper, decrying my classmate's insults. Of gay people, I said that they—a ten-foot-pole of a pronoun—should be just as worthy of respect as other minorities.

After my letter was published, I was invited for coffee by the head of DaGLO, the Dartmouth Gay and Lesbian Organization. Bill reached out and placed his hand a scant inch from mine. "Almost no one takes our side," he said. "Why did you?"

The café patrons stared at Bill—I was sure they did—with pity and revulsion: they could tell. "Aren't we all on the same side?" I said, losing my nerve. "In the end, aren't we all just human?"

When I next fooled around with Allen, I told him about the conversation with Bill.

"Maybe we could go to one of those DaGLO meetings," he said.

"Yeah, maybe," I said. "I don't know."

That week, I visited Stefan; after getting my letter about the Amish, he'd invited me to camp. Driving over, I was nervous—I barely knew the guy—but when I got there, Stefan smiled and handed me some snowshoes, and soon we were bounding up a ridge in knee-deep powder; Harold, beside us, dolphined through the fluff. Afterward, Stefan suggested that he would vouch for me, but only once he knew me better: "I'm protective. The Beilers are my family." So I brought him to Dartmouth and toured him through my haunts: the music and religion departments; Cabin and Trail, the hiking club; the ritzy English library. (I didn't show him the café where Bill and

I had met.) The sanctuary of our church had wonderful acoustics. Stefan had brought his guitar, and I got out my banjo; we sang together late into the night. "No music at the Beilers', though," he warned. "You're gonna miss it!"

After he left, I was thumbing through the college paper. I stared at the events calendar (DaGLO, Mondays at 9:00), feeling spineless. Then an ad for a play caught my eye: "Do you know someone with AIDS? You will . . ." The play was called *The Normal Heart*. I hadn't heard of its writer, Larry Kramer.

I went alone and sat in the back row. The show followed a gay, Jewish writer named Ned Weeks, who, after watching his friends sicken and die, becomes an AIDS activist. "The writer fellow who's scared," a doctor named Emma calls him. "I hear you've got a big mouth."

NED: Is big mouth a symptom?
EMMA: No, a cure.

In the theater's darkness, I wept. For Ned and all his friends, and for myself. Ashamed of my silence. Terrified to change.

An usher saw me wiping my tears and handed me a flyer: David Pickford, Dartmouth class of 1965, former assistant secretary of the treasury, was giving a talk on AIDS. Would I go?

I did go—and sat again in the back. Pickford's Midwestern voice was flat, which made his message all the more startling. "Fifty-nine percent of Americans," he said, "think AIDS is God's punishment for being gay, like I am."

He was modest looking, with a trim brown mustache, wearing slacks and a plain Oxford shirt. But to me, he radiated a pulsing, awesome aura. He was the first gay adult I'd ever been in a room with. The first, at least, I had known was gay.

He shared a story about his lover, Stephen, trying to hail a cab. The cabbie, recognizing his illness, wouldn't take him and, instead, provoked some teenage punks to torment him. "Die," the teens yelled. "Die, you fag!"

"Stephen did die," Pickford whispered. "Seven months after his diagnosis."

A beeping split the hush. I shifted, ready to run if someone hollered "Fire."

"Sorry," said Pickford. "Time for meds." He fished pills from his pocket. Only as he held a glass of water to his lips, his trembling hand making the liquid slosh, did I see the frailty and the fear beneath his courage. "Maybe they'll buy me a little time," he said. "More than Stephen."

That night, I couldn't sleep, my ears ringing as though someone had slugged me. Ringing with the sound of his alarm.

Allen came over later that week, and we went up to the organ loft. Before we kissed, I held his face. "Let's go to the next meeting," I said.

The meeting was in Robinson Hall: the same building and same night as Cabin and Trail's weekly get-together. After C&T, I walked out with my hiking pals, then snuck back and vaulted upstairs with Allen. We were met in the DaGLO room by Bill's knowing smile.

I don't remember what was said, but I can still feel my mesmerizing mix of anxiety and relief. The dozen students seemed mostly "normal" (that's how I thought of it), but stylish in a way I didn't get. Whereas my pals wore chamois shirts and pinesap-stained Carhartt pants, these kids wore shiny Doc Martens, pegged jeans, and T-shirts touting bands I hadn't heard of. Their laughter (at what, exactly? I couldn't parse the irony) billowed with the scent of cigarettes.

I couldn't stop staring at a sophomore named Gregorio, his hair in a flawless flat-top fade: he had twice the flair in one of his bold eyebrows that I had in my whole oafish body. Then, who should walk in but my Modern British Drama prof—apparently, the faculty adviser!—who, within this friendly space, got all the more stagy, as if playing a Noël Coward production. How much did I have in common with him or with Gregorio? Could I be part of C&T and also part of this?

After the meeting, Bill peppered me with spring-term possibilities: a gay-student dance at Boston University, a new "alternative" nightclub in Northampton.

"Sorry, I can't," I told him.

"Oops—I'm overwhelming you?"

"No, not that," I said, although I did feel overwhelmed. "Thing is, in three weeks I'm moving to Pennsylvania. To live with an Amish family."

"The Amish?" Bill looked horrified. "*Why?*"

AFTER STEFAN left the Beilers', the bungle of my response to his confession ate at me.

During my years and years of only longing for guys, I had not contemplated having to reject one; the boys I had longed for had never expressed interest and, as far as I knew, weren't even gay. But what of two guys who *were* both gay, who even loved each other—must they automatically be lovers? The question now seems simple, but, at eighteen, I had never considered it. I'd been weighing questions only about my own sexuality—straight or gay, closeted or out—thinking the answers would lead to clear sailing.

I wish Stefan's anguish had offered me a kind of fellowship, reassurance that even the strong can struggle. But I'd been shaken to see my friend so needy, nearly broken. If he—gutsy, thirtysomething, a staunch nonconformist—if even he was tortured by gayness, what did that bode for me?

But none of that could account fully for how I'd treated Stefan. Not until I talked with Elam one evening a week later and learned about a certain Amish practice, was I able to pin down my feelings.

We had spent the afternoon training his newest horses. Even among the Amish, Elam was known for his talent with the animals. Days earlier, we had seen a neighbor, Noah Zook, about a gelding Zook had deemed hopeless. "Hardly lets me get within ten feet of him," he said, "let alone hitch him to the buggy." To show us, he lifted a bridle warily toward the gelding; its kick missed his kneecap by an inch. Elam took the bridle and set it on the ground, then padded up to the horse and circled it once, twice. On tiptoe, he murmured in its ear. Soon enough, the horse backed up between the buggy's shafts.

Freed from the grind of dairying, Elam would now cash in on his horse-whispering prowess. He intended to pay bottom dollar for problem horses, then train them and sell them for twice the price. He had bought an old wooden freight wagon with steel-wrapped wheels, planning to drive the back roads like an old-timey peddler, horses to sell or trade tethered behind. It was a nutty notion—and, for Elam, that seemed half the point.

That afternoon, we had finally taken the wagon out, hitched to two new purchases, a Saddlebred and a Morgan. "Like my hotrod?" Elam said, knocking the wagon's side. "Needs some paint, but the engine's got two horsepower!"

As if on cue, the horses sprinted. Had Elam's knock spooked them? The wagon thrashed, bounced my body skyward.

"Brake!" he yelled, yanking the lines.

I stomped the pedal. The wagon started to capsize.

Leaning like a yachtsman trimming his sails, Elam righted us and steered the team into a new-plowed field. We hurtled over dirt clods the size of bowling balls, inches from a taut electric fence. Elam hauled and hauled, his boots braced on the buckboard. Just when he'd seemed to gain control, he slacked the lines. The horses ran and rollicked, dashed in figure eights.

Soon their hides frothed with the effort of their freedom. They cantered, then trotted, then walked. We turned for home.

That evening, in the farmhouse, Elam and I sat in wooden rockers. The kids played with model tractors; Beulah pumped at her foot-powered Singer. These calm hours had come to be my favorite times with the Beilers—no TV or telephone; the big hand of the rural sky enclosing the house in darkness—but this evening felt extra special. Elam and I, together, had survived.

Maybe that's what gave me the nerve to pry. I started simple: "How did you know what to do with those horses?"

"About the same as raising children, not?" Elam said. He reached down and tousled Jakie's bowl cut. "Sometimes, keep 'em tight in the lines. Other times, let 'em run their hearts out. That way, when they come back to their senses, the choice is *theirs*. It sticks."

"Horses, okay, maybe," I said. "But children?"

The runners of his chair went *crick, crack.*

"Do your kids—" I lowered my voice. "*Do* they have a choice? In being Amish?"

"Sure they do. They only join the church when they're adults. Eighteen, nineteen"—he grinned slyly—"just about your age."

The evening's dark had closed its grip. Elam twisted the valve on a nearby propane lamp, struck a match and held it to the mantles.

"This," I said, gesturing to the barely lit room, "this is all your kids ever know. It's beautiful. But how can you say they've chosen?"

That was when he explained rumspringa. Nowadays, it's better known, but back then, few outside the Amish had heard the term. When Amish teens neared the age of baptism, he said, they could venture out a bit, without their parents' censure. Some got "fancy" haircuts, installed CD players in their buggies. Bolder ones might even drink or drug. Because they weren't yet baptized, there would be no punishment. Then, if they did join the church, they did so more conscious of the world they had renounced.

"*What am I ready to give up?*" he said. "That's what we all ask ourselves before we take our vows. Makes you stronger—the church stronger too—to have that time-out."

I don't know if my head snapped back but it felt like it might have, as though Elam had jerked on hidden reins. A time-out—exactly! Now I understood that this was what had drawn me here: to get about as far away as I could go from gayness, away from Allen and Bill, from sex and AIDS and DaGLO; to pause before committing to all that. Would I retreat to the closet? No, I'd come too far. But I was wanting, one last time, to feel my life *without*—without sexuality, all its joys and burdens—so that when I did come out, it would truly be my own good choice. Peach Bottom was my rumspringa in reverse.

But Stefan, with his confession, had messed everything up. Now I lurched through every day gripped with apprehension. What should I do when he came back: Keep my secret, to justify my coldness to his come-on? Sleep with him, to spare his feelings? But what about my own?

ON THE first church Sunday after Stefan left (the Amish hold services every other Sunday, the "off" week saved for family visits), Elam pulled me aside at morning chores. "Maybe," he said, "you would like some time at home? Alone?"

The Amish communication style often flummoxed me. When was a question a velvet-wrapped demand? Looking back, I suspect Elam was being kind, sensing my funk and offering me a break. At the time, I took it as a vote of no confidence. I felt sure that he'd been keeping tabs on all my foibles: my toilet trips, my runny nose, my clumsiness with the horses. (The day before, when he had left me alone to mow for just a minute, I had steered the horse too close to a fence and snagged the blade.) More to the point, I wondered if I'd offended him with my prying. I'd been dying to see the Amish at church—their most unguarded—but Elam, I feared, might be saying: *I don't think you're ready.* Or maybe, worse: *We're not ready to have you.*

The Beilers took off, and I was by myself for the first time in three weeks. Left alone in someone's house, I had often fizzed with a furtive energy. But now, as the hoofbeats of the Beilers' horse faded, I could scarcely muster the urge to snoop. I tried on one of Elam's austere black frock coats but struggled with its hooks and eyes; I hung it back on its peg.

In the hutch, next to the Bible, I found a thick university press book, *Amish Society*—the "definitive study," according to its cover. Imagine owning a treatise on yourselves! It must give such comfort, I thought, to have your way of life spelled out, to know your part in a capital-S Society.

I sat awhile, reading about the Amish tenet of *Gelassenheit*: humility and yielding, surrender to the community. Those who transgressed (for example, by using banned technology or seeking higher education) were disciplined, if they didn't repent, with total "social avoidance." Other church members, even their kin, could not share a table with them or take any object from their hand.

It was hard to picture the Beilers meting out such punishment. What if Christy (watchful Christy!) wanted to go to college when he was older; would Elam literally not break bread with him? I thought of my own father, in far-off California (since the divorce, we saw each other a few times a year), and wished we had clearer rules to follow. Elam's kids, if ever he shunned them, would know he'd done so out of their faith's tough love. If my father avoided me because of my "transgression," it would be his choice and his alone. What love was that?

Agitated, I walked outside, into a chilly fog, and found myself heading to the phone. My thoughts had turned from my father to my mother. Her home was only two hours' drive, and I was hoping she might visit soon—because she'd love the Beilers but also because a visit here was safer than one at school, where we might encounter DaGLO folks. I dialed her number, missing the ease I'd used to feel between us. No answer.

Another thing I'd been missing, just as Stefan had warned, was music. At school, I played every day: banjo, guitar, trumpet. But the Amish (as I had just read in *Amish Society*) frowned on musical instruments because they fostered self-expression. I couldn't argue with that; music had always made me feel the most like myself.

Like myself: Wasn't that the feeling I was chasing?

Back at the farmhouse, I got out the pennywhistle I had kept hidden. Playing it in the Beilers' house, especially on a Sunday, felt wrong. Better to head into the woods—or no, I thought, the silo. I had watched Christy climb to the silo's top each morning, to shovel out steaming heaps of fodder. "It's a perfect hideout," he'd confessed.

The silo was made of concrete staves, a shaky ladder bolted to its side. Whistle in my pocket, I climbed up and squeezed through the porthole-like door. I was hit with a boozy, green smell of fermentation. Alfalfa dust danced in the fuzzy light.

On the whistle, in truth, I was just a trifler. I played one of my only songs, a bouncy old march, the notes rising and swirling in the silo's domed roof. I recalled the acoustics in our church, back at Dartmouth. Singing there with Stefan. Allen in the organ loft.

All at once, a whomp of misery sent me to my knees. I had never felt so all alone.

Before I knew what I was doing, I was masturbating. Thinking not of Stefan or Allen—of nothing, really, beyond self-soothing.

Climbing down afterward, my legs dull with shame, I considered telling Elam that he should send me home.

LATER THAT WEEK, as I came in from chores, Sadie sprinted up. "Mike, look! A letter for you. From Stefan!"

The message, in his careful script, was brief. He had been reshingling a roof and slipped, tumbled down; X-rays revealed two broken ribs. "Now I'm on a 'forced vacation,'" he wrote. "Doctor's orders. Guess I won't be coming back so soon."

"Bad news," I told Sadie, even as I loosened with relief.

My dread of his return had been a looming storm, but here was a clear-blue barometric lift—a high that, remarkably, lasted for days, then weeks, all the time I stayed in Peach Bottom.

THERE WAS the day I hunted groundhogs with Christy. (Their holes were a tripping hazard for horses.) He went barefoot, so I did too. The squidge of mud between my toes felt primal. As we paced the pasture, peering into the holes, Christy asked how to say groundhog in Spanish. I had regaled the Beilers with tales of the Costa Rican ranch where I had worked one summer during high school, and Christy had then asked to learn Spanish animal names; ever since, he could be heard striding around the barn, calling, "Hello, *vaca*!" or "Hey, there, *caballo*!"

"I don't know," I told him now. "I didn't meet any Costa Rican groundhogs."

"That's okay," said Christy. "The ones here probably don't speak Spanish anyway."

Did he know how funny he was being? He was easily as

bright as the summer-camp kids I'd counseled—children of New York lawyers and Harvard physicists—his curiosity so propulsive it seemed almost to lift him from the ground. Whenever a visitor left a copy of the daily *Intelligencer Journal,* Christy would wait for Elam to "read" it—a quick check of the auction ads—and then study every inch of the paper.

"I could teach you some other words," I offered.

"Please!" said Christy.

I was about to add "if your father says it's fine," but he grabbed me and pointed: a groundhog at fifty feet, periscoping out of its hidey-hole.

We had left the rifle at home, choosing to test our luck with rocks, and I was shocked when the one I hurled nailed the creature squarely on the skull.

"No one's ever done that!" Christy yelled. "Dad'll pay you a whole quarter."

I proposed we split the reward, and Christy's hug almost knocked me down. "If I was ever English," he said, "I would want *you* to be my brother."

ANOTHER TIME, the boys clamored to watch the creek for muskrats—not to hunt, only to admire. Secretly, they finished all their chores before supper, and then begged for the evening off.

We tiptoed through the woods as a shard of moon ascended, and then, at the creek, we crouched to scan for bubbles. "What's a muskrat look like?" asked Jakie, but Amos shushed him. Talking was poison; we needed perfect silence.

For forty minutes, we huddled, one big holy being. The creek flowed with infinite persistence.

Not one muskrat did we see, not even any bubbles, but the boys, skipping together later back to the house, said they'd never had so much fun.

GAINING IN self-confidence, I stopped drinking the Beilers' milk; my guts almost instantly calmed down. Somehow this also quelled the worst of my horse allergies. Mornings, when Elam called, *"Zeit uf shtay!* Time to get up!" I was raring.

I began to understand more Pennsylvania Dutch. "Toss some hay down," Elam might say, or "Put your hands in your lap," and I could follow. At breakfast, I would ask to have my eggs *"lawf-y"*—*lawfa,* as a verb, meant "to walk"—because in Dutch, yolks don't run, they stroll.

I was also improving with the horses. Elam started sending me for solo drives in the *hundscart,* a small two-wheeled sulky; at dawn, I would zip through dewy, pink-streaked fields. One Friday, we visited his brother William's farm as William disked behind a team of six. Elam let me sub in for a pass across the field, showing me how to guide the horses, three lines in each hand. My arms thrummed as if I were steering the solar system.

Then there came an afternoon with stabbing shafts of rain, when Elam said the "scholars" (as the Amish call schoolchildren) would get soaked walking home. "Why don't you go fetch 'em in the carriage?" he suggested—as if it were no big thing to trust me with their lives.

WE'D BEEN using the freight wagon according to Elam's plan: clopping through the countryside, horses tethered behind, trying to entice farmers to buy. Some days, we covered fifteen miles. Even though the labor consisted mostly of sitting, it was grueling, tailbone-bruising work.

Then one morning, as I was pinning the doubletree to the wagon's tongue, Elam said, "How's about a different form of transport?" and led me to his neighbor Ray's farm.

Ray was an English guy with big, ungrudging eyes. In his barn: a red Ford mini pickup. "Only a '78," he said. "Mileage is

99,999 point five. You can have her," he said to Elam, then turned to me. "*You* can have her"—he winked—"for three hundred."

"Pretty good price, not?" asked Elam.

"Hard to beat," I said.

He hadn't asked if I wanted a truck. I didn't—not here in Peach Bottom! But Elam counted the money out for Ray.

Days later, Elam announced a trip to northern Pennsylvania. A Mennonite had listed a pair of Percherons for sale that might be perfect for Stefan's covered wagon.

Starting the truck, I throbbed with umbrage. I resented how Elam had forced me into complicity, using me to get around the *Ordnung,* and how in plotting his own freedom, he had discounted mine. Plus, I dreaded the drive—six hours round trip—and Elam, of course, couldn't share the burden.

As we motored up through the Susquehanna Valley, the rhythm of the speeding truck started to lull my nerves. It was early May now; the sun, as if atoning for months of stingy pallor, lavished light on green new fields of soy.

Elam rolled his window down and leaned way out of the truck. The wind split and lifted his beard and mashed it to his face. He yelped something wordless and euphoric.

"Go on, Mike. Try it!" he urged.

How could I stay angry? I rolled down my window, too, and yodeled.

The Percherons were a dud—Elam doubted they'd make it to California—but the trip still counted as a triumph for our friendship. Driving home, we pulled off at a rest stop for a snack. Sharing doughnuts and pizza, we drew blatant stares. A rubbernecker aimed her camera, and Elam ducked his face, joking that the tourist must be crushed to catch him here. "'Bad *Ay*-mish!'" he barked, mispronouncing on purpose, playacting the woman's disapproval.

"Well, I'm just as bad," I said.

"What kind of bad are *you?*"

I had meant only that I was scarfing junk food too, but now Elam's question loomed large. Chewing pepperoni, I almost said *A bad Jew*—a thought I still could not escape whenever I ate something so unkosher. *A bad friend,* I also thought, picturing Stefan's stricken face. *A bad gay.* Someone who could leave his comrade suffering.

What I said was, "I'm supposed to be your chauffeur, right? I didn't even want to make this trip. I hate to drive."

"Hate to drive?" He clutched his chest. "Good-for-nothing English!"

By the time we hit the road, it was 9:00 p.m. We were still forty miles from home.

Elam slapped the dashboard. "Can't this thing go faster?"

I was starting to tell him that the engine was too dinky, when Elam thrust his left leg onto the driver's side and set his big boot atop my gas foot. Mashing it, he shouted, "Giddyap!"

SOMETIMES, THOUGH, he could be severe. One morning, when I came back from driving in the *hundscart,* Elam stood in the barn's forebay, tying his newest colt. The colt reared, and Elam said, "Oh, you want the persuader?" From a hook on the wall, he grabbed a leather crop. He whipped the colt's hock, the barrel of its belly—blows that only made the horse grow madder. It lunged leftward, nearly pinning Elam against a trough, and Elam whipped and whipped—a sickening slicing sound—until the colt's flank ran with blood.

The Beiler boys, drawn by the noise, gathered in the doorway.

Elam landed another blow. The colt fell to its knees. Then, jumping up, it broke free and bolted from the barn.

Christy asked, "Shouldn't we chase him down?"

Elam gripped the bloody crop. "If he knows what's good for him, he'll be back."

"MAIL CALL!" sang Sadie one day, handing me an envelope.

I smiled, hoping she couldn't sense my apprehension. Had Stefan sent an update, saying he was coming? (How awful, to hope a friend's healing might take longer.) But no, I saw, the sender's name was not Stefan but Allen, to whom I had recently mailed a card.

"Mike," said Sadie, "aren't you going to read it?"

"Later," I said. I stuffed it into my pocket.

The next day—the kids at school, Elam at the blacksmith's, and Beulah weeding asparagus in the garden—I climbed up the silo ladder, into its sultry cave. I opened the letter.

"Dearest Mike (my peach-bottomed buddy)," Allen began. "I loved your postcard. I also love the H-word: HOMO HOMO HOMO HOMO HOMO." I pressed the page to my chest, as if to mute his voice, imagining it could echo to the garden. The sweet smell of silage made me woozy.

Allen wrote that he was already a budding activist. He'd organized a screening of *The Times of Harvey Milk,* a film about a murdered gay leader I hadn't heard of. He had also gone with Bill to the gay dance at BU, bopping in a packed hall with two hundred fifty beautiful sweaty men. Such a scene was inconceivable, more exotic to me now than steering six horses abreast or hurling rocks at groundhogs. And yet I could conjure up a foretaste of the pleasure, the way you can sometimes whiff a rainstorm hours ahead.

"I did it!" Allen also wrote. "I told my mom I'm gay." He had sprung the news in person, during parents' week, after which his mother admitted she had long suspected. "Anyway, she still loves me. That's what counts."

I refolded the letter and squeezed it to my palm. The silo's strange acoustics amplified my breathing. It sounded like a congregation of men had encircled me, all their lungs quickened with shaky hope.

THAT EVENING, I hiked to the phone. In the hut was a notebook for logging long-distance minutes. So, despite my mother's fervor—"*Sweet*heart! Tell me *every*thing!"—I said we should save our conversation for her visit. We settled on a day the next week.

The prospect left me dizzy with anxious expectation. What would she do to my rumspringa-in-reverse?

I was about to hang up, when she said, "Oh, your banjo came!"

At spring break, just before moving to the Beilers', I had ordered a custom-made five-string from Utah.

"I can bring it," she said. "Aren't you dying to try it?"

"Yes!" I said. "Can't wait to see you!"

THE BEILERS bathed—or bath'd, with a short *a*, as they said it—once a week, Saturdays after supper. Behind a hanging bedsheet, they took turns in a small steel tub filled with water heated on the stove. After washing, they would trade the shirt and pants they'd worn all week for fresh ones to use in the week ahead.

There came a Saturday, just as I was ducking behind the sheet, when Elam said, "Church tomorrow's up at Bennie Fisher's. If it suits, you're welcome to come along."

"Only if it's no trouble," I said, trying not to sound so eager that he might reconsider.

The next morning, at seven thirty, all our chores dispatched, we walked up the hill to Bennie Fisher's. (The Amish, who have no church buildings, worship in members' homes and barns, with every family hosting in rotation.) Outside Bennie's, there was much amused consternation as the men, who always entered church in a strict order, based on marital status and seniority, debated where to place me: with the older single boys or the married men. I wasn't married, but I was bearded. Was I a guest, or part of the Beiler family? Finally, I was given a spot of honor with the boys, second in line, just behind the oldest.

The Fishers' home was decorated exactly like the Beilers': feedstore calendars, green window shades. For church, all their furniture had been removed to the barn, the house filled with backless wooden benches. Men and boys sat in one room, women and girls another, with ministers in a doorway between, visible to all.

The service, though I hardly understood it, was captivating—Bible readings in High German; spells of silent kneeling; two tearful sermons in singsong Dutch—but when I now summon up the feeling of that day, I think only of one thing: the hymns.

I'd learned their history from *Amish Society*: sixteenth-century poems penned by Anabaptist martyrs imprisoned in a Bavarian dungeon; the verses collected in a hymnal called the *Ausbund,* the music passed down only by voice and ear. The hymns were sung exceedingly slowly—originally to prevent the guards, so the story went, from dancing in mockery of the martyrs.

None of this prepared me for the sound.

A man in the middle of the crowd sang out "O" in an eerie, unrefined voice, and then he trilled embellishments—up, down, up again—stretching the vowel across five, six, seven notes. After the slightest pause, the congregation joined: "Go-o-o-o-o-tt!" A gush of sound, in ragged unison.

I was tracking the lyrics in my copy of the *Ausbund,*

struggling with the German Gothic script. The pace felt unendurably slow, but I could sense the pointlessness of pushing against the hymn, a planet with its own gravity. The tune droned on, dirge-like but not entirely mournful. To sing just the first line—"*O Gott Vater, wir loben dich*"—took the congregation a full minute.

The chants sounded tempting, full of affirmation. But I was too self-conscious to add my voice.

As the German poetry flowed past unfathomably, I felt as I had as a boy in synagogue, intoning Hebrew I couldn't comprehend. Stefan had compared the Amish *Ordnung* to a musical key, a consonance resounding through their lives. What key was my own life in? Could anyone else hear it? I had long been torn between craving a tribal bond and chafing at the fear that it might choke me. Again I tried to picture Allen dancing at BU, amid the sweaty throng of gay men. What music had they moved to? Would I have felt in step?

The Amish boy beside me, seeing that I wasn't singing, pressed his thumb to our place in the *Ausbund*. Six or seven minutes had passed, but only now was the first verse concluding. The hymn leader belted out the next line's first syllable, and then, when the church chimed in—so as not to offend the boy—I joined. At first I only whispered, worried I'd botch the German, but soon I found that singing the wrong sound was not possible. The hymn moved so slowly, with such communal force, it tugged all my notes into place.

The next line began, and voices rose in unison, my own lost—and found—in the chorus. I knew the Amish were not my people; this was a taste I'd savor but not swallow. My ribs rang like struck tuning forks.

MY MOM drove up one morning, her white K-car gleaming;

it might have been a spaceship from Mars. "Sweetness!" she called, stepping out, and threw her arms around me—an open show of emotion, as alien here as her car, that seemed to give the Beiler kids permission. They swarmed her, tugging her sleeves, fighting to be her guide. Sadie led her into the house to show off a quilt-in-progress, explaining that they'd price it by the yard of thread used, a literal measure of all their hours sewing. "Isn't that the *most* stunning quilt you've seen?" said Mom. "Actually," Sadie said, "I liked our last one better." Mom guffawed and pulled her new pal close.

Elam suggested I take her out in the *hundscart*. We hitched a laid-back Standardbred, and Mom said to Elam, "Really? You trust my kid to drive?"

He smirked. "Maybe not. But I trust God!"

We embarked on a grand tour, rolling past Ray's barn and the creek with no muskrats. The phone hut, the Fishers' house, the field where we'd almost crashed the wagon. Pointing it all out to Mom, I was shocked by how much I had learned in just two months. I felt a weird fast-forwarding: a blur, then a snap into focus.

"Come up now," I called to the mare. The horse started pacing—lifting her front and hind hooves on each side together—and I taught Mom the difference between a pacer and a trotter. "Isn't this great?" I said. "Feel the speed!"

"I'll tell you what's great," she said. "When your kid gets better than you at something or does something you've never dreamed of doing. That's when you know that he's grown up. It's the best part of being a parent."

Was this my moment of truth? *Mom, I have to tell you who I am.* The wind in my face, the whirring wheels, the hoofbeats' fast applause.

The impulse passed. Not the time or place. But I felt sure

that there would be a time and place—soon. I knew I could steer us through that passage.

Back at the farm, I walked Mom to her car to say goodbye. Simultaneously we said, "But the banjo!"

I took it from the trunk and opened the hardshell case. It was the most beautiful banjo I had ever held, a Vega Little Wonder pot with a red maple neck. Sitting on the hood, my feet atop the bumper, I plucked "Blackberry Blossom" and "Boil Them Cabbage Down." My fingertips, from all the farm-work, had stayed good and callused.

The Beiler kids, who'd followed us out, scuffed their feet in rhythm, as if scratching an itch within the earth—or in themselves. Somehow only now, with Christy dancing before me, did I think of a silly classic tune about groundhogs. Lifting my face, I sang with all my might:

Whet up your axe and whistle up your dog,
Whet up your axe and whistle up your dog,
We're off to the woods to hunt groundhog.
Oh, groundhog!

Christy danced harder, and so I kept on going: verses about the killing and the cooking of the critter, about a gal named Sally with "groundhog gravy all over her chin." The boys hurrahed; they couldn't get enough. I loved how much they loved the song, just as I had loved their hymns at church.

"Look at them fellers," I sang out, "they're about to fall. They ate till their britches won't button at all!"

The kids, pretending gluttony, staggered and puffed their cheeks—looking just like Elam, back on my first day, mimicking the man who'd bought his plow.

And now here was Elam himself, squinting in the sun.

"Children!" he shouted. "Chore time. Say goodbye." Then he added something in Dutch that made the kids scram.

Elam told my mom she was welcome back whenever. Then he made the slightest upward motion with his chin—the way he bid at the New Holland horse sale—and strode away. I knew I should follow.

At first, he just stared, his gaze flat and blunt. "It would be better," he finally said, "if your mother took that thing away."

That thing. As if even to say *banjo* was sinful.

It had never occurred to me that I might keep it here—of course I would send it home with Mom!—but now that he had shamed me, I burned to fight back. *Sure, you can buy a secret truck,* I longed to say. *But a banjo? God forbid!*

I packed the banjo back into the car.

I hugged Mom, holding on a beat longer than normal. Her hair's scent was so familiar, I could not have said it smelled like anything other than my life.

ANOTHER CARD from Stefan: his ribs had healed; he would fetch me and drive me home to Dartmouth.

Reading his words, I expected dread again to seize me but found myself instead feeling ready to work things out, almost restless. Allen's letter, the church service, the banjo, my mother's hug: I'd been getting clearer about which kinds of belonging belonged to me. My rumspringa was coming to an end.

When Stefan arrived, he shook Elam's hand, then reached for mine, but I embraced him. "Can we go talk?" I said.

For privacy, we walked down to the creek, with Harold trailing. What I would say, and how, I still wasn't sure; I was trusting my clearer self to lead me.

Stefan asked how Elam was doing. Did he regret selling the dairy herd?

"Honestly?" I said. "I think it's been a weight off. I didn't know him before, of course, but he seems sort of . . . new?" I recounted our trip to northern Pennsylvania: Elam's goofy howling in the wind. "The horses were no good," I said, "but he says he'll keep looking."

No need, Stefan said: the covered-wagon trip was off for now.

"But why? Your plan sounded awesome."

"I'm gonna *bike* to California," he said. "By myself."

My flare of disappointment was followed by an upswell of respect. This was not the broken-seeming man I'd seen the last time but someone who'd gained clarity, like me. Maybe the pain of our previous talk had pushed him toward a new self-reckoning.

"Stefan," I said, "I owe you an apology. I'm gay too. I just didn't know how to tell you."

"Ha!" A gasp of anger, or maybe satisfaction. Harold anxiously nudged Stefan's calves.

"Thing is," I said, "I'm not really 'out.' I've only ever been with two guys. And so," I added, dodging his gaze, "I'm not ready to be anything more than just good friends."

Stefan stopped. He gripped my arm. "Thanks," he said, "for telling me. But come on, if we're being honest? Don't say you're 'not ready.' Say that it's not—*I'm* not—what you want."

Now I heard the hurt beneath his anger. The hurt of having asked a friend's help to cast off shame, only to have him pile on to the load. I sensed there was little I could do in reparation, but I vowed to myself that from here on out, I would do my best to battle shame—in myself and in my classmates, maybe even in people I'd never meet.

We started hiking back, the air between us tense and magnetic. Now that we had said the truth, I could see his dazzle again, see the man I wanted to emulate.

"We won't tell the Beilers?" I said.

"No. No, of course not. Some things are for our world, not theirs."

That was when I told him about the banjo incident.

Stefan was sympathetic, if not much surprised. "Wouldn't it be great," he said, "to blow Elam's mind? Play him every kind of music—not just folk. Punk! Heavy metal!"

I laughed. "He's a natural for the mosh pit."

"There's so much I know he'd love," said Stefan in all seriousness. "Singing and dancing. Movies. *Harold and Maude*!"

The dog yipped at the sound of his name, and something dawned on me. "Harold" had always made me picture the character who sulks throughout the film, driving a hearse, faking his own death. But maybe Stefan, in picking the name, had thought more of the ending, when Harold's car plunges off a cliff but then we pan back up and see him alive, banjo in hand, skipping to the film's signature song.

That was the song I joked about now, knowing Stefan would get it: "Don't you want to say to Elam: 'Hey, if you want to sing out, sing out!'"

Together, then, Stefan and I belted out the lyrics, about being free if you wanted to be free because there were a million things to be. We sang all the way back to the house.

THE NEXT DAY, Stefan wanted to go and buy some cheese, but his station wagon wouldn't start. Elam said, "Pop the hood. Let me have a look once."

"It's not a horse," said Stefan. "You can't whisper to it."

"Don't be so sure!" said Elam, who cupped his hands around his mouth, pretending to confide in the engine. He took off the distributor cap. "There's your problem. Corroded."

He scraped the rust with his penknife, replaced the cap. The car hummed to life.

"What a relief," said Stefan. "I was seeing us getting stranded halfway to New Hampshire."

Elam grabbed my shoulder. "You're not going with Stefan, though."

"Course he is," said Stefan. "Why do you think I came?"

"But Mike," said Elam, "aren't you driving back in your own truck?"

"Oh," I said, "I guess I thought—"

"Thought you could ditch your truck on an Amish farm?" He kept a straight face, but his eyes were smiling.

When Stefan left to get his cheese, Elam added, "You've earned it, Mike. Thanks."

STEFAN DROVE home that afternoon. I stayed one more night.

It had been the hottest day of the year so far, mid-80s, humidity like a steam press on our necks. After supper, the Beiler boys were playing "calling over"—tossing a ball over the roof from opposite sides of the house—but Christy and I, soaked with sweat, had quit.

"Next time, I'm going to bring an air conditioner," I said. "Rig it to run on propane. Or horses."

"Yes, please!" said Christy. "And maybe an ice machine?" He had perfected his deadpan delivery.

"Ice machine? You think too small," I said. "Ask for a swimming pool."

"But we could make our own pool now," he said. "The bulk tank!"

The bulk tank was a remnant of their dairy: a 400-gallon stainless-steel vat for cooling milk. Left unsold in the auction, it now sat empty in the milk house.

"Better ask your dad," I said, so Christy went and got him.

Elam popped his dentures out, then flipped them back and nodded.

At once, it was a Beiler family production. Everyone crowded into the milk house, the tank's top was lifted, frigid water hosed at full blast.

Amos and the younger boys had already shrugged out of their suspenders. I had never seen them naked or anything even close. Neither had I bared to them more than my feet and forearms. The boys shucked their shirts and pants, revealing pale chests, touchingly yellowed briefs. One by one, they dunked themselves, then bounded out, shouting that they'd never been so cold.

Sadie tenderly toweled each brother dry—as close as a girl could come to all the fun.

Christy went last and came up spitting, his hair plastered to his skull like a newborn's.

Now the attention turned to me. The kids cheered, "Mike! Mike!" I didn't want to be unseemly. Was I too old? Too English?

Beulah, on her bobbing legs, waltzed across to me. "Tonight you're one of us yet," she said. "Go ahead."

Stripped to my briefs, I felt exposed but also irreproachable. I splashed into the water and made a show of shock. When I climbed out, the kids huddled around me.

"We're gonna miss you, Mike," said Amos.

Jakie said, "Please stay?"

Then the whole chorus of boys: "Stay!" They crushed me in a shivery group hug.

Elam said it was bedtime. The kids moaned and groaned but turned in.

Christy, though, got permission to linger. He and I sat on the ground against the milk house wall. At half past eight, there was plenty of dusk left in the evening—not far from the longest of the year.

"What are you gonna do back at college?" Christy asked, his accent rendering it as *cull-itch*.

Be more honest, I thought. Be bolder. Be myself.

"I'll be busy with classes," I said. One on a writer named Shakespeare, another on the nuclear age.

Christy looked off blankly into the pinking sky. Guessing he didn't understand the phrase *nuclear age,* I was about to define it, when he spoke.

"I heard they have missiles in Moscow aimed at Washington, and Washington has its own aimed at Russia. Now they're putting something in the middle of the ocean to stop them both from burning up the cities." He sighed. "I hope we have a future."

"How do you see your own future?" I asked.

Christy tipped his head back. I thought he might say he dreamed of going to college, like me. I shouldn't get his hopes up—such a path would be painful—but maybe I could pledge to help when the time came for his rumspringa. When Christy reached college age, I'd be twenty-five. Where would I be living then? With whom?

"I would like to have a herd," he said, "like before. Get this milk house up and running again."

"Really?" I said, not hiding my surprise.

"What did you think? Horses? No—I want to be a dairyman."

I couldn't help smiling at how far off I'd been. "Set your sights," I said. "You can do it!"

MY DARTMOUTH CLASSMATES, that summer, must have found me strange. I wore zipperless Amish pants with black leather suspenders, a broad-brimmed Amish straw hat. Everywhere I went, I went barefoot.

Looking back, I cringe. So contrived! But I can also see how sincerely I was trying to signify something about myself. For the Amish, clothing marks their separateness from the world, and I think that was my spirit too: *I'm a part of you, but I'm apart from you.*

Often, as I strode shoeless across the college green, my banjo or trumpet case was slung over my shoulder. I holed up in the library, poring through *King Lear,* but also danced the toyi-toyi at anti-apartheid protests. I'd been named the summer co-chair of C&T, the hiking club, and led ascents of White Mountains peaks.

The steeper climb was coming out to those outdoorsy friends. I started with one of my roommates, Ian, a Nordic skier from rural Manitoba. (He had once remarked of our sleepy college town, "How will I get used to all this *traffic*?") Ian lay in bed one night, mooning about a girl, and I interrupted: "My crushes are on guys."

"Really?" he said. "Always, or just sometimes?"

"Almost always," I said. "I'm gay."

"Oh, okay!" He sounded puzzled but full of wonder, as if I had spoken of some odd American food—Jell-O salad with cottage cheese and Cool Whip—as yet undiscovered in Manitoba.

Next I turned to Thomas: one of the very guys I had a crush on. We were fond of long soul-baring walks along the river. I had not dared to hope that he'd return my feelings, but I was ready to show him who I was. All the more gutting, then, when Thomas promptly put an end to our walks. Maybe he didn't like feeling he couldn't give me all I wanted from him.

Word began to spread, which took some pressure off: less need to talk with everyone. Still, things were hard in ways I hadn't counted on—or, at least, didn't ease in ways I had hoped for.

I had dreamed of coming out as a quick cure for loneliness. But in my entire class—more than a thousand students—only four or five men at the time were openly gay. I had heard of closeted students meeting up for sex, but now, as an identifiable queer, I was toxic; those guys wouldn't be caught dead with me. (It seemed a sick joke that they, in hiding, found each other, while I, in the open, found no one.)

I had discovered *The Advocate,* a gay magazine the library subscribed to. Every two weeks, as soon as the new issue hit the shelves, I would sit in the reading room, holding it up and hoping someone, anyone, might notice. In some ways, I felt even lonelier than before, dispossessed of my main excuse for lacking true romance. *If only people knew,* I'd thought—and, well, now they did.

And yet, I was also catching glimmers of affinity, learning in *The Advocate* about the liberation movement I was now part of. It was this sense of shared purpose, over the next two years, that would chip away my solitude. I would bond with a small bunch of fiercely queer students: taking over the president's office to protest homophobia, hijacking the Dartmouth Hall lights to turn them pink. Among those fellow outcasts, I would find kinship—and finally, late in my junior year, a boyfriend.

ALLEN, a class behind me, wasn't on campus that summer. Because of our leave-term schedules, it was a full year before I saw him. Our lust had dissipated.

I also saw Stefan less after I returned. He biked off for California, his bike sporting plastic jugs in which he sprouted lentils for snacks. He was still my hero.

After he came back east, we picked up where we'd left off.

In April 1993—five years since driving to Peach Bottom—we drove south together again, this time for the March on Washington for gay and lesbian rights. We stomped past the White House, chanting, "We're here. We're queer. We're not going away."

Larry Kramer—now more famous for founding ACT UP than writing *The Normal Heart*—gave a fiery, inspirational speech: "The future we have waited so long to live is here on this Mall."

Stefan and I went to see the AIDS Memorial Quilt and walked weeping among the hand-sewn panels. I couldn't find the one for David Pickford, who had died only a year after his Dartmouth talk. (Decades later, I would find it: a tribute both to him and to his partner, Stephen Scott, it shows a ladder rising into the heavens.)

My most vivid image of Stefan from that weekend: him in my mother's kitchen, haloed by clouds of flour. We and four of our queer pals were crashing at the house, taking over her guest beds and the family-room floor. Stefan, as a gesture of thanks, decided to bake bread, and turned the kitchen into a charming chaos. The house filled with the wheaty smell of friendship.

I HAD come out to my mom at my junior-year winter break. All through that vacation, I'd vowed and failed to tell her. Before I knew it, we were driving to catch my plane to school. *So much for that,* I thought, which filled me with such shame that I blurted out, "I need to tell you something."

I don't recall her making any scene. It's hard to be dramatic when you're driving to the airport—probably why my subconscious picked that moment.

At the airport, she said she loved me and made me swear to call her when I got safely home.

I did call that evening, and every day for a while. She was squeamish but knew to blame herself for that, not me. Within weeks, she would check out all her library's books on gayness; within a few months after that, she would join PFLAG—Parents and Friends of Lesbians and Gays—and then would wind up serving on its national board of directors. She was still her judgmental self but now aimed her venom at "those fucking homophobes."

MY DAD'S embrace, after my graduation speech, was slower but still emphatic. I think he even came to regret my grandmother's exclusion from that occasion—and from the truth.

Standing that day at the podium—my SILENCE = DEATH pin on my gown—I had resolved never again to closet myself to anyone I loved.

OR, WELL, not anyone but the Beilers—ironic, given that my speech had featured them.

The talk was titled "Conformity and Community." I began by contrasting the pomp of Dartmouth's ceremony with Christy Beiler's plain graduation, a month before: he and his classmates had finished the eighth grade—and thus their education—celebrating with little more than handshakes and homemade soda. No big fuss of community affirmation had been needed, because the Amish had already agreed on their shared culture, agreed to dress and pray and think alike. At Dartmouth, however, I said, belonging wasn't contingent on conformity, and we could not simply shun dissenters. Building cohesion was harder for us, especially since we'd grown diverse in race, class, and gender—and even, I added, sexual orientation. At which point I mentioned I was gay.

The Beilers were my friends, I said, and I deeply respected their religion. But while their community depended on obedience, Dartmouth's would thrive only by being challenged. To bind a new community, we would need new traditions, rooted not in sameness but in celebration of difference.

I DIDN'T TELL the Beilers about the speech. If they'd known, I was sure that they would cut off contact. In a culture where sex of any kind was rarely mentioned and gayness was an excommunicable sin, my coming out would have crossed a line.

But keeping our friendship, I decided, was worth making a carve-out to my rule. The Beilers' world was so radically different from my own that I let go of normal expectations when I was with them. I withheld not just my gayness but lots of things about my life that they would find mystifying—just as I knew they kept aspects of Amish life from me.

More than three decades later, the Beilers are still my friends. Years ago, they left Peach Bottom and moved to the Midwest, but Christy and I—we've kept the closest—exchange occasional letters. The *Ordnung* in his church district has marginally evolved, allowing him to install a phone in his barn, and so we also sometimes call each other.

He never became a dairyman—the acreage proved too pricey—but worked instead building barns and fences. He's a father of ten and recently a grandfather. His children, along with all his siblings and their kids, have stayed Amish.

If Christy was ever puzzled that I hadn't married a woman, he chose mostly not to bring it up. In one long-ago letter, mentioning for the first time his soon-to-become wife, he wrote of making trips "to visit a special friend." Then he added, "I wonder if you've found yourself a friend, or is she hidden in the stars?" After that, he never asked again. Respecting my privacy, probably. Fearing he'd poke a sore spot.

I wondered, though, what he made of my answering machine message. In 2006, I had bought a house with my then-boyfriend, whose voice on the recording said, "You've reached Michael and Scott, leave a message." Christy had met Scott once—presented as just "my pal"—when Scott and I were driving cross-country. Maybe Christy truly believed that Scott was just a pal. Maybe he believed that for a while.

Eventually, though, after years of hearing our joint message, Christy started making a point of asking after Scott, in ways that suggested he knew more. If I told him I'd traveled abroad, he might ask, "Did Scott go along?" When I talked of visiting my mother for the holidays, he would say, "I hope Scott could join!"

Christy is wise—he must be—to how our values clash. If I've staked my life on the freedom to be myself, Christy has staked his on the freedom from that freedom, on giving himself up to God and church. And yet, he still believes, as I do, in our friendship: insurmountably separate, exhilaratingly stitched.

Face the Music

SUN RA claimed to hail from Saturn, but he and his far-out band, the Intergalactic Arkestra, still suffered the hassles of earthly travel. Because of a snafu, they would arrive on campus a day early, before their hotel expected them. His agent, in a panic, called our group's director. Could we help him rustle up some beds?

We were Barbary Coast, the Dartmouth College jazz band. Every winter, our director invited in a guest musician—Max Roach, Slide Hampton, Lester Bowie—who'd teach us for a week and guide us in a Saturday-night performance. Each of them had mastered the master-class circuit; none had needed help with where to sleep.

We turned to Adam, our piano player, who lived in an old frat house called Panarchy. Bucking its Greek identity, the house had become a refuge for students too weird to fit in at our tight-assed WASPy school. Adam told his fellow Pan-archists about our bind, and they were stoked to host one of the world's wildest bands. Mattresses and questionably clean bedding were dredged up, dusty couches cleared of detritus. Adam's girlfriend, Angela, commandeered the kitchen, churning out hundreds of dumplings for dinner.

I must have come late, because I found my bandmates

already cross-legged on the floor, gazing up at an armchair in which, as if enthroned, sat Sun Ra. He looked like no entity I had ever encountered. Said to be seventy-five, he seemed a hundred, until I peered closer: childlike, impulsive eyes; puffy cheeks. His goatee was dyed an uncanny shade of orange, that of a Dinka tribesman's hair or maybe a punk's mohawk. His bulk, shrouded in a floor-length poncho, appeared almost weightless, ectoplasmic.

". . . get the planet ready for space beings," he was saying. "People need to be *tuned up*. They're out of tune with the universe. That's why they have to hear my songs: *cosmos* songs."

His voice came in lispy, whispered bursts; we all leaned in.

"My music is *power*-ful," he went on. "Few months back, we played some gigs behind the Iron Curtain." This was the very start of 1990. "And?" he said. "What happened? Y'all saw: the Wall came down!"

On and on he speechified, his brown skin purpling as his vehemence increased: *history versus mystery—his story, my story—knowledge of the ancient unknowns* . . . Part lecture, part homily, or maybe schoolyard brag, his spiel was both baffling and bewitching. The other Arkestra members (he'd come with eight or nine) hovered at the room's margin, gobbling dumplings, chiming in with the "Mm-hmm" or "That's right!" you'd hear at a Baptist church.

And the students at Sun Ra's feet? Some were nodding, brows furrowed, as if in a foreign-language class; others were trying not to bust up laughing.

Sun Ra had never done a college stint like this, let alone at a place as conventional as Dartmouth. Even at Panarchy, you could sense the instant culture clash. Sun Ra looked as comfortable as a parrot in the Arctic.

Or maybe I was projecting.

At twenty, I'd played the trumpet for fully half my life:

thousands of hours of embouchure training and finger drills and scales. I was proficient, and loved to play, but what I truly excelled at was excelling; musical discipline was part of my whole strive-for-straight-A's MO. But now, four months from graduating, I wondered how the trumpet would fit in my new life. Without the structure of school, without the earning of brownie points, would musical achievement lose its meaning?

Really, I was wondering about much more than the horn. The striver in me had increasingly been losing faith in the worlds I'd sought praise from. Coming out as gay had sealed my distrust of standard power structures, and landing at the top of my class seemed to cast doubt on my integrity: fishy to succeed within the very system I questioned. The compass I'd been steering by had scrambled; did I need a new north?

Enter Sun Ra, brimming with eccentric insurrection, claiming his music's power to topple walls. He kindled in me a combination of skepticism and jealousy: I didn't think I wanted to believe what he believed, but he sure made me long to believe something.

SUN RA was a visionary, according to our director, Don. In the 1940s, going by his birth name, Herman Blount, he'd played in Chicago with the famed big-band leader Fletcher Henderson. Then, in the '50s, proclaiming he'd had an out-of-body experience in space, he transformed into Le Sony'r Ra—or Le Sun Ra, or Sun Ra—and started making "music of the spheres."

A pioneer in using rhythm machines and synthesizers, he'd put out maybe two hundred albums, revered by a range of artists, from Herbie Hancock to Sonic Youth. He and his "Arkestra" had toured the world, performing in flamboyant robes and floppy wizard's caps.

"It's a kind of cosmological cult," Don had told us, the

day he announced Sun Ra's visit. "Science fiction mixed with ancient lore, Egyptology."

"What about this coming-from-Saturn stuff?" Adam asked. "Are we supposed to think that's true? Does *he*?"

"I don't know," said Don. "Does it matter?"

Then he told us how he thought about it: Imagine growing up in the 1920s and '30s. A dreamy boy, a musical genius, different from all your peers. A dreamy Black boy—in Birmingham, Alabama. Brutal Jim Crow segregation. Lynchings. That boy—Herman—looked around, saw that there was literally *no place* in that world for him, and decided he was "not of this earth."

"Maybe it's a myth," said Don. "Or maybe a kind of drag. But who's to say it's any less true than what's beneath the costume?"

The band was quiet. Everyone looked as hesitant as I felt.

Don said, "If it's not your thing, don't get stuck on the 'spacey' stuff. The *music* is what's really out of this world."

NORMALLY, in advance of his visit, the guest would send us charts: full arrangements, with parts for trumpets, saxes, 'bones, and so on. But Sun Ra demurred; first, he said, he had to see what we looked like.

Don mailed him a photograph. We waited.

A curiously thin packet finally came. He'd sent a dozen single sheets; on each was scrawled a title and an unadorned melody, like jingles from a kindergarten songbook. Had Sun Ra clocked our strait-laced looks—and seen that all but one of us were white—and thought this was as much as we could handle? Don phoned and asked what we should do.

The pages turned out to be the alto sax parts. Sun Ra said to transpose them for every other instrument. "Then play 'em all in unison. *Real slow.*"

Dutifully we plodded through the simple melodies. The longer we rehearsed them, the less sense they made, like words repeated so often they crumble into nonsense. Was this some kind of avant-garde joke?

MY DOUBTS about Sun Ra mirrored qualms I had about the very nature of jazz. My childhood trumpet training had been classical: right notes vs. wrong. Later, in high school, when I had first tried jazz, I found improvisation terrifying. If all the notes were mine to choose, how could I ever know I got them right?

I fashioned an escape hatch: whenever my part called for an open trumpet solo, I'd go home, compose some riffs and practice them to death, then perform this faux improvisation at the concert. Eventually, obeying the music's letter if not its spirit, I rose to the rank of first trumpet. I even made the all-state jazz ensemble.

Then I scored a spot in Barbary Coast. The music was intimidating—funk and bebop, Afro-Caribbean—but Don was patient, somehow both meticulous and mellow. He pushed us toward ad-libbing, and I embraced the challenge: boning up on blues scales, rehearsing rhythm changes, hoping to make up in perseverance for what I lacked in feel. By senior year, most of the time, I could ad-lib adequately, without leaving behind a song in ruins.

Adequately. Does any word in the language have less jazz?

TUESDAY EVENING, when I arrived for our first rehearsal, Sun Ra was sitting at the piano. He wore the same poncho, and also a woolen skullcap. He seemed subdued. It turned out he'd stayed at the hotel after all (Don had found the last available room), while the other Arkestra members had partied at Panarchy, shooting pool until dawn. Three of them had crashed on the floor in Adam's room—he'd woken at six to find them passing around a bottle of wine, saying, "Hey, now, give me some of that mouthwash!"

At the piano, Sun Ra looked to be in a kind of exile. Someone should be tending to him, I thought . . . but not me. I feared getting closer, nervous that he'd sniff my doubts—about him, and about myself. He plinked around on the keyboard, then smiled arcanely. Time to start, he said.

His voice was barely audible. A song with "space" in the title? That hardly narrowed it down: he'd sent tunes called "Island in Space," "Sons of the Space Age," "Spacelore." I was searching through my folder when he mumbled, "One-two-three-four-five-six-seven-and—"

I whipped my trumpet up to my lips in time to muff a note. A beat later, a sax squawked, and then the trombones.

Sun Ra let his hands go still, and all of us stopped playing. He gazed up, away, as if to a distant nebula, and then, in a voice as thin as tracing paper, went, "One-two-three-four-five-six-seven-and—"

Now we came in together, but all at different speeds.

Beside me stood Laura, our trumpet virtuoso, a freshman who played with silky sophistication. "Excuse me, um . . . sir?" she said. (She and I had debated: Should we call our guest Mr. Ra? Mr. Sun?) "Excuse me," she said again. "Can I ask something?"

Sun Ra looked more or less at her.

"When we rehearsed," she said, "we did this four times slower."

He seemed to consider this. He nodded.

"But now you're counting it off super-fast. Which way's better?"

A gleam livened his eyes. He was a jester playing a bod-hisattva, or vice versa. "Depends," he said, "on what you want to hear."

The rest of the rehearsal was only more unnerving. Pronouncements blazed forth from him but evanesced, leaving only contrails. The Arkestra members tried to guide us: Marshall Allen hunkering with the saxes, counting rhythms, Michael Ray kibitzing with us horns. "Watch his face," Michael said. "Always just keep watching. Anything else, I'll be here to translate."

Translate seemed too tame a word. I gave up and slumped onto a stool.

"Listen!"

It was Sun Ra, his voice aimed at me. I looked into his dark, dilated gaze.

"Your ear's a harp," he said. "A harp made of strings. My music vibrates strings in there that never moved before. It's gonna make your head hurt. Don't worry." With that, he stood and shuffled to the door.

I should have stayed with my bandmates; there would be strength in bellyaching together. But I was so wrung out, I just packed up my horn and took off.

In the bitter New Hampshire night, my skull ached with tight, tectonic pressure. *Depends on what you want to hear,* he'd said—an empty riddle. As if *wanting* were all success required. I stomped home, mad at him and madder at myself (why should I let this total quack tip me off my hinges?). I crunched snow in a steady, stringent beat.

THE SECOND REHEARSAL didn't go much better.

Sun Ra had decided against playing the tunes we'd practiced. Instead, he'd spent the day composing new material.

Jothan Callins, another Arkestra trumpeter, tried to calm us: Sun Ra did this *every* day, and used the date for a title. During a concert, he might call out, say, "April 6," and you'd have to locate that date's tune.

Jothan seemed agreeably nerdy—less astro-jazzman than small-town postal clerk—but his attempt at reassurance backfired. If at first I'd felt the rug was being pulled from under me, now I doubted there'd ever been a rug.

Sun Ra played each section's part, then asked us to play it back by ear. Without written notes to follow, I flailed. Laura managed to jot the trumpet part into a notebook, but by then, Sun Ra's riffs had changed.

After an hour, it was time to try our parts together. Sun Ra counted off, and we came in.

Disaster. A multicar pileup.

What he hadn't explained was that he'd written the parts in conflicting time signatures: saxes and trumpets in 4/4 time, drums and bass in 3/4, piano in 7/4, 'bones in 5/4. He seemed peeved we hadn't figured it out. "Not just that you're *playing* wrong," he said, "it's that you're *thinking* wrong. Exercise the muscles of your brain!"

Afterward, I battled a headache twice as sharp as the previous day's.

THE NEXT REHEARSAL was Friday, a day until the show. Surprise, surprise—Sun Ra opened more musical cans of worms: songs that, for all we knew, he was making up on the spot. Diplomatically, Don suggested we work on tunes we'd played before.

"Y'all seem so worried," said Sun Ra, "about playing the *notes*. But you can play more than just notes on a page, you know. You can play the river. You can play the sun rays."

What a cop-out, I thought. If anything goes, nothing needs perfecting.

But fine. He was the visionary.

And so, during the next song, I decided to beat him at his own game. I came in a millisecond ahead of or behind each note. I'd like to say I did this out of open-mindedness, but cussedness was closer to the truth.

Strangely, my mischief-making failed to wreck the music. For every phrase I sabotaged, Sun Ra changed his playing, widening the song's sidelines to keep my notes in bounds. *You're right, it's a game,* the man seemed to be saying, *but all of us are on the same team.*

We moved on to a stumper of a song called "Friendly Galaxy." Before, I'd been thrown by its herky-jerky melody, but now I let my knees and shoulders act as shock absorbers, and found I could bodysurf the song.

Among the band, a fissure formed: who was in on the music's fun, who wasn't.

Sun Ra wrote a vamp that the saxes couldn't seem to learn. "The problem," he declared, "is you don't *want* to know it. The 'bones look like *they* do. Let them try."

Matt, an Asian studies major, led the trombone section. Pale and blond, as placidly compassionate as a chaplain, he huddled with Pete, a toothy, earnest grad student in chemistry. It was hard to picture two less probable avant-gardists, but after some transposition, they both nailed the vamp.

Adam, on piano, also found the groove. "See?" said Sun Ra. "He used his *ears.* Just like Jesus Christ did. Used his ears and listened to the people."

Sun Ra's patter was growing only weirder. The less I took him seriously, the more seriously I could take him—which seemed, to my delight, like one of his own riddles.

It was still unclear how we'd throw a show together, but

after rehearsal I was buoyant with imagined Sun Ra–isms: *The less you grasp for something, the more you'll come to grasp it. The less you think you know, the more you know.*

I was halfway home before I noticed I didn't have a headache.

SOUND CHECKS were normally just a quick test of the mikes. But Saturday afternoon, Sun Ra, wearing a huge Russian-style fur hat, launched another full-scale rehearsal. Now that he'd begun to get a sense of us, he said, he was matching the songs to our "vibrations."

Discontent began to percolate among the band. Sun Ra didn't notice, or didn't care. The check stretched beyond an hour. Then two.

The first to leave was Laura. She muttered something, maybe an excuse about homework, and stalked offstage. Jothan asked what the trouble was. Way too long, I told him.

"Two hours? That's nothing," he said. The Arkestra often practiced for *fifteen.* "Night or day," he added, "Sonny can call rehearsal. You just have to be there. Be ready."

Maybe that worked for the Arkestra, but not for Barbary Coast: minutes later, another defection, and soon a steady stream, until more than a third of the band had bolted. Now Sun Ra couldn't help but notice. He looked like a Santa Claus, tired from hauling gifts, who'd learned none of the children liked his toys.

Well, maybe not none. Matt and Pete had stuck around to rat-a-tat their vamp. Were they truly digging the style or just being charitable?

I found myself, for the first time, feeling bad for Sun Ra. The week here must have been as hard for him as it was for us—harder, maybe, since he was on our turf. I considered what

Don had said about Sun Ra seeing he had no place in the world around him. I'd often felt that way, too, in my family and also here on our beer-and-frat-boys campus. I'd assumed that fitting in required changing yourself. But Sun Ra said: Change the space around you.

I stayed for the whole sound check. I had started to like his music—or to like the notion that I could like it.

FOR GUEST-ARTIST concerts, we split the night in two: first set by the Coast and our guest, second by the guest and his own group. I wish I could remember the first set more sharply, but the shock of the second half has skewed my recollections, like wall-hung art rattled by an earthquake.

Feeling encased in a body cast of nerves: that I remember. Nerves for myself but also for the band, considering all the walk-outs during sound check. But once we took our places onstage, everyone found their manners. (Laura had even purchased a multicolored cap and donned it now with good sportsmanship.) If anything, we all behaved too well—Sun Ra included.

He strutted out in a gold lamé cape and bejeweled velvet hat—they looked nicked from a Renaissance Faire—and gave the crowd a Grand Panjandrum bow. But then, when he turned around and sat at the piano, he sent us an anxious-looking grin. At the time, I supposed he worried we'd make him look the fool, but now I wonder: Did he worry *he'd* make *us* look bad? He played the first tune timidly, and so we inched out after him onto the music's tightrope, everyone scared of knocking the others off.

It was Michael Ray who cut the tension. (Along with Marshall and Jothan, he was sitting in on our set.) On "Love in Outer Space," he pranced about the stage, crooning with evangelical or maybe self-mocking charm: "Sunrise! Love for the world to see. Sunrise in outer space. Love for every face!" When he soloed, he screeched a streak of higher and higher notes, pretending to tug one leg up on a long invisible string, as if his leg's rise controlled the music's.

Oh, right, I thought. The point is to have fun!

And we did, for the rest of the set, an aural tickle fight that drowned out the memory of rehearsals. After our last tune, Sun Ra seemed pleased. Or not displeased. Relieved?

I was too: I'd played well, I'd let myself enjoy it. We followed Don downstairs to our practice room, high-fiving.

I had buffed my trumpet and laid it in its case—antsy to claim a seat for the next set—when Michael Ray materialized at the door. After a brief consultation with Don, he beckoned to me and Matt and Pete.

Michael was now in costume—orange tunic, satin dunce cap studded with ruby sequins—transformed by his garments, like a priest. "Grab your horns," he said. "Sonny wants to see you."

No time to gauge the other students' reactions. (Envy, I'd guess, in equal measure with pity.) We scrambled upstairs, into Sun Ra's dressing room. Surrounding him were acolytes who tinkered with his outfit. Piles of composition paper spilled from old satchels. On the table: a battered Disney songbook.

He said nothing but somehow used his silence to convey that we were meant to join him for his set.

If I'd been taut with nerves before, now I was unstrung. On noodle legs, I stepped back onstage. The Arkestra's ranks had doubled with late-arriving veterans: June Tyson, vocalist and dancing violinist; John Gilmore, so inventive a tenor saxophonist that John Coltrane had asked *him* for lessons.

At last Sun Ra sashayed onstage. He raised his arms (but wait, I thought, what *music* are we playing?), then *whap!*—whipped his hand at the air, as if swatting an insect; the band, at the instant of the phantom insect's doom, pounded out a massive, motley chord. Without quite having known it, I was playing too. How had I chosen my note? No idea.

When Sun Ra hurled his hand again, we struck another chord. Every player had chosen a new note, no one had consulted, and yet the sound was ringingly coherent.

Sun Ra twirled, his arms and wrists as fluid as a showgirl's. *Pa!*—he flung his fingers, now like someone shooting craps—*pa! pa!*—with each fling, we forged a different chord. Even the notes that shouldn't have fit within each cluster did. Dissonance and harmony, consonance and clash: the sound kept swallowing its own tail.

I felt attached to the band, like one foot of a centipede: as it moved, so I must move; as I moved, so must it. The song—if that was what it was—tumbled toward a climax, Sun Ra's antic directions arriving ever faster, until *shh!* His arms shot down; the Arkestra cut to hush; the hall tremored with complicated silence.

I would have liked to bask in it, but Sun Ra now started banging something on the piano, and Jothan whispered, "Watch. Follow me." Sun Ra's intro wandered, appealingly arrhythmic. Then a frenzy as all the players rifled through their music. (Had they caught a signal I had missed?) Just in time, Jothan slapped a page onto the music stand we shared.

Soon the song evolved into a daisy chain of solos. Gilmore's tenor gushed, demonically divine. Next went Marshall Allen, hands on his sax like feral scrabbling mice.

I almost didn't notice Jothan jabbing at my arm. Crap. Had I missed another cue? I dared a glance at Sun Ra, whose eyebrows waggled minutely in my direction.

Jothan said, "It's *you.* It's your solo."

His smile brought to mind his statement yesterday: *You just have to be there. Be ready.* How often, attempting jazz, had I failed to do that? Terror trampled through me, but there was no time to fret: Sun Ra had shoved me off the ledge, and now I fell and fell and—

Whoa . . .

I floated!

A fresh feeling: pregnant with pure space. Nothing for me to do now but fill that space with sound. Instead of trying to live up to a music I'd heard before, I decided just to *play,* and found out that I could. I played, splendidly dazed, until I knew to stop. The song swept on. Now I swam within it.

The next tune was new to me: a cross between a Count Basie stomp and a *Sesame Street* rhyme. The band danced in a conga line, up into the crowd, singing the admonitory lyrics:

What do you do when you know that you know
that you know that you're wrong?
You've got to face the music!
You've got to listen to the Cosmos Song!

As we sang, Sun Ra chanted a descant from the piano: "You in the Space Age now . . . ain't no place you can run . . . you can't run away . . . Space Age is here to stay . . ."

The band paraded on, daffily proselytizing: *Face the music!*

At some point, Jothan told us students we were done. Back in the dressing room, we hugged and pumped our fists.

I was giddy with disbelief, with pride at my ad-libbed breakthrough. I grabbed a pencil, an unmarked sheet of composition paper. "I'm not sure I could say I've been to Saturn," I wrote. "But tonight, playing with you, came close. Thank you. Your music has changed my life."

I slipped the note into the middle of Sun Ra's Disney songbook.

I WAS EAGER to carry something of Sun Ra forward with me, but it was hard to keep hold of my bliss. The all-involving week with him had left me so behind—I hadn't touched the thesis I was writing—that I could focus only on catching up.

I was on a Senior Fellowship: a year free from courses, in order to pursue my own project. I'd applied in a tantrum of frustration, claiming to be sickened by the academic treadmill, but maybe, too—if I'd been honest—sickened by my talent for sprinting on it. I'd proposed to write a novel, promising a draft by year's end.

Writing a novel, it shocked me to learn, involved its own drudge work. In fact, as the year progressed, my thesis had come to seem like a classic office job. Every day, I sat at my desk and poked some words around: less like bolts of inspiration, more like nuts and bolts. Should this have been a disappointment? Was it?

For now, I had to knuckle down and grind out the novel's ending—a big task on a bigger list for my last months at school: print an issue of our queer newspaper; plan a radical alternative commencement; prepare for the Coast's Senior Show.

I was thinking only about that show—what song to choose— when I arrived at rehearsal a month later. But Don pulled me aside with Matt and Pete. Sun Ra's agent had called, he said. Something about a secret message, stuffed inside a book? The Arkestra was heading out on tour soon, to Europe, and Sonny wanted the three of us to join him.

"Oh, my gosh," said Matt.

Pete said, "That's insane!"

Dorkily, we danced around the room.

After we'd calmed down, Don divulged the hitch: the tour would take us away for the school year's last weeks, meaning we would miss exams and also all the end-of-college parties. Dartmouth students simply didn't do that.

"But we have to," I said. "Don't we have to?"

One last thing, said Don: the agent had mentioned a show in Boston. Could we play that gig first, a warm-up for the tour?

Yes, we said. Yes to it all. It was in our stars.

THE DAY OF the concert, I wore what passed for wild within my wardrobe: a faded purple button-down, a Guatemalan patchwork vest. Matt picked me up for the two-hour drive to Boston (where Pete, going separately, would meet us).

The ride to Boston was always a culture shock—speeding from our sheltered, rural campus to the city—but this time, it launched us toward an inconceivable distance. What new worlds would Sun Ra show us? Who would I end up being?

We headed to an address at Northeastern University. A group of students were waiting for a promised preshow workshop, but the Arkestra, they told us, was nowhere to be found. Uncertainly, we joined them in their vigil.

Evening fast approached; still, we waited. Could we have been roped in to a conceptual performance? Maybe to one-up John Cage and his infamous four minutes, thirty-three seconds of silence, Sun Ra had composed a piece for a band that never comes.

Half an hour before showtime, a bus pulled up and out straggled the bleary-looking Arkestra. Jothan saw us and shook our hands, as did Michael Ray, but Sun Ra scuffled by with an air of depthless blankness.

Matt and I tailed the band backstage. Had Sun Ra forgotten his invitation or, worse, had a change of heart? Panicking, I wondered if I'd done something (my purple shirt?) to prove I was unworthy. When Pete arrived, we didn't know what to tell him.

The show was already twenty minutes past curtain time

when we were ushered over to Sun Ra, who sat in a love seat, pasha-like, a heap of garments before him. June Tyson, the vocalist, picked out a robe for me. No, too short, said Sun Ra: "Can't be 'earth clothes' showing." Finally, he consented to a baggy saffron toga and a purple toque that made me look like one of the Seven Dwarves.

I felt silly, but Sun Ra's solemnness kept me from cracking up. In truth, I wanted *not* to laugh; I wanted to be transformed.

Sun Ra's aides helped him up, and we all followed him out into the lights. The hall was rife, I knew, with jazz cognoscenti: students from nearby Berklee College and the New England Conservatory, who'd mastered more music theory than I had ever heard of. But I was the one onstage. I tried to look convinced.

The show was a volcano: creating itself out of itself, all flow. A smash of drums, a piling-on of horns. Meanwhile, an oldish guy (Art Jenkins, I later learned) skulked around, acting out some cryptic melodrama. He "sang" in the spookiest, most sublime voice I'd ever heard, a goblin with a tracheostomy tube.

Sun Ra was simultaneously impish and imperious, bossing us with wiggles of his hands. He played behind his back, with his elbows, his knuckles—the man was having furious fun.

At last came a moment I'd hoped for and dreaded: Sun Ra gave me the scantest wink; I lifted my horn to solo. But Michael Ray elbowed me. "Not here. Go up *front*."

Alive with fear, my skin throbbing, I threaded my way forward and peered into the crowd: a black void. Could they see past my costume, inside, to the iffy impostor? Behind me, the drummers beat an ominous jungle soundtrack. I answered with some anxiously honest notes.

Soon I heard another horn, and spun to find Jothan, aiming his riffs at me like a lance. I aimed my own notes back, and we jousted. A spotlight hit us, or maybe I imagined that toasty glow. The crowd cheered—grading on a curve, was my first thought. But they didn't know I was just a student.

The rest of the show, I rode a stream of jittery amusement, juiced by the inch-close risk of failure. We played Sun Ra's undulating take on a Chopin prelude, a Wes Montgomery cover, cosmic jazz. Miraculously, I managed to keep pace.

A gust of applause ended the show, strong enough to blow us out into the Boston night. The Arkestra said to chum along, the party was only starting. The name of the place we ended up, Café Amalfi, rang with all the glamour of the world I now guessed I might be part of.

THE NEXT DAY'S *Boston Globe* had nothing about the show. The keenness of my letdown was dismaying.

But the following morning, there it was: "Sun Ra and his Arkestra play some imaginative originals and a few surprises."

I skimmed past the praise for Marshall Allen's flute work and zeroed in on a line I immediately learned by heart: "Aside from one sideman dancing with a black ventriloquist's dummy, the most surprising visual aspect was the presence of three Caucasians in what has heretofore been a resolutely nonwhite ensemble."

I loved the line's loftiness: confirmation that what we'd done might be as momentous as I hoped.

DON WOULD LATER say Sun Ra's visit changed his life. When Michael Ray formed an Arkestra offshoot, the Cosmic Krewe, he asked Don (who'd mostly been teaching, and not performing, for years) to play "jazz funk of the future" on trombone.

Adam, on whose bedroom floor the Arkestra had crashed, also joined the Cosmic Krewe and became a full-time pianist, including tours as a US State Department "Jazz Ambassador."

Matt, the trombone player, didn't pursue a jazz career, but Sun Ra's pull on him remains strong. He recently emailed from China, where he works in infotech but also still performs music, for fun: "Played a gig last night that had definite tones of Saturn."

As for me, I don't play Sun Ra's music anymore—not even in an amateur group or by myself at home. In fact, I haven't played my horn for more than thirty years. Its case, in my closet, gathers dust.

THREE WEEKS after our Boston gig, Don announced distressing news: Sun Ra had had a stroke. The tour was off.

And that, as it turned out, was that.

Life went on. I finished my thesis and my other tasks. I performed with the Coast one last time—the Senior Show—and I was back to being nothing more than what I truly was: a decent dabbler in a solid college band.

WITHOUT BARBARY COAST, my trumpet playing dwindled; it was hard to practice when I didn't know what for. Eventually I moved to Boston, where my neighbors, I told myself, would have made a stink about the racket. True, I could have found a group to join, rented a practice space. Hell, I simply could have used a mute. Maybe the trumpet was something I just outgrew.

But all these years it's irked me that I lost my drive to play the horn so soon after our near-miss with Sun Ra, that my brush with the big time led to . . . well, to quitting.

Led to. Why am I so tempted to draw a link?

The tour's cancellation certainly sapped our spirit, but for me it also brought relief. As much as I'd longed for adventure in the abstract, I'd feared how the actual trip might go: the foreignness of the places, the people. Easier just to stay at school, enjoying all the parties.

Maybe I already knew what would make a better story: the whopper that got away. It's a tale I've told and told again to scores of friends who didn't even know I played the trumpet. Especially now, in middle age, I love dropping Sun Ra's name. And yet the story rings a little false. I've billed it as a tale about coming *this close* to something, when really, I can see now, the lesson was how far away I always really was.

RECENTLY, through the uncanny magic of the web, I found a bootleg recording of the Boston show; in no time, MP3 files landed in my Dropbox. (Imagine Sun Ra's joy—his music beamed through space at the speed of light!)

For days, I couldn't bring myself to listen. What if I'd actually flubbed my solo? What if my playing ruined the performance? But when I finally summoned the guts, what I heard was maybe more disturbing.

There are licks that sound like mine, and then another horn: Jothan, I figured, coming downstage to joust. But no—the second horn sounds even more like mine. Did Jothan go first, and then I joined? All these years, have I had it backwards? I've listened a dozen times, and I can't tell. Maybe that seems a good thing: when it counted, my playing passed muster. But Jothan was a pro, a lifelong jazz master. Shouldn't I be able to tell his solo from my own? Shouldn't *any* listener hear the difference? The fact that I couldn't distinguish his licks from mine typifies why jazz couldn't have been the path for me.

Not that Sun Ra's music wasn't exacting. Often mislabeled

"free," his style required control: methodical open-mindedness, rigorous relaxation. And yet the music's power, like that of all true jazz, depended on heart-not-head abandon. Which is how an amateur, clad in a borrowed toga, could feature in a concert as notably as a seasoned band member.

It was my own unlikely success that bothered me the most: if I was going to succeed at something, I wanted it to demand skills that couldn't be pretended. As much as I might gripe about the grind of meritocracy, it turned out I couldn't thrive without it. Sun Ra had believed—and made me, too, believe—that he'd awoken a cosmic spirit within me, but maybe what he'd triggered was my same-old striving self: follower of directions, teacher's pet. Which meant I'd gotten his message exactly wrong. Conforming to someone else's style: that's what Sun Ra scorned.

But playing with him did help me nail down my own nature: I wanted to be spontaneous, but not *that* spontaneous; wanted a calling where ad-libbing didn't count for quite so much. Better for me the nuts-and-bolts march toward expertise. Jazz had been an outlet when my life was full of strictures and I liked to think of myself as offbeat; now that I was starting the open solo of adulthood, I had to face the truth of my own music.

Used-Car Salesman

ON THE PHONE, the possible buyer, despite his Spanish accent, had seemed not uncomfortable with English: Was the car still for sale? Could he come and see it? But now that he was standing here, scuffing his feet in my driveway, I sensed he understood almost nothing. Asked if my directions had been clear enough, he shrugged. The car's condition—just as I'd described? Another shrug. Mostly he just smiled with a Buddhist's calm detachment, as if from heights of enlightenment beyond my feeble reach. Odd, I thought, that he could grasp so little but seem so knowing.

Maybe the call had been an act, akin to how I've faked my way through cab rides in Paris, brandishing the few French phrases I've burnished smooth. Or maybe on the phone it had been a different man, a friend with better English, standing in.

He looked soiled but tidy, like an old-time factory hand: oil-stained shirt trimly tucked, black hair in a boyish cut but clotted at its ends, as if he'd shampooed with creosote. A grubbiness I envied—it seemed earned.

"What country are you from?" I asked.

He grinned. "Guatemala."

Normally, I might have said, "My dad's a Latin Americanist!" or bragged of having gone to Costa Rica; I might have tried to wow him with my Spanish. Three months out of college, I was a pro at small-talk-as-grandstanding. But something about his workman's looks, his halting comprehension, made me too self-conscious to show off. Plus, I'd botched a similar situation the week before and feared making a fool of myself again.

I asked his name.

"John."

"Juan?" I said.

"No, John."

I felt guilty that he might think he had to Anglicize himself. (I'd taken a sociology course called "Prejudice and Oppression.")

John got busy with the obscurely authoritative things men do in evaluating cars. He tickled something that popped the hood, then leaned into its maw, a lion tamer proving to the beast that he was boss. He sauntered around the body, brushing it with his fingertips, phrenologically reading its dents and bumps.

Exam concluded, he asked just one question: "How long it's yours?"

"Long enough?" I mustered a chummy laugh.

I wondered if he understood my joke or its evasion, but surely he knew a used-car salesman always fudged his story. In fact, I'd had the car for only three weeks. Also, it wasn't exactly mine.

I WASN'T in the habit of selling things I didn't own, but what had happened was this:

My boyfriend, Chris, and I, after graduation, had worked at a summer camp in Vermont. Days before camp ended, as we were readying to relocate to Northampton, Massachusetts, my old Ford pickup's transmission conked out. Coincidentally, the camp director—a stand-up guy named Dave—had just bought a showroom-fresh Subaru wagon but hadn't yet traded in his old one. "Take it," he said. "Use it till you get yourself set up, then sell it. Send me what you make."

I'd have wheels, and Dave would avoid the bother: win–win.

Chris and I arrived in Northampton without jobs or even much sense of the jobs we might like. I only knew I wanted to be a writer. I already had notes for a couple of what I considered winningly hard-nosed short stories, based on real-life situations: one about a woman who masturbates stallions at a stud farm, another about a man so fat the cops have to cut him out of his bedroom.

This was 1990, when "dirty realism" was the rage. I worried that my own life was too squeaky clean to ring with realness. What I'd have to do, I thought, was go out into the grungy world and borrow other people's hard truths. Wasn't that what my role models, Orwell and Steinbeck, had done? Orwell had scrubbed dishes in a Paris hotel's basement; Steinbeck had hit the road with Dust Bowl refugees.

It makes me want to laugh now, and also want to slug myself in the eye, that I imagined quaint Northampton might offer what I was seeking. Chris and I had chosen the town for its lefty atmosphere (two years later, in a notorious *National Enquirer* article, it would be nicknamed "Lesbianville, USA") and because two friends there needed housemates. The four of us went in together on a cute two-bedroom cottage. I liked our modest neighborhood: near the fire station and the Bluebonnet, a classic '50s diner. Our back fence abutted a Stop & Shop parking lot, from which the roar of delivery trucks sounded like a summons to adventure.

The morning after we settled in, I walked downtown to find a seedy restaurant to toil in. Orwell had taught me that restaurants teemed with sordid drama; waiters' hours would leave me mornings free to do "my" work.

First I tried a burger joint. The manager, with all the humor of an underfed guard dog, asked if I had any experience.

"I only just finished college," I told her.

"Huh," she said, and gave me an application.

I filled it out. Then, seeing all the blank space remaining, I added parenthetically, in the section for Education, "Double major in English and Religion."

I left and went down Main Street to a bunch of other spots—pizza place, hole-in-the-wall Chinese—thinking that the more I applied, the better would be my chances.

That week, as I waited, I tried to start my story about the stallion masturbator, but each morning my concentration was cracked by the sound of the phone not ringing. By ten o'clock, I would ditch my pallid paragraphs and walk to Stop & Shop for the newspaper. None of the Help Wanted positions seemed to fit. Warehouse watchman? Laundromat attendant? I was willing to put up with a certain degree of drudgery, but couldn't it be a bit more dramatic?

Afternoons, I'd sink into the borrowed beater Subaru and drive myself literally to distraction: the smear of passing scenery cleared my mind. Summer was holding on by a thread, the cornfields dark and ready, the sky so utterly sky blue it resembled nothing but itself.

Then one day, crossing the Connecticut River, the car made a pitiful creak that shot up through my feet. Or maybe I imagined the feeling: a twinge of premonition. I decided to list the car for sale right away, lest it meet its end on my watch.

At home, Chris was in the mudroom, about to walk to his new job as a prep cook at a music club. I asked if there were messages.

"Nope," he said.

"Not one?"

"Why don't you call *them*?" he said. "Squeaky wheel gets the grease."

I dialed the burger joint, mentally loading arrows into my quiver: *I'm a quick study. I'm good at math, so I could help with the books.*

The manager, hearing my voice, said, "Ah. The college boy."

"Now, look," I said, "I know my background's maybe not the usual. But if you're worried I'm overqualified, I can assure you that—"

Her laugh was so sharp it stung against my cheek. "*Over-qualified?* You think I'd ever hire someone with zero food-service experience?"

Before I could fire a comeback, she hung up.

And so it was Chris, later that night, at whom I aimed the thought that finally came: "If you can't get a waiting job without having *had* a waiting job, how does anyone ever start?"

"How do you think?" he said. "They lie."

TWO WEEKS LATER, and here I was, urging John to get behind the wheel. I climbed in on the passenger side, and watched him check the headlights, the hazards. Toggling switches but going nowhere, we could have been playing at adulthood. I had to stifle the urge to say, "Vroom!"

John pantomimed turning the ignition.

"Right," I said. "Want to hear how she runs?" *She.* Who was I fooling?

The engine had sat idle since the day it made that awful creak, but now, when John turned the key, it growled. I flashed him a thumbs-up.

He just grinned his knowing grin and said, "Okay? We go?"

"Go?" I asked. "Go where?"

He pointed to the street.

"Oh, like a test drive? Of course."

Before I could buckle my seat belt, John had slammed back out of the driveway.

Through our quiet neighborhood he squealed at madcap speed. "Whoa," I said—not sure if I meant to chide or cheer.

John paid no attention to me. He turned right, then right again, onto a bigger road.

"Got some good years left in her," I spieled, patting the dashboard. "Only been a country car, you know? In the mountains?" My hands fluttered, suggesting the shapes of peaks.

Now I saw that John was headed straight for the interstate on-ramp. "Big highway," I warned him. "You understand? Fast!"

Doggedly he nodded. "Yes. Fast!"

Up we zipped onto 91 and darted into traffic, gravity hurling my guts against my spine. John drove nimbly, switching lanes, overtaking semis. The speedometer tipped past seventy, seventy-five.

I wanted to say slow down, but the words caught in my throat. A language-challenged immigrant, a humble low-wage worker (or so his oil-stained clothes made me think): surely his life was filled with guys like me telling him "Don't."

Also, he might guess I feared the car would fall apart.

"Geez, you really . . . drive," I said. "Is driving part of your job?"

"Yes," he said. "My job." He gestured toward the road, as if our very speed was his vocation. Or maybe what he meant was that the car was *needed* for his job. Or to *get* to his job?

I didn't care. I cared about making the sale.

I was feeling pleased with myself for pulling this off so smoothly. All we'd have to do now was trace an equal distance home, then John would take the car away—its coming death *his* problem—and I could turn my energy back to writing and finding work.

THE WEEK BEFORE, I'd finally found a promising job listing. *Counselor for at-risk teens. Spanish-speaking ability preferred.* It sounded enticingly wrong-side-of-the-tracks.

The director, Mario, interviewed me in his office. "So," he said, "tell me why you can do this."

I cited some previous do-good work: a conservation corps for urban youth in San Francisco, a community group in Spanish Harlem.

"Glad you mentioned Spanish," he said. "You speak?"

"*Más o menos*. I worked in Costa Rica, on a ranch."

"Wow, an actual cowboy? Do tell!"

I'd herded cows, I told him, and helped to castrate calves. Slashed acres of brush with a machete. I lived with a farmer's family, sleeping head-to-toe in a narrow bed with one of his three sons.

With Mario rapt, I added a bit about the family's parrot, who, whenever we came back from another hard day's labor, would gaily insult us: "*Puta! Puta!*"

Mario beamed. The room seemed tilted in my direction. "How'd you ever get that chance?" he asked.

Why did his question catch me so off guard? Other times I'd told the story, I'd included its genesis. But now, angling for street cred, I didn't want to cop to certain details. "My dad was friends with the owner," I said, and winced at the spoiled-kid sound of that. "The owner, he was . . . well, he was the president."

"The *president*? Like, of the whole country?"

"The ex-president, but yeah."

On Fridays, I explained, he'd fly up from the capital, landing his private plane on a strip cut from a cane field. My boss would hand me off for a weekend of being pampered: sailing the Pacific coast, a butler serving shrimp in silver bowls. Then, Sunday evening, *el presidente* would leave. "The farmer picked me up and it was: wham, bam, back to the life of labor."

"Unbelievable!"

"Right?" I said.

"I'm just curious. What was this guy's name?"

That was when I'd botched everything.

ON 91, as John held the Subaru at its limit, I gazed at the bucolic landscape: silos and tobacco barns, magnified by cusp-of-autumn light. This was my first September since kindergarten with no school. I saw myself as a character in a well-constructed story, coming to the hinge between two chapters.

The exit approached. The world felt loose, weightless.

But John was still in the passing lane. "John," I called. "The exit!"

Too late. We flashed past it.

"This is really far enough," I said. "Don't you think?"

"Little more, okay?" he said. "My friend?"

I would not have said I was feeling like his friend, but what could we do but head for the next off-ramp? Gripping the armrest, I started to count mile markers.

Half a mile from the exit, I said, "You're getting off here, right?" My knee had started to jitter. My voice was jittery too. "John," I said. "You have to pull off. Now."

He rapped my knee playfully with his knuckles. "Okay. No problem."

To my relief, he did pull off, and joined a local highway, aiming the Subaru south, toward home. We passed a garden center that whiffed of mulchy rot, a farm stand with apples and ornamental corn, pyramids of cherubic early pumpkins. I'd been here on a previous drive, I thought.

Next: a muffler shop, seemingly long-shuttered; a roofless house, half its rafters charred. Neither seemed the least bit familiar. A twinge of dread, up through my feet, just like when I'd driven across the river—but now it wasn't the Subaru's death I pictured, it was my own.

"You sure of where you're going?" I asked.

John just said, "Is fine."

He turned onto an unmarked road, then, a minute later, onto a dirt lane darkened by looming maples. My thoughts began to whirl, but they only came to gridlock, the way a wheel can spin so fast it looks like it's not moving. Don't be crazy, I thought; there's nothing to worry about. Then I thought: thinking there's nothing to worry about—*that's* crazy.

Trying not to provoke, I asked, "This road heads to town?"

"Little more," he said. "Little more, okay? My friend?"

I tried to track landmarks—a picket fence, a flagpole—but everything seemed generically rural. No house numbers or street signs. No traffic. The car sped on, its odometer like a blood pressure monitor, marking my anxiety's upward tick.

Then, as the taste of panic trickled down my throat, John braked and pulled up to a trailer propped on concrete blocks. No one had tried to prettify the yard with plastic whirligigs or tire planters sprouting marigolds. The porch could've used a few planks.

"My friend," John said again. He looked at me insistently.

No, I thought. Still not your friend. Not just because you finally stopped driving.

The Subaru's engine, cooling, went *tsk, tsk.*

"My friend," he repeated, pointing to the trailer. He married his thumb and forefinger in the standard sign for money.

The fingers, more like rubbed-together sticks, lit a spark. I saw I'd been reading him all wrong! He wasn't trying to soothe me with this business about "friend" but only naming our destination: the home of his friend, right here.

"Oh, *your* friend!" I said. I showed him a hopeful smile.

Did John need to borrow money, in order to pay for the car? Maybe he was undocumented and barred from having a bank account. That must be it: he'd come to pick up cash.

I wanted not to think the worst of him. Wanted not to be a person who would. How could I write stories that mattered—weighty, real-world stuff—if I so distrusted a guy like John?

Gently, as if to a puppy, he said, "Stay."

Before I could say anything, he got out and walked up to the trailer.

I sat there, suspended in uncertainty. If only we could hash everything out in a common tongue, I was betting that John could justify his odd behavior. Should I try to speak to him in Spanish when he came back?

No, I couldn't. The thought made me queasy. Because of my fucked-up interview with Mario.

"What was this guy's name?" he'd asked about *el presidente,* after my account of Costa Rica, and I had stammered, "His name? His name was . . . um. His name . . ." A mystifying memory lapse. My skull felt as empty as a magician's hat after he's yanked the rabbit.

All I could conjure up was Chris's phrase: *They lie.* That's what people did, he'd claimed, in order to get their jobs.

I *hadn't* lied. Everything in my story of Costa Rica had really happened.

Still, I'd skipped over parts of the truth. I had failed to mention the shame I'd felt those Sunday evenings, coming back to the farmer's plain home. His sons would ask for details of the luxuries I'd tasted on *el presidente*'s butler-serviced boat, and I would dodge, saying I preferred their rice and beans, then joke about the parrot's potty mouth to change the subject. Later, in bed beside those sweaty, wrung-out boys, I'd wonder if they smelled the ocean's freedom on my skin.

Mario said, "You can't remember? Really?"

"Daniel," I managed to say. "I called him Don Daniel. His last name was—" Why could I not summon my patron's name? The man who'd been so generous a host. "—Ortega!" I blurted out. I sensed this was wrong but, in my panicked amnesia, doubled down. "Of course. That was it: Daniel Ortega."

Mario squinched his nose, clearly convinced he'd smelled a fraud. "Gimme a break. You said this all happened in Costa Rica? Ortega was the president of Nicaragua."

"Wait!" I cried, as finally the actual name came back to me, resolving my inexplicable mix-up. "What I meant to say was Oduber. His name was Oduber."

To Mario, surely, even the honest truth now sounded fishy. He told me to find my own way out.

WAITING in the Subaru, all these days later, I still felt sullied by my fraudulence. And it was this feeling, I realized—not our language barrier—that had kept me from standing up to John. The problem was, no matter the language, I would still be myself: someone whose brushes with hardship were really another form of privilege.

After ten minutes, John strolled back. He sat down in the driver's seat, gave me his hand to shake—a great big hand but graceful in its grip. "Is good now, we go home," he said. "Is finished, okay? Sorry."

The effortful apology made me sympathetic. My fear that he might harm me went to dust. We started back to town in cordial silence.

This time John drove calmly, and I, no longer choking the armrest, watched the roadside beauty. I let my mind turn to the coming negotiation: If he bargained hard, how firm should I remain? What was the lowest price I would take? I was inclined to go easy, to compensate for having pictured him as a murderer. I owed it to Dave, my ex-boss, to strike a decent deal, but there was still a way, I thought, as John sent me a friendly look, that all three of us could end up winners.

Faster than I expected we were back in Northampton: the Bluebonnet Diner, Stop & Shop. John eased the car into our driveway.

Before he'd even killed the engine, I leapt out to the solid ground of home. "Now you know how she runs," I said. "Ready to make an offer?"

I had started to make my way around to the driver's side— bubbly with entrepreneurial zeal—when the car shot back and out into the street. A shriek of smoking tires, and it was gone.

At first I stood there laughing, the car's disappearance as perfectly timed as a punch line. I waited for John to circle back and tell me he was kidding, to offer a wad of cash, call me "friend."

Soon my laughter petered out. Beyond our fence, grocery trucks droned.

THE REST of the day, I sat staring out the kitchen window, listening for the Subaru's return. Maybe I'd misunderstood John; I hung on to that hope. He couldn't *steal* the car, I thought— not in daylight, not from my own driveway. He knew I could call the cops and tell them what he looked like. What kind of fool would dare a heist like that?

Two hours passed, then four. Still no sign of John.

Yes, I could report him to the cops, but saying what? I

knew no last name to tell them, no phone number, no address. I guessed I could tell them about the trailer in the woods, but I hadn't seen who lived there. Could I even find it?

The facts, then: a stranger named John (really? had I believed that?) had taken exactly as much as I'd allowed.

WHEN CHRIS HEARD, he tried to help: Maybe the phone company could somehow trace John's call? But no, I was sure that wouldn't work.

Nothing to do but contact Dave, tell him I'd been robbed. Figure out a plan to pay him back.

"But hey," said Chris. "Now you have an amazing story to write."

I scowled. Should I really tell the world how I'd been duped?

After some days of brooding, though, I thought I could see how to make the facts gleam. John, the car, the trailer—their realness would be foolproof, but I would give myself the final word. I sat down at my desk to get to work.

And sat there. And sat there. Shrinking so far inside myself that everything went dark. Although I'd lived through its events, the story's meaning shied away. If John had always planned the theft, why detour to the trailer? If the theft had been spontaneous, what incited him? My image of him, distressingly, had already started to fizzle. The more I thought about him, the less I understood him, the less I could summon up his face; I'd flattened him into a cliché villain.

Worse yet—worse, at least, for my own self-regard—I also saw myself as a stock character: the sheltered little prince who tries to be a man of the people, but who, out in the real world, face-plants in the mud.

No matter how exactingly I tried to mold the plot, something about it ended up off-center. I wanted to find a hero, but this story didn't have one. It seemed at once too simple and too finally confounding, a parable with no lesson.

I CALLED DAVE and told him that the Subaru "had been stolen"—letting the passive voice hide my blame. I'd pay him back, I pledged, but I might need a while.

"Forget it," he said. "Wasn't worth much anyway."

"But Dave," I said, "you trusted me, and—"

"No big deal. Happy to have it gone."

I was relieved but also ashamed of having slipped the noose so easily.

Plus, this made writing the story even more confusing. That neither John nor I would suffer any consequence undermined our narrative's catharsis; now that we were both scot-free, where could the facts take me? I still thought of storytelling then as selling a bill of goods, instead of letting honesty prevail. If ever I wrote the tale, I thought, I would have to make it fiction, in order to find a harder-hitting, morally certain outcome. One of us should be made to come off better, and one of us worse—but which should be which, I couldn't say.

A WEEK AFTER my call to Dave, I finally got a job: dishwasher at the club where Chris cooked. I joked about following in Orwell's sudsy footsteps, but my work was nothing like the grind he described. The servers who brought me dirty dishes were sweet and playful, like the butch named "Julie *Wheeler* . . . you know, as in 'eighteen-.'" The hothead chef never took his anger out on me, but vented stress by merrily slinging empty plates out the back door.

The club's nightly music shows were intimate, intense: Richard Thompson, Béla Fleck and the Flecktones, Taj Mahal.

I couldn't see much through the dish-room door's porthole, but speakers had been mounted on the wall above the sink, so I could hear the action from onstage. Scrubbing pots, I'd stroke a Brillo pad to the music's beat, dancing on my anti-fatigue mat.

I was too embarrassed to admit it to my friends, who expected tales of sweat and toil, but I was having a pretty good time.

You Don't See the Other Person Looking Back

THEY SAY dogs resemble their owners, so I shouldn't have been shocked when Tommy's Seeing Eye dog humped my knee. But at least Oscar was easy to deter with a rawhide chew. His owner proved considerably more persistent.

Tommy was my roommate on the Rainbow Bear Valentine's cruise for blind gay men and friends, in February 2002. I had decided to share a room to save on the expense, and told the trip's planner, a blind gay travel agent, to pick my companion; he chose Tommy. When I called Tommy to say hello, we spoke about our hobbies, our hometowns (I was talking from Massachusetts, he from West Virginia). He was glad to hear my voice, he said, so that when we met onboard, he would recognize me. His voice herked and jerked with an Appalachian accent, inflected up on odd syllables. He asked if I liked to cook, what types of books I read, and then, just as nonchalantly, "Do you like massages?"

I answered with a lengthy *hmm*.

Tommy, showing no sign of sensing my apprehension, pushed the broom of small talk again: Was Boston getting much snow this winter?

For weeks, I didn't hear from him. Then, two days before our sail date, a message on my machine: "Mike, it's Tommy. I was wondering if you'd bring some cream for your skin, so I can massage you. And I like a rectal thermometer, if you could bring one along. I like the feel of one going up my ass, but that's entirely up to you. Anxious to see you on Sunday. Take care."

MONTHS EARLIER, when a friend had asked what I thought it would be like to be gay (as we both are) and blind, I hadn't factored in rectal thermometers. Never having considered the sex lives of the blind, I reacted at first, I'm sorry to say, with pity: attraction must be faint, I thought, without the sparkle of flirty looks and smiles. Soon, though, my pity mixed with a nervous envy: What if, with my "normal" vision, I was the one in the dark? This was the same sort of irrational sexual jealousy that I had often felt regarding women, whose orgasms, unlike men's procreative spurts, seemed more purely about pleasure for pleasure's sake. When blind people felt the burn of sexual desire—felt it without needing visual cues—was that desire deeper, more authentic?

And what about the blind *and gay* specifically? Tricky enough for sighted gay people, in the face of heterosexual norms, to recognize our same-gender attractions; how much more fraught must it be to go against those norms if you couldn't see what gender looked like? The more I thought about it, the more compelled I got, building up a fantasy of the blind and openly gay as sexual bravehearts: people who, despite their double disorientation, felt their cravings so clearly as to risk everything to fulfill them.

To validate my intuition, I searched the library for information on blindness and homosexuality, but I found not a single citation. I wrote to the editor of the journal *Sexuality and Disability*; in his sixteen years in the job, he had not received any submissions on the topic.

The most extensive discussion I could locate was a brief subsection of the 1933 text *The Blind in School and Society*. Writing about homosexuality among students at residential schools for the blind, the author deemed it "a problem of environmental causation . . . a perfectly natural, although unfortunate, result of the conditions under which the children live"—hardly aligning with my dream of dauntless sexual heroes. But the more I searched in vain, the more I took scarcity as indicative of magic.

I puzzled over my growing fixation. Why should blind folks' sex lives matter to me? My mother's father was blind, but he had died when I was a kid, before I really knew him; my own eyesight was fine. I had recently separated from my longtime boyfriend, or tried to—scared of moving on but also of falling back. How were you even supposed to know what you wanted? Were gay blind people sure of their wants? Mustn't they be? But how?

I came upon the website for BFLAG: Blind Friends of Lesbian, Gay, Bisexual, and Transgender People. The group, I learned, had been founded in 1996 and now, after six years, counted forty members. Then, on their listerv, an ad appeared for the Rainbow Bear Cruise: a sail along the Mexican Riviera. Right away, I knew I had to go. Maybe a week at sea with this group of blind gay men could help me glimpse some truths about desire.

IN SAN DIEGO, waiting in line to board Royal Caribbean's *Vision of the Seas*, I scanned the two thousand passengers for a group of visually impaired men. The crowd formed a catalogue of futile attempts at beautification: women with penciled eyebrows like appliquéd licorice, face after hypertanned face.

And yet, they all seemed happily coupled; I felt like the only one alone.

After boarding, I headed to Tommy's and my stateroom on Deck 4. I hadn't spoken with him since getting his phone message, but I had left a return message explaining that while I hoped we'd be friends, I was not looking for physical intimacy.

The *Vision* was still firmly moored, but I felt something like seasick as I walked in calling, "Tommy?" The cabin was hardly bigger than my galley kitchen in Boston. Tommy was not there, but his clothes crowded the tiny closet.

I unpacked my own clothes, then went out to walk the ship, telling myself I was searching for Tommy, but hardly looking. I lost myself in the warren of hallways, then hiked upstairs to the solarium, the Casino Royale, the pool.

I ended up at the Viking Crown Lounge, where a man sat at the bar, gulping a margarita, his Seeing Eye dog—adorned with a rainbow neckerchief—curled around his stool. I steeled myself, preparing to offer my most platonic handshake, then recalled Tommy saying his dog was a young golden retriever; this one was black, its muzzle gone to gray.

"So, this guy comes to read the meter," the dog's owner said to the man beside him. "And when I show him in, he goes, 'You blind people are amazing—all the things you can manage by yourselves!' I wanted to say, 'That's right. I can even *jerk off* by myself. Don't like to, but I can if I have to.'"

The man waggled his swizzle stick. Although seated, he radiated the pratfallish energy of a physical comedian. His skin was acne-scarred, his nose the bulbous knob seen in cartoons of Bill Clinton, but his brashness was sexily magnetic.

I introduced myself as part of the Rainbow Bear group. Turning toward my voice, the man offered his hand. His name was Howard, and his friend was Steve, a sighted Brit with

close-cropped hair and a snaggletoothed smile. They had met
last year on a Caribbean cruise and decided to be roomies on
this trip.

"And who," I asked, "is this old boy at your feet?"

"His name's Harvey," said Howard. He felt for the dog's
neckerchief. "Accessorizes wonderfully, don't you think?"

WAS HOWARD what I'd expected, after my months of research
about blind gay men? Research that had only redoubled my
hankering to project special powers onto them.

Blindness, I'd learned, has long been associated with sexual
deviance. In the Middle Ages, blinding was a common punishment for sexual transgressions, a not-so-subtle symbolic cas-
tration. The same held true in literature—think of Oedipus,
Tiresias, and even Peeping Tom—and also in superstition: masturbate too much and you'll go blind. And yet, as much as the
sightless have been shunned (blindness was often thought to
be contagious), they have also been revered. From Greece to
China to Ireland, the blind have been hailed as bards and seers,
mystics and soothsayers—individuals who, lacking sight, compensate with insight and/or foresight.

Compare this with gay people's position: denigrated, accused
of spreading scourge, but also not infrequently esteemed. In
some Native American traditions, gay and two-spirit members
have been honored as shamans. And in even the most repres-
sive cultures, queer people have been disproportionately lauded
for their creative (if not procreative) talents: as court jesters,
artists, and musicians.

So maybe I'd been on to something, looking to the blind
and gay for guidance. Doubly marginalized, might they also be
doubly visionary?

APPROACHING our dinner table in the Aquarius Room, I came upon a man being tugged by a tawny dog, bobbling behind the animal as though it were a child and he the child's wind-tossed kite. His neck was thicker than his mostly bald head.

"Tommy?" I guessed, as he nearly bumped a waiter bracing a tray of eight salads.

"Mike?" he said. "How'd you recognize me?"

He appeared as off-kilter as his phone message had sounded. "It was Oscar," I fudged. "He looks just the way you described him!"

The rest of our group was already at the table. I sat next to Bill, a natty lawyer with more than a passing resemblance to E. Lynn Harris, the novelist whose new potboiler, he told me, he'd been listening to. Next to Bill sat Robert, the trip's organizer, a large man (his Yahoo profile mentioned a fifty-four-inch waist) with a whispery voice and glaucomatous eyes. Robert's sighted partner, Tim—partner in both their travel agency and their eight-year relationship—was heavyset but, in Robert's lee, looked tiny.

Carl was next, his Mississippi drawl and his corrective glasses both as thick as any I'd ever encountered. Then catlike Doug, whose buzz cut flashed with silver, as did his opaque, squinted eyes. And finally Steven, Doug's sighted boyfriend, a Texan with a wry, friendly smile. (Howard and Steve, whom I'd met earlier, were seated at the next table over.)

I struggled to keep track of everyone; the blind men, going by voice, suffered no such problem. They called to one another across the table while simultaneously running their fingers along the Braille menus, reading about "tagliatelle gifted with portobello mushrooms." Our waiter, oblivious to their multitasking prowess, appeared to panic when he noticed their blindness. As if the blind men were infants or invisible, he addressed only us sighted guests. I wanted to feel outraged, but in truth the waiter's gaze, directed squarely at me, helped ease my own anxiety.

Tommy's weirdness had left me watchful; I kept waiting for someone to propose a group massage. But the meal proceeded as meals do: Doug and Steven swapped bites of food; Carl rated the coffee; Bill, citing his figure, skipped dessert.

A *Vision of the Seas* crew member, in eye-patched buccaneer regalia, came from nowhere and pressed a plastic cutlass to Robert's neck. "Argh, matey!" he growled, while a colleague snapped photos. Robert, unable to see the farce, flailed in self-defense, but the pirate had already skipped ahead. "Argh," he repeated, assaulting each next unsuspecting victim.

DINNER went past ten; I was pooped. While Tommy brought Oscar to the custom-built "mulchboxes" on Deck 5 to relieve himself, I retreated to our room. I stripped to my underwear and climbed into the bunk near the door, which we'd agreed would be mine. With the lights off, our windowless cabin fell to a darkness I'd experienced only once before, on a tour of Alcatraz, in solitary. Lulled by the ship's rocking, I dropped asleep.

It felt like weeks later when the hands awakened me. Through the blanket, they touched my ankle bone, then my shin.

"This is *my* bunk," I blurted. "Yours is farther."

Louder and louder breathing, then, as Tommy (I sensed) knelt and shuffled closer. His hands reached my face. I grabbed hold of his arms.

He said, "I just want to see what you look like."

Get away! I wanted to shout. But would Tommy think me scared of his blindness? Was I?

Keeping hold of his wrists, I let him rove. "Sorry—I haven't shaved in a couple of days," I said, then wondered why I was apologizing.

He handled my features like a sculptor with clay, as if he weren't appraising my face but shaping it. He lingered at my outsized nose, the feature most people find unsightly but that for some seems to be a fetish. It was what had smitten Scott, the boyfriend from whom I was ambivalently separated, and I could never forget my shock when he and I were first alone, and he had sucked it all into his mouth.

I wondered if Tommy, too, had a nose fetish. If so, how else but with his groping could he have rated me? I'd read about the challenges of sex ed for blind people, whose learning often relied on tactile exploration. In the 1970s, blind-rights activists had advocated sex-ed classes with live nude models, and in Scandinavia such courses had been tried. Elsewhere, though, the plans were squelched, for fear that the participants would derive sexual thrills.

Thrills? I was clammy with discomfort. How much farther did I have to let Tommy explore, in order to assuage my guilty conscience?

Just as I approached my breaking point, Tommy quit. He undressed, climbed into his bunk, and started snoring.

Tommy's snores or no, I couldn't have slept. I was mad at him for using his blindness to take advantage of me, mad at myself for assuming that was the case, and madder still not to know the truth.

The cabin was so dark, I couldn't even see my own hands. I lay there, my pulse subsiding, and thought about things unseen but alluring. A book editor had called me once, wondering if I'd heard of a writer named Vestal McIntyre. I hadn't, but instantly I was certain we'd hit it off. *Vestal McIntyre!* I could only explain it as love at first name. I found his number and asked him out. The sex was even better than I'd imagined.

Handwriting had given me hard-ons: not the look but the feel, the stippled loops and slashes on the backside of anything penned by Scott, who wrote just as forcefully as he loved. Smells too: like vetiver, the smoky scent Scott dabbed on his neck. But these things aroused me because they made me think of him, and I already knew how hot he looked.

What if I'd never seen Scott? What if I'd never seen anything?

DOUG HAD BEEN born three months premature and kept in an incubator, where overexposure to oxygen caused a condition known as retinopathy of prematurity and left him fully blind. I spoke with him on day two of the cruise, at a retirement party for Robert's guide dog, Zeppelin—a poolside affair, replete with a frosted rum cake and testimonials ("Zeppelin knocked me back, away from the car, and saved my life!").

At dinner the night before, Doug had struck me as shy but fiercely curious, the curiosity apparent not in his misdirected eyes but in the alertness of his posture, his head's tilt toward unfamiliar voices. Now, when I took the initiative, he seemed eager to tell me about his life. For years, he had been a professional computer geek, but recently he'd been licensed as a massage therapist. I flinched, feeling the ghosts of Tommy's snooping hands, but Doug added, "It's tricky. You say 'massage' and people assume it's sexual." His practice, he promised, was legit.

Doug was thrilled just to be sitting among a group of blind gay men. Until a few years ago he hadn't known of any others, despite having been involved with gay culture since the early 1970s, when, as a high-school senior, he had first gone to a gay bar.

Later, I asked Doug how—with no visual sense of gender,

and knowing boys were meant to like girls—he had realized he might be gay.

"There was never really a question in my mind," he said. "There was always something more appealing when you said 'boy' versus 'girl.' Boys smelled better."

"Like what?" I asked.

He thought a second. "Like outside: grass and dirt and sweat."

And boys, it seemed, were readily available. Throughout his early teens, Doug had enjoyed frequent trysts with boys, in which his blindness was "not in the least" an issue. "In the bathrooms at school," he said, "we checked each other out"—which, for him, meant sizing up the others, literally, with his hands.

In college, at Texas Tech in 1972, Doug had overheard some rednecks talking about how "the faggots are going to be out in full force tomorrow," and, after calling the student center anonymously to gather information, he found himself at the very first meeting of a gay campus group. "I had to work really hard to become part of that group," he told me. "I think it was mostly the blindness. People were a little standoffish."

In the years since, Doug had encountered this unease about blindness throughout the gay world, which, in his view, was overly focused on questions like "Does my butt look good in these shorts?" Nonetheless, he had been involved in a number of relationships, all with sighted men. I asked about his current boyfriend, Steven.

"I know that most of y'all pick people by the way they look," he told me. "And I know that's how I *don't* operate. I couldn't tell you what sort of jawline Steven has, or what sort of nose. I mean, I could tell in comparison to myself—his nose is a bit longer and more squared off. He's told me that his hair is sort of red-blond, but that doesn't really mean anything to me."

If he could, would he want to see Steven?

"Selfish as this sounds," Doug said, "if I could see for just ten minutes, I would want to see what *I* look like. I could be hideous or I could be okay, but I don't know. And there are *things* I'd like to see. The house I used to live in. My cat. I would like to see a giraffe, because the concept is just so bizarre. As far as how people look, it may be kind of important, but not terribly."

"CAN YOU get a photo of me blowing?" Bill asked. "I know it's *personal*, but . . ."

We were in Cabo San Lucas, our first port of call, at a mom-and-pop glassblowing factory. The owner had offered to let Bill try his hand at the craft, sparking one-liners about long hot rods. Now Bill drew a deep breath and huffed with all his might; the molten blob at the end of his rod globed.

"Ooh, me too," said Howard. "If it's an oral thing, put me next!"

I'd woken that morning groggy—after another fitful night, nervous about Tommy—but now I was having a ball. The guys were cracking me up, especially Howard, with his raunchy, perfectly timed wit.

Howard had also been masterful at guiding my guidance of him. At first I'd called out every obstacle (*Steps coming up, six of them, okay, you're almost there . . .*), but Howard had said, "Just let me hold your elbow! I'll feel everything, and you won't need to say a thing." Instantly our balance of power improved: Howard was the craftsman; I was just the tool.

At our next stop, a stucco church in San José del Cabo, I described everything to Howard: the plain but beautiful wood-work; the Mexicans, heads bowed in prayer; the altar statues of Jesus Christ and Mary.

"What colors are they?" he asked.

Mary was blue, I told him, and Jesus was pure white.

He sucked his teeth. "If Jesus was with *twelve* men, should he really be wearing white?"

I led him and Carl to the confessional, thinking they'd appreciate the feel of its latticework. I described the thronelike seat for priests, the bench for penitents.

Howard dropped to his knees and ran his hands on the wood. "Are there glory holes? Bless me Father, I've sinned *a whole lot.*"

"Yeah, Howard," said Carl, "that's why you're blind!"

IN FACT, Howard was blind from retinitis pigmentosa. As a first-grader, he'd had 20/200 vision: legally blind but still able to see the blackboard from the front row, if the teacher used special thumb-thick chalk. By the end of high school, he couldn't read even large-print books up close, and now, at forty-six, he retained only the barest light perception.

Howard's early sexual stirrings had been similar to those of most gay men. "You knew the boys in your class that you just wanted to be in the proximity of," he told me. "It wasn't even a sexual thought. But there was an attraction. You liked the way they talked." In 1970, after he transferred from a public junior high to the Western Pennsylvania School for the Blind—where dorms were gender-segregated—he had sex with a number of his classmates. By eleventh grade, everybody at the school knew he was gay.

At that point, Howard had felt driven to join the larger gay world. "I would walk past the Holiday Bar in Pittsburgh," he said, "which I knew was a gay bar. I used a cane to travel in those days. I had to learn which side of the street [the bar] was on. I had to ask a stranger"—scary, he admitted, but his yearning trumped his fear. Too young to drink legally, he never went inside; he simply wanted "to be near."

After graduating, Howard moved to Harrisburg and became a barfly at the city's gay clubs. This had been fun and, more important, a strategy to attract sexual attention. "People would say, 'I know this blind guy in Harrisburg . . .' *Everybody* in those bars knew Howard. They also knew he was a sleaze. And he still is!"

I asked if he'd worried about people judging him: *Poor guy's blind, of course he takes all comers.*

"I've heard that," Howard said. "But if I was sighted and engaged in the same behaviors, it wouldn't be because I need to take anything I can get. They would just say I was a slut."

He had eventually fallen in love and spent fifteen years with a sighted partner. They had split up four years ago, partly due to the difficulties of maintaining a "mixed marriage."

Howard had worked in social services for almost two decades—most recently as the founder of a computer resource center for the blind—but his passion was the gay community. For years he'd run the gay-and-lesbian switchboard in Harrisburg and had been involved in "every gay organization" in the city. If he weren't blind, he would be "a sighted *gay* person," he told me, meaning that his sexuality would be his prime identity. "Never wanted to be anything but gay."

AFTER THE CHURCH, our group split up: some hunted for tacos; the half-dozen rest of us looked for the Rainbow Bar & Grille, a gay club that Howard had found online.

Our local guide, Doris, declined to accompany us but pointed to the address, a block away. We trooped over, a traffic-blocking column of men and service animals, but we could see no club, only a hotel. We about-faced and retraced our steps. Still nothing.

The group reversed once more, now attracting attention. I jogged into the hotel lobby and asked in Spanish for the Rainbow Bar & Grille.

The clerk glanced outside to the blind men and their dogs. "You sure?" he asked in English, clearly thinking I'd gotten my Spanish wrong. "The Rainbow . . . that's a *gay* bar."

Yes, I said. That was what we wanted.

The bar, it turned out, was in the next building, its door marked only by a tiny notice of its hours of operation, which, unfortunately, did not include now. (What a scene we would have made, barging in to such a hush-hush spot!)

As we trudged off, disappointed, I mulled over the clerk's surprise that a group of blind men might be gay. I could have mounted a high horse with which to tromp his bigotry, but the truth was that the men in our group barely pinged my own gaydar. Sure, Doug's ears were pierced, and Howard's dog wore his rainbow neckerchief, but when Doug had asked me, "Do we blind guys 'read' as gay?" I had told him I didn't really think so.

Gaydar has always been at best a slippery concept, dependent on cultural context. (A classic conundrum for queer Americans abroad: "Is he gay or is he just European?") And yet, although signals of sexuality do get scrambled—especially nowadays, as identities grow more fluid—gay folks still have ineffable ways to recognize each other. On one level, it's all in the eyes, the glance that balances daring with trepidation. Blind men can't send or receive such signals.

There's something else too: call it "self-consciousness." Growing up with the dread of being unmasked, and thus a paranoia about being scrutinized, many queer people become overly conscious of their appearance. This manifests in various ways: mannered, theatrical gestures and gaits; overly groomed hair, skin, and clothes. The blind gay men I met, although of course they knew they could be watched, never actually saw themselves being seen, and seemed less prone to such self-consciousness. My sample size was tiny, but none of the men were stylized in the ways that usually triggered my gaydar.

But if these men didn't "look" or "act" gay, did that reflect essential differences, or did it say more about the constructed nature of gay culture? Many components of the prevalent gay "lifestyle," in 2002, were inaccessible to the blind: noisy gay bars were tricky to navigate; gay novels and newspapers were rarely available in Braille or audio, and most gay websites were incompatible with screen-reading software; even porn movies, which for legions of gay men had served as sexual primers, were largely useless (try just listening to the dialogue). If much of "gay style" was a marketing contrivance or the result of aped behavior, these men were less likely to feel its influence. As Doug told me, "I could never pick up a *GQ* or an *Advocate* and look at pictures and tell what people are wearing." In terms of stereotypically gay gestures, he added, "If you haven't seen it, how would you know how to do it?"

But Doug had had an early experience that suggested a more intrinsic source of gay identification. When he was a boy, not yet in his teens, he had accompanied his mother to a Dallas shopping mall. As they sat sipping sodas, Doug had been riveted by the voices of two men at the next table. "I was fascinated by the way they sounded," he said. "I don't know that I knew why. I just knew that they sounded interesting. And when they left, Mom was like, 'Those two men were fairies.'"

DORIS HAD SAID we'd need to hire cabs back to the dock,

but Bill suggested we walk. "How far can it be?" He marched ahead with his dog.

The marina was clogged with pushy touts and peddlers of souvenirs, but Bill pretended not to notice—a perk of being blind, he gloated. Typical of him to emphasize the benefits of blindness. A lawyer specializing in Americans with Disabilities Act litigation, he was well aware of the hurdles faced by blind people, but also aware that those hurdles were often societal, not inherent.

As we strolled the waterside, Bill told me his story. He hadn't fully lost his vision until he was twenty-one, by which point he'd already come out as gay, so he'd experienced some visual flirting and cruising. "I'm really glad I had that," he acknowledged. Still, he was adamant that his blindness had not limited his sex life. He'd had two significant relationships, one for five years and one for seven. Neither boyfriend had been blind, but Bill said he was "not exclusively into sighted guys, that's just the way it's happened." And although he'd be happy someday to find another partner, he would always guard his independence. "I would *never* live with someone I was involved with," he said. "No way."

Bill had relished training his boyfriends to be more aware of nonvisual sensory input. The notion that sight was necessary for attraction, he said, was laughable.

What about sex itself, I asked: Was the act different when you couldn't see?

Bill bristled. "If anything, being blind is an advantage. If you're prone to feeling uncomfortable, it helps, because you don't see the other person looking back."

His implication—that sometimes the best things are not seen but felt—reminded me of what had happened at the glass factory, after Bill had tried his hand at blowing. Doris had arrayed glassware samples on a table, which Bill and the other guys inspected with their fingers, palpating every ridge and curve: beer steins, margarita glasses, a blowfish-shaped candy jar. Everyone's favorite was a tequila shot glass featuring matching dimples on either side: a built-in grip for thumb and index finger.

The shot glass was passed from hand to hand. "It just *feels* right, doesn't it?" Bill said. He dispatched Doris to fetch a dozen for him to buy.

She returned empty-handed. "Hate to tell you, but that glass? It was defective. Wasn't supposed to have those indentations."

Bill, who'd had his heart set, groaned. Defective was in the eye of the beholder. Or in his hand.

"DOWN, BOY. Down!"

I kicked Oscar's rawhide chew toy across our room, fending off his humping while I struggled with my tie. Tommy and I were dressing for the captain's formal dinner.

Tommy stood before the vanity, dabbing CK 1 onto his wrists. Naked but for his forty-inch-waist Calvin Klein briefs. "Mike," he asked, "are you a skinny guy?"

My tie came out wrong, wide end shorter than the thin. "Oh, I don't know," I said. What should I have told him? My waist was eight inches smaller than his, but in my gay circles, I was considered average-bodied, maybe a little flabby.

Tommy pulled on his slacks and an Oxford-cloth shirt. "It's just in my stomach where I put on weight," he said. "I know I don't look near my age—I look much younger." The man he'd been seeing for almost a decade had told him this.

Tommy's chin sagged; his hair had ebbed to nothing but a horseshoe. To me, he looked every one of his forty-five years.

I frowned at my own hair loss in the lighted mirror: At

thirty-two, was I aging badly? If Scott and I stayed broken up, would anyone else want me?

I had bungled my tie again; I tried a third time.

As Tommy worked on his own tie, he asked, "Are you a hairy guy?"

"More than some, I guess. Less than others."

"Wow, Mike, you sure are evasive!" He knotted his tie perfectly in one go.

I *was* being evasive. Why shouldn't I tell him what any sighted passerby could gauge at just a glance? I'd divulged more intimate facts to strangers I'd met in bars. In that context, doing so was implicitly seductive; the last thing I wanted was to lead Tommy on. Still, dodging his questions felt crummy; this time, I was the one exploiting his blindness. Maybe I also wanted to punish him.

"Would you look at that!" he said, apparently dropping the issue. "Six o'clock and it's still light out!" He retained some light perception, he'd told me.

"You're in front of a vanity," I said. "Our room has no windows."

GAY MEN are often dinged for being obsessed with superficial beauty, and, like most stereotypes, this one holds some truth. Mainstream gay culture—constructed mostly by media and porn—can be a skin-deep body cult. How do blind men fit into such a world?

Some people's blindness is not outwardly evident; others have conditions—cataracts, glaucoma—that make them "look" conventionally blind. Either way, blindness challenges the body-perfect ideal that many gay men furiously strive for. If sighted gay men's identities depend to some degree on being *looked at,* blind gay men's mere presence can be unsettling.

But blind gay men, judging by those I met, are not immune from worries about their looks. Bill was a regular treadmill user, and more than once I heard Doug, lamenting recently added pounds, recommitting himself to the NordicTrack. Aside from Robert, who identified as a bear (a term for hefty, hairy gay men), all my cruisemates seemed to feel they'd fallen short of a body-image ideal.

Weight gain can be a special concern for the blind, often stemming from restricted mobility. Another factor may be their desexualization by the sighted. Many blind folks rely on others to help with their appearance—to check their clothes for stains, for example—but because the sighted might not consider blind people as sexual, they neglect to offer beauty advice. "That's why there tend to be a lot of overweight blind people," Doug told me. "Nobody says to them, 'Maybe that's not the way you want to be.'" When I asked Doug about his own self-perception, he said, "I know other people have much better bodies. But people don't scream and run away from me, so that's a good sign."

THERE ARE gay realms in which other attributes count for more than body-fat percentage or 20/20 vision—for example, the hookup site that Howard was devoted to. (It took two special software packages for him to use the site, but he considered it well worth the trouble.) His profile was up-front about his blindness, but when he chatted with horny men looking to hook up, he touted himself as "46 years old, 5'10", 195 pounds," and, using gay shorthand for his manhood's mammoth size and circumcision status, "9.5 cut."

"I'm going to use that asset to my advantage," he told me, "because I'm trying to level the playing field. They don't care then if you're blind."

Howard himself, scrolling the site, vetted men as superficially as anyone else cruising for zipless sex; he couldn't see profile pics, but he could type questions. "The first thing I want to know," he said, "is height, weight, if there's any facial hair. Then I go to 'Are you smooth or hairy?' To feel sexually aroused by that person, the smoothness is such an issue."

What about the men he met in person—say, in a bar? Would he ask those same questions out loud?

We'd been sitting across from each other in my cabin—I on my bunk, Howard on Tommy's—but now he came and settled next to me. "My little ploy would be that I would sit down," he said. "I've finally got a barstool. And I go, 'Boy, beautiful day out there today!' And if the person doesn't just say 'Yeah'—if I get a sentence or two—now I realize this person's comfortable talking to me. Plus, now I know there's not an empty chair beside me." He laughed.

"And if you're continuing to talk to me, then it allows me to go"—Howard patted my thigh—"'That's *exactly* it,' or 'I can't believe that, that's *awful*!' I'm gauging your body language. When a person tenses, I'm reading that. I'm trying to get a sense of the person."

What sense was he getting of me right now? Was this simulation itself a ploy? (Earlier, he'd mentioned that he found my voice "intriguing.")

He went on, "I may well say, 'You're really tall, aren't you? Because your voice is coming from way up here. You about six-two?' Then I'm going to make a point like this"—he gripped my shoulder, twice as hard as he'd felt my leg. "Now I've got stature. I've also got how he carries himself: 'Oh, he's a barfly, he's hunched over, he's in here *every day*.' That just told me a lot.

"Now they're going to say, 'It's okay if you want to feel my face and see what I look like.' I don't! I mean, *oh yes*, I want to touch their face. But when people say that line? That's like squeaking a Styrofoam cooler. I don't know where *that* ever got started."

Maybe, I thought, I should ask him to bring this up with Tommy.

"But under *my* initiative," Howard continued, "I'm going to find out, so my next move is probably going to be this"— he touched the side of my face. "Okay, now I know he wears glasses. Then I'll find out if he has a mustache. I'm not going to ask how hairy his chest is, but somehow I would find out from this"—he grabbed the back of my neck—"that he's smooth.

"I'm not the one to put the pressure here"—he pressed his leg to mine—"and hold it there to find out if he moves *his* leg over. I don't do that. If we're talking and we're both starting to get touchy-feely, okay, then it becomes just as physical as anybody else, but that's *after* you've already gotten all that positive feedback that the person doesn't mind your attention."

I realized, to my surprise, I didn't mind Howard's machinations. His scheming was so unabashed as to seem almost guileless. (Whereas Tommy's purported naïveté was only creepy.) Howard, with his stratagems, was marvelous and poignant, a spider tuned to his web's slightest pulse.

His hand, once again, rested on my thigh. I laid my hand on top of his and squeezed.

IN HIS MEMOIR *Touching the Rock: An Experience of Blindness,* John M. Hull writes that for the sighted, desire and vision are so closely connected that "it becomes difficult to distinguish between 'I feel hungry' and 'I want to eat that food which I see there.'" When blindness disrupts this connection, Hull says—referring to hungers both physical and sexual—desire can become merely "the restlessness of an unformed longing."

But just as the sight of food is not a prerequisite for hunger, the sight of a sexual partner is not a prerequisite for arousal. I wondered how my new blind friends fantasized. Were their longings, as Hull says, "unformed"?

When I asked Howard what he thought about when he jerked off, he said he most commonly relived the stages of meeting someone, "like seeing the comic strip beginning to end. It isn't visual. I'm not seeing their facial expression. I'm not seeing the color of their hair. But I'm seeing *position*."

Doug, having been born blind, did not fantasize visually, he told me. Sometimes he thought in terms of touch ("those thin, young body types, smooth"), but mostly it was "scenarios. Lots and lots of scenarios. People with accents. Going to a country where I don't know the language and meeting somebody and trying to see if we could make a rendezvous happen without words." I was struck by the speed of his shift from palpable sensations to a dream of freedom from the limits imposed by blindness. But aren't most fantasies a blend of what's reachable and what's not? Isn't that precisely what makes them potent?

In Mazatlán, our second port of call, I stopped to watch a swan-diving daredevil. The young macho scaled a crag—fifty feet to the top—then crossed himself and spread his arms and leapt, a soaring bird. I gasped, then gasped again when the boy emerged from the water.

"Tell me what he looks like," Doug whispered.

"Teensy waist, teensy Champion gym shorts," I began, straining like a sportscaster to keep pace with the action. "The shorts are so clingy, you can see *everything*. Brown skin, and dark brown hair—oh, the way it rippled when he was soaring!"

"Thank you," said Doug. "God, that was great! For that, I think I owe you a margarita."

"Nah, my pleasure," I said—but then I stopped to think about Doug's pleasure. What had my description meant to a man who'd never beheld *brown,* who couldn't hold *soaring* in his hands?

"HOW'S IT rooming with Tommy?" he asked on a later evening, when he and Steven invited me to their stateroom.

"Fine, I guess?" I hadn't told anyone about the groping or the proposed rectal thermometer.

"You don't think he's kind of strange?" said Steven.

"Well, he is a little, uh . . ."

Doug told me then of a phone service that some of the men subscribed to, through which they exchanged recorded messages. When Tommy had joined the network, said Doug, he had seemed to have no sense of limits. "You'd come home and there would be a dozen messages from Tommy. He wouldn't wait for you to return the first before leaving another. And each one got more and more explicit. I mean, I'm not easily shocked, but hearing those things from someone I'd never met? I couldn't believe it."

"I almost wonder if he's got developmental disabilities," said Steven.

It felt immensely satisfying to have my own misgivings validated. I confessed to knowing something of Tommy's message-leaving.

"Geez, why didn't you say anything?" asked Doug.

"Didn't want to embarrass him," I said, which was true. "And if we were rooming together, I didn't want to make things *more* uncomfortable." Also true.

What I failed to add—the realization clenched my throat with shame—was that I'd excused his antics because on some level I must have *expected* a blind gay man to be perverted.

THAT NIGHT, I couldn't sleep. My doubts about me and Scott clamored in my mind, but there was also the noise of Oscar, panting below my bunk, liable to molest at any moment. Worse, Tommy's snoring. I stuffed earplugs into my ears, buried my head in pillows.

"Tommy," I called. "You're snoring."

No response.

"Tommy!" I clapped my hands. "Please! You're driving me insane."

At the last word, Tommy stirred, and I realized my error: now awake, he would start the scratching.

When I had first heard the scratching, a few nights before, I had assumed it came from Oscar. But then, in the morning, when I turned on the light, I had seen that the culprit was Tommy. Since then, he'd scratched himself constantly in our room. He lay in his bunk, sometimes in his briefs, sometimes naked, his hand on his belly or just lower. Scratch scratch. Pause. Scratch scratch. As though he were trying to rescue someone buried alive inside him.

Crabs, I had guessed. Scabies?

Sure enough, now that I'd roused him: Scratch scratch. Pause. Scratch scratch.

He had persisted lately in making his advances: pawing at my leg under the dinner table, and saying, just that morning, as we were getting dressed, "Mike, I'd really like the chance to see what *all* of you looks like."

Thinking now of what Steven had said, I suspected that Tommy's clawing might be less physical than existential.

It was well past midnight. I hissed, "Shh!" There was no more scratching.

IN PUERTO VALLARTA, we finally collided with gay

culture—literally. At the Blue Chair Resort, a gay beach, our gang galumphed across the sand, stumbling into clusters of bikini-waxed men. Attendants, fearing more collisions, arranged our chairs at the property's edge. Even so, some nearby sighted patrons moved away.

The blind guys were spared the sight of strangers turning their backs. Unaware, they settled in and ordered frozen drinks, propped umbrellas to shade their loyal dogs.

Everyone seemed to have a fine time. Howard and Carl frolicked in the water, then wandered among the klatches of tattooed musclemen, trying to find their way back to our group. If you didn't know they were blind, you'd have thought they were browsing the hustlers.

Later, Carl led Tommy to the surf's edge, and Tommy asked me to hold his sunglasses. He waded into the water, radiant in his flower-patterned yellow bathing suit. Now that I had drawn a line more firmly between us, I could find him almost endearing. When the first big wave hit, it knocked him on his ass. He leapt up, grinning, a jackpot winner.

I strolled to the bar, where Bill and Doug had gone to get beers. They asked me to describe the scene, and I did my best—the rising surf, the haughty flexing hunks—but I left out the Mexican dude two tables over, his shaved head showing off a dozen sexy scars, who'd looked at me, looked away, then looked back and winked. It was exciting, even if he was more Scott's type than mine. I wished Scott could be here to enjoy it.

"Isn't this nice?" said Bill, oblivious to my flirtation. "Just the right amount of breeze."

"Best place we've gone so far," said Doug.

"Uh-huh," I said, as I winked back at the Mexican. Now that I no longer took my healthy sight for granted, I'd have expected to revel in this visual dalliance, but all of a sudden I went jagged with loneliness.

At first, I thought my loneliness was vicarious, for Doug and Bill. They were the ones who'd missed out on the moment. But what had they missed, really? The chance to wink at a stranger we'd never see again?

Doug and Bill, I had to admit, possessed no heroic powers, no prophetic wisdom about desire, but they seemed, despite whatever they missed, mostly happy. So, no, my sadness wasn't for them. Or, rather, it was for them and their gay blind compatriots—but also for me, for Scott, for all of us in this world who crave connection and never get enough.

OUR LAST NIGHT, I sat in the cabin. I had packed my suitcase and left it with the porter; I had filled out the customs form.

Tommy was at the mulchboxes, offering Oscar a last chance to poop. One more night, I thought. Just one more.

But as taxing as rooming with Tommy had been, I held no grudge. Mostly, I felt sympathy—especially since I'd learned more about him. Howard had told me that Tommy, until just recently, had been a member of Homosexuals Anonymous, trying to "cure" himself of being gay. And the man Tommy had boasted of, the one he'd been seeing for a decade? Howard said the guy was married and only exploited Tommy for sex. Also, twice in the past year, Tommy had picked up strangers who then robbed him.

The door opened and Tommy clunked in. "Hey there, Mike!" he called out sweetly.

The thought hit: maybe those strangers hadn't really robbed him; maybe Tommy had *offered* his money. He was that good-natured, that simple.

Tommy unharnessed Oscar, who, as usual, latched on to my leg. I let him thrust a moment, then shoved him off. "What am

I ever going to do now?" I asked, mock-serious. "Go home to my lonesome life, no puppy dog to hump me?"

Tommy plopped down onto his bunk. "Oh, there can't be many times *you're* lonesome, Mike," he said.

"There are," I said. "There are. More than you think."

"Really?" he said. "I always thought it would be different if you had twenty-twenty."

Loss of Orientation

IN EDINBURGH, in 2002, I danced at a party called Joy at a club called Ego, where for five pounds you could buy a pill to boost both. Fun enough, but the horde of shirtless homosexuals was too much like the ones back home in Boston. What I'd once found liberating had landed me in a rut.

The next morning, I rode a bus to Perth, where I switched to another, for Inverness, then took yet one more, to Ullapool, where I hopped a ferry for the three-hour sail to Lewis. The northernmost of the Outer Hebrides, the Isle of Lewis has long been a bastion of traditionalism. Just that week, the place's hidebound ways had made headlines: "Islanders Invoke Wrath of God as Airline Schedules Sunday Flights" proclaimed *The Guardian,* noting that when Loganair announced their Sunday service, the Lord's Day Observance Society had made a zealous stink.

I should have been leery of such an illiberal place, but when the boat's horn blasted, I found myself thrilled to be going where gayness would be unspeakable. Not that I thought it should be, in Lewis or anywhere else; if I lived there, I would surely chafe. But sometimes—and I can say this only because I live in a place where it's safe to be gay, and because, when I choose to, I can often pass as straight—sometimes I crave a break from sexual orientation. On the ferry, I ordered some haddock, then sat alone, happily out of place. The locals around me gossiped in Gaelic, with its otherworldly, abracadabric lilt.

In the morning, I set out hitchhiking. I hoped to make it to the ancient standing stones of Callanish and to a rural restaurant I'd heard was worth the trek, but my true destination was remoteness. My first ride came from an off-duty "estate watcher," a quick-eyed twentysomething whose job, he said, was to hike the coastline looking for salmon poachers. Neither of us was in a rush, so we detoured for a sympathy call at the home of one of his colleagues (chestnut hair, pale cheeks with riotous bursts of freckles), whose wife had recently miscarried. We talked about their comically ill-starred woodcock hunt last winter; the fickle weather; the nature of God's mercy. They asked where I was from and what I did for work. Beyond that, they didn't probe, but in our easy warmth I felt real friendship.

Eventually, the estate watcher dropped me at a fork in the road, and I was soon picked up by an excitable carpenter ("Well, now—a visitor. Must be my lucky day!") who drove me out of his way ("Can't just let you tramp along") to a blackhouse preserved from the 1800s. He sent me off with a pat on my shoulder, assuring me that the pleasure had been his.

My next ride also took me miles away from his route, wanting to show me Dalmore, "the prettiest beach on Lewis." He was a salesman of some sort, his trousers neatly creased. At the beach, we stood together—the salt breeze scouring off our reticence—and spoke about the beauty of untouchable horizons. We talked for only twenty minutes before he had to go, but I was sure we'd each glimpsed the other's essential truth.

But could we have, really, when I had said nothing of being gay? (Neither had he mentioned his own orientation.) On the other hand, we might not have bared *any* truths—I might not have bonded at all with him or the other islanders—if I had decided to come out.

I wanted not to think that my silence was a lie. Maybe the version of me they'd met, far from being false, was actually more nuanced than the one I show at home, where sexual orientation tends to trump all other traits. Often, when I say I'm gay, that's the last thing someone hears, as if the word short-circuits their capacity to take in anything else.

From Dalmore, I hiked a path along dramatic clifftops, the tireless sea slapping itself below. I felt both exposed and utterly unnoticed; in two miles, I saw nobody else. Skirting boggy patches and the carcass of a sheep—its big, incurious eyes rolled skyward—I reached the road to Carloway, population 493.

I had to thumb it only a minute before a car pulled over. Its driver, a bald man with a friendly, scrubbed-potato face, waved me in. "Headed to Callanish, are ye?" he asked, his accent making the words a lullaby. "Everyone wants to see those old stones."

Yes, I told him, and I was also looking for a restaurant. I'd heard the chef served wild scallops her husband dove for early every morning.

"Right, right—Tigh Mealros," he said. "Lovely food, but, well, a touch dear."

"Really?" I asked. "How much?"

He pondered as we paused to let two ewes cross the road. "I would say . . . twenty-five pounds, at least."

In those days, I traveled overproudly on a budget and never would have allowed such a splurge. The B&B I was staying in—a cozy room and a Scottish breakfast that left me stuffed all day—had set me back only fifteen pounds.

I shook my head. "No, that's way too much."

"Och," he said, "there's plenty to see for free."

As if to prove his maxim, he took a sharp right turn—not

the way to the ancient circle, according to my map—and rumbled up to the ruins of a massive stone tower. "Built two hundred years before the Christ," he said. "Imagine the isolation!"

"Still seems pretty isolated to me," I responded.

"Aye," he said thoughtfully. "That's the joy of living here. And, you might also say, the sorrow."

Back on the road, we passed homes where men were weaving tweed, visible through their open garage-shop doors. The air was peppery with peat smoke.

Soon we saw a sign for the Callanish standing stones. The driver steered us up a lane, into a parking lot.

"Thanks so much," I said. "Take good care!"

"No goodbyes just yet," he said. "I'll wait."

He had already gone so far above and beyond for me. "Really?" I said. "I can catch a lift with someone else"—even though his car was the only one in the lot.

"You might wait for hours," he said. "Go and see the stones. I'll stay here."

A sign gave the rundown on the site: a Celtic cross of standing stones, four hundred feet across. Older than Stonehenge, older than the Pyramids of Giza. Its purpose? No one knew for sure. Something about the moon and time, the turning of the stars.

I walked a lane of megaliths into the cross's heart, where the tallest stone—more than twice my height—stabbed the sky. I leaned in and kissed it; it had no taste but stone. I stared up, then closed my eyes, grateful to be alone, to not have to perform any version of myself. Everything whirled, everything stilled: a loss of orientation that felt like finding something.

Back on the road, my new friend said he'd take me to Tigh Mealros.

No, I said, I really didn't want to spend so much. I'd just grab a cheap snack in town.

"Nonsense! You should try it. When will you be here again?"

If "here" meant Lewis, he was right; I would not soon return. But I was still reveling in my inner sense of hereness.

We drove on in silence, down to the center of Callanish, a gathering of maybe twenty homes. Passing by one bungalow, the driver jabbed his chin. "See that B&B? Managed by two men." He raised his eyebrows. "Some here say they're gay."

The word was so jarring, I barely recognized it. It might have been a riddle told in Gaelic.

"Terrible," he said, "isn't it?"

I said nothing to contradict him. Not for years had I heard someone's raw, uncensored views when they thought no one queer was within earshot.

"Although, I suppose," he added. His gaze flicked to the rearview. "I suppose some folks think that kind of thing's all right. People do it for all sorts of reasons."

I was nervous to look at him. I stared instead at roadside piles of peat.

"Like you, maybe," he ventured. "A hitcher on a budget?"

An arrow on a handmade sign pointed to Tigh Mealros. The driver pulled to the shoulder and poked the hazards button. *Lick-lock, lick-lock, lick.*

"For twenty-five pounds," he whispered, "would you do it?"

His hand, on the gearshift, trembled. I was trembling too. Sex for money? It would make a cheeky tale to tell back home. It would pay for my wild-scallop dinner.

The driver gulped: a dry, panicked sound. "Or," he said, "maybe thirty pounds?"

Now I looked at his face, his affable, shame-filled face. "I don't think so, sorry," I said. I thanked him for the ride and clambered out.

He sped off, and I stood in a swirl of car exhaust. Looking back, it's easy to say that he had overstepped; I owed him nothing. But standing there, breathing in the fumes, I reeled with guilt. I hadn't wanted sex with him, for money or otherwise—his middle-aged drabness didn't appeal—but couldn't I at least have told him that I'm gay? How lonely he must be on that churchy, uptight island. It would have cost me nothing to show him I was a kindred spirit.

Were we kindred? Just because we both liked sex with men? That was the kind of cliquish thinking from which I'd wanted a break. *I'm gay too,* I might have said, *but it's complicated. The bonds you crave are what I came so far away to flee.*

"Complicated," even as the thought arrived, rang false. It was a luxury to have kindred spirits to run away from.

Tigh Mealros looked more like a private home than a restaurant. My knock on the front door summoned the owner. Although she was flattered I had come so far to find her, unfortunately, she was closed that night.

Now that I couldn't have her food, I wanted it all the more. Twenty-five pounds? I'd have paid fifty.

It was only a mile or so back to the stone circle, where odds of getting a lift would be better. Making my way back through the village of Callanish, I considered the driver's fib about a gay B&B. I'd employed such ruses myself when I was a closeted teenager, concocting any excuse to bring up the word *gay,* hoping someone might pick up the hint.

Then I spied, on a small dusty sign hung from a mailbox, a three-by-five rainbow-flag decal. Every June, when rainbow flags emerge on Boston's streets, I'm inclined to roll my eyes: community by lowest common denominator. Here, though, the emblem filled me with pride and tribal yearning. Could there really be gay men in this village?

I marched up to the house, where a stocky man, seeing me, came to the porch's edge. He was puffing a fat cigar, shrouding his face in smoke.

I had nearly lost my nerve and made to turn away, when the man asked, "What can I do for you?"

"I've got a story that might amuse you," I said, then wondered: Would it? Or would my story instill fear or anger? I didn't want to rattle the man; neither did I want to harm the driver. Maybe I just wanted to tell the anecdote to someone who would get it.

Another man appeared on the porch: barefoot, with a gone-to-seed beard, a jolly paunch.

"Saw your sticker," I told them. "You know, the rainbow flag?"

The second man smiled guardedly. "Why don't you come inside a wee while."

We drank tea in their kitchen—stuffy and small but brightened by eccentric painted accents—and I unspooled the story of the driver's proposition, the way he'd used their "terrible" presence to broach a taboo subject.

They pelted me with questions. What did he look like? What about his car: make and color? Their voices swelled with titillation and something else, more somber, which I heard as urgent cautious hope. The hope of finding another one like them.

But I couldn't think of outing the driver to whom I hadn't even outed myself.

"Right, of course," the cigar smoker said. His name was David. "We were only keen to find out, because, as I'm sure you've heard, there *are* no gays on Lewis." He and his paunchy partner shared a laugh.

I took this as a chance to pry: How long had they lived here? Were they natives?

David explained that no, for their first decade together, they had lived on a *more* remote island. "For us," said Tom, his partner, "Callanish is practically the big city!"

They had never proclaimed their gayness, but never hid it,

either. They just went about their business: tending their flower garden, cutting peat. The rainbow-flag sticker had been a kind of coming out, but few of their neighbors, Tom complained, seemed to understand it.

"Still, it worked," said David. "It brought you here to us."

He poured another round of tea, and we fell into a gab-fest, debating the merits of the British and American versions of *Queer as Folk,* and whether here in the land of redheads, "ginger" was more compliment or insult. Although at times I struggled with their porridge-thick accents, I could tell their sense of humor matched my friends' at home: sidewise, averse to sanctimony.

I felt, as I had that afternoon among the stones, that I was both far from what I knew and at its center. How could I have imagined there were places beyond gayness, that sexual orientation was a thing to be outrun?

The phone rang: a neighbor whose ram had caught his horns in a fence. Could David and Tom come to lend a hand?

The men pulled on their wellies, and I said I would leave them. David asked if I needed directions back to my B&B.

No, I told him. I could find the way.

Unmolested

I'LL CALL HIM Ricky, which sounds almost right: boyish, sort of innocent, sort of insolent. Why did it take me twenty years to think of tracking him down?

In 2002, I'd published a novel starring a boy inspired by him and then tried to smother thoughts of the real one. After all, I'd taken only a small seed of his life and grown a magic beanstalk of *what if?* Whenever I was asked if the boy was based on an actual kid, I hedged: protecting Ricky, I liked to believe, but more truly protecting myself from old, dismaying questions.

Then one day, at my desk, creating another teenage boy— my stories are overcrowded with them—I was struck by a truth I'd stifled: by now he'd be findable on the web.

His name got half a million hits; I braced myself for a long wild-Google chase. But when I searched it along with the state where he grew up, the first link was a YouTube thumbnail showing part of a face I knew was his. The shade of his biracial skin, like something just this side of burned, was more vivid than I'd let myself remember.

The video, a decade-old clip from a local newscast, begins with a solemn anchorwoman. Above her shoulder, a graphic:

a fist smashing apart the symbols for male and female, and the stark blue letters of Assault.

Then there's Ricky, standing on a lawn, more filled out than when I knew him but still remarkably skinny. His buzzed hair is thinning at the temples, even though, in the video, he was only twenty-five—almost as old as I was when I knew him as a fourteen-year-old.

The camera pans to a shirt and pants laid out on the grass like Sunday clothes set on a church boy's bed. We zoom in: the clothes are spattered with blood.

Ricky says that a stranger at a nightclub had mocked him: a campy, effeminate flip of the wrist. When Ricky asked, "Why would you do that?" the man up and punched him. He tried again: "Why are you hitting me?" There his memory ends. His lip and chin needed twenty stitches.

The victim is sure, a reporter says, that he was attacked because of his sexuality.

I was soberly satisfied to hear his gayness confirmed, but sad to know his sexuality was still causing pain. I felt, above everything, a charged expectation. Ricky, whenever I'd thought of him, had been ambered in place, never progressing past his teenage self, but here he was, older, evolved—which meant we might finally be able to talk through what had happened.

The reporter interviews a policewoman, who says she's studied security footage and seen nothing to match Ricky's claims. Witnesses were drunk; accounts of the fight conflict; police, therefore, can't yet deem it a hate crime.

Ricky comes onscreen again; his doleful, seductive eyes well up. His lip wouldn't be split if he weren't gay, he says. Is he blaming the basher or, in a sense, blaming his own gayness?

His tears took me back to the summer when I knew him: his honest anguish, his canny machinations. And, just as I'd been back then, I was torn between the urge to throw my arms around him and the conviction that I should keep my distance.

IN 1997, my friend Colin, who'd become director of the boys' camp where we'd gone as kids and then worked on staff, asked me back for a weeklong stint as a kind of "guest-star counselor." His putative reason was that I was a Pathfinder. This was the camp's name for its highest achievement rating, awarded for mastering a list of survival skills (catching a fish without a hook, lighting a fire with a bow drill). The designation carried zero worth beyond the camp, but in our little world, it loomed large. In fifty-eight years, fewer than ten boys had earned the title.

"Think we've found the next one," Colin said. "We need you to teach him!" Over the phone, his rah-rah voice jingled. I could picture his crinkly smile, his swell of sandy hair.

It had been seven years since I had worked at the camp; my skills were rusty, to say the least. At twenty-eight, I lived in Boston, my summer booked with writing gigs wedged between all-night bouts of clubbing. Before I could lob these excuses, Colin repeated, "We need you," and I suspected he meant something deeper.

Three years earlier, a former director—the man who had taught the man who'd trained me for the Pathfinder—had been convicted of molesting a teenage boy. Afterward, a dozen more alumni came forward, citing abuse from during my time as a camper and before. Almost as distressing as the revelations themselves was the blatancy of what we must have willed ourselves to overlook: that parts of the camp's core culture had helped enable abuse.

The place combined Quaker values (simplicity, social justice) with back-to-the-land ruggedness and flower-child free spirit.

Campers milked goats and helped construct the rough-lumber cabins, quoting Kahlil Gibran: "Work is love made visible." From this distance, I can roll my eyes at the hippie-dippiness, but for a kid like me—reared in the selfish suburbs—the camp was thrilling. Most especially its flexible masculinity: counselors yelled "Attaboy!" to watch us chop a tree but cheered just as much if we talked about our fears. At "meeting for worship" every morning, we were urged to share our private thoughts. It took two years for me to muster the courage to rise and speak; when I did, I found my truest voice.

But the camp had an even weirder side.

Its founder construed the Quaker tenet of "that of God in everyone" to mean that human bodies are divine, so we shouldn't feel ashamed to bare them. At camp, then, we always swam unburdened by bathing suits, and also canoed, and roughhoused, and grubbed in the garden, nude. Our group showers, which had no walls, stood in view of passersby, and our outhouses were multi-seaters with no doors and no dividers between the holes.

Did this seem kooky, even cultish? Sure. But cults thrive by offering a great sense of purpose. Regular camps, we told ourselves, were vapid (who cared about "color wars"?), but ours was a freeing force, liberating humanity one tan line–less body at a time.

All too freeing, it turned out. Our beloved liberation had offered cover to predators.

The camp now forbade nakedness; staff received abuse-prevention training. But how much of the program's unsafeness could be erased without killing off what made it special?

My old pal Colin was tasked with rebuilding, serving as a bridge from the defensive old-timers to a dynamic new generation. I think he asked me back to camp (did he say this, or just imply it?) because I, too, straddled a seeming chasm: as a Pathfinder, an avatar of the camp's macho ethos, but also unapologetically gay.

For all its bohemianism, the camp had never been immune from homophobia; the nudism, if anything, made it worse. Picture a tangle of naked boys wrestling on a dock, shouting "Quit staring!" and "Don't be queer!" lest anyone impute sexuality to the scene. (As a camper, attracted to boys but scared of what that meant, I had found the mixed messages torturous.)

When I had last been a counselor, my then-boyfriend had worked in the kitchen. We had made no big announcement of our coupled status, but everyone knew; the boys took it in stride. In 1990, that had felt like a major step forward. But now, since the scandal, Colin feared the worst: given our culture's tendency to conflate gayness with predation, any same-sex affection—especially from counselors to campers—might be censured. But I could use my big-fish-in-a-tiny-pond prestige to show that it was possible to condemn sexual abuse without playing in to homophobia. Just by being my gay self, I could spark discussion, an antidote to the willful ignorance that had enabled abuse.

Colin did say something like this to me, I feel sure; he was always scrupulously honest. I was the one who wasn't quite straightforward. I thanked him for his leadership and told him I would do my part for a place I loved so much. What I didn't tell him: I'd been trying to write a novel about a camp rocked by sexual abuse, but I was stuck, with nothing but aimless notes. Given this opportunity to immerse myself in camp, maybe I could find the novel's heart.

Why did I keep this from Colin? If you'd asked me then, I might have cited a writerly fear of being seen as a scavenger. But what really muzzled me was thornier. A novel about abuse would necessarily feature an abuser. To write him, I would have to sustain sympathy for him, and I felt unready to defend that sympathy—not to Colin, and maybe not to myself.

COLIN INTRODUCED ME on the dining hall stage, at lunch, hyping me like a movie star who moonlighted as an Olympic sprinter. Boys stood up for better views, squinting as if at sunlight. Their stomps of acclamation shook the wagon-wheel chandeliers dangling from the rafters.

We went back to eating, and I could sense the campers tracking my every move. *That's how a Pathfinder takes a sip of juice!* The adulation felt troubling—the glorification of favored counselors had helped them get away with crimes—and also not a little ludicrous: in Boston, I was just a freelance writer piling up rejections.

Maybe what troubled me most about the campers' worship was that it felt great. I loved it.

After the meal, I was swarmed by ten-year-olds, tugging at my belt loops, my wrists. This was so much of what I treasured about boys their age, the propulsive intimacy they hadn't yet learned to be ashamed of. The gang of scruffy, shirtless kids hauled me onto the lawn to play "slack 'em": two competitors stand some yards apart on wooden stumps, holding ends of a thick Manila rope, and try to knock each other off by yanking or slacking the line. One boy after another took me on; I trounced them all. Daring me to play with just one hand, then just my weaker hand, they quizzed me on my Pathfinder achievements. What animal had I trapped? How had I managed to cook it?

My next opponent—a geek with pointillist freckles on his nose—asked where I lived, and did I have a girlfriend.

I had planned on coming out, of course—why else was I

here?—but I had only just begun to bask in the campers' worship. By saying I was gay, would I blunt their adoration? So soon?

But no, I reminded myself: the goal was to *use* their adoration.

I pulled the rope, then reeled in more, forcing the kid forward, until he teetered along his stump's front edge. "I live in Boston," I said. "But my boyfriend? He's in Manhattan. It's such a pain to go back and forth!"

Without warning, I slacked the rope; the boy flew off his stump. All of the other kids wore expressions just like his: weightless, wide-eyed, scrambled with surprise.

GOSSIP TRAVELS fast at camp—a truth I'd counted on. By morning, it seemed, the boys all knew. They weren't repelled; if anything, the news stoked their interest.

I met with Reid, the Pathfinder candidate, a pale boy with preppy hair and suspiciously clean clothes. When I ticked through his list of requirements—killing a critter, crafting a birch-bark pot to boil it in—his lips curled with a red-blooded fervor that forged our bond.

Next, I hiked to that summer's cabin-in-progress and grabbed a hammer. "The trick," I told the clutch of kids gathered like paparazzi, "is letting the head's weight do all the work." This was a scene I might use in my novel, I decided, to show how fast counselors could inspire godlike reverence. "Don't choke up and peck," I said. "Hold the handle low. One and two"—I pounded a sixteen-penny nail—"and *done*."

The campers itched with a question: *You're an ace at* this, *but you like to kiss* boys?

Or maybe I only imagined it. Soon their attention shifted, and they all bolted off to an Ultimate Frisbee game.

Except for one, who puppied me wherever I went that afternoon.

Ricky.

He was almost as tall as I, his legs elastically overlong. But there was something babyish in his face and in his plaintive, unfledged affect. Later, I learned he was fourteen.

The next day, I snuck out of the lodge during announcements, hoping to avoid the post-lunch crowd. Forgoing the usual sawdusted path, I opted for a slippery steeper trail. I was watching my feet when a crack of twigs made me turn around. There was Ricky, beaming with his big galootish grin.

"Figured you'd take the shortcut," he said. "*Path*finder, right? Ha ha."

"Guilty," I said. I grabbed a sapling for balance.

"I heard you live in Boston?"

"Yup. For three years now."

"Wow," he said. "Just wow!" He confessed that he was from a dumpy rural town. "Is Boston wicked cool?" he asked. His voice was on the brink of changing; it echoed within a hollowness it couldn't yet quite fill.

The camp now had a stringent prohibition: a counselor should never be alone with a camper. "Can't talk now," I said. "Catch me later?"

I scrambled down the trail and ducked into my cabin, where I lay on my bunk, wrestling with why, even without the prohibition, I might do my best to sidestep Ricky.

THE RULE against one-on-one time forced me to rethink the Pathfinder. Back when I was gunning for it, my mentor and I had spent hours alone in the woods, like followers of a secret faith. But now, mentoring Reid, things were different. He was getting ready for his orienteering test, when he'd be driven, blindfolded, miles away from camp, then try to hike back aided by just a compass and four topographical maps. I had to dragoon another kid—a pudgy prankster who'd never held a compass—to bushwhack through the backcountry with us.

On my third day, Ricky saw me as I was finishing a swim. The sunny air, pouring onto my taut, lake-chilled skin, tickled like a dousing of champagne. But my swimsuit reminded me of how the old camp ways had been erased.

"Mike, hey!" called Ricky. "What're you up to?"

I was about to fib my way out of chatting with him—*Sorry, I need to find a towel*—when I saw that I might appease him and solve the problem with Reid at the same time. Did he want to hike with us later? We would dig up fern roots and weave them into fishnets!

Ricky pouted. That boy-scout stuff didn't interest him. He would rather ask me about my life in Boston. What did I do for fun?

"Go to the movies?" I said. "Maybe to a party." I steered us toward a bench where other campers and counselors sat talking.

"What kind of party?" Ricky asked.

"I don't know. A dinner party."

"A dinner party! With what kind of people?"

I had recently dined on the roof deck of a memoirist whom Edmund White, in a cover blurb, had called "the most famous piece of ass of my generation."

"Oh, you know," I said. "Just people." I wanted to model matter-of-factness about my gay life, but something about Ricky—as clingy as my swimsuit—provoked me, and I withheld.

"You have a boyfriend?"

"Yes," I said.

"What's his name?"

"Scott."

"What's he like? Older than you or younger?"

Later, I would understand that Ricky, in asking this, really was asking something about himself, but in the moment, I feared he had sussed out my weak spot and was jabbing. When friends asked about Scott's age, I said he was three years older but looked, and often acted, much younger. In other words, my type. I was attracted to boyishness—to bratty braggadocio and adolescent preening, redolent of the hotshots who would've snubbed me in high school.

Boyishness, yes. That's true. It's also an artful dodge. I was attracted not just to adolescent preening but, sometimes, to actual adolescents.

Copping to these attractions is easier for me now: I'm past fifty, and I will never be a counselor again. But back then, I was nervous even to let myself feel such stirrings, worried they might be legible on my face.

To my relief, I didn't find Ricky that attractive. He had a youthful magnetism, and his on-the-verge-of-something lankiness intrigued me. But his charm felt forced, the chipperness of an old Hollywood hayseed. He was too needy, too ready to please. Too much of a reminder of myself at his age.

"I said, what's Scott like?" he asked.

"He's . . . he's a writer, like me," I said. "He lives in New York."

"The city that never sleeps! Gosh, I'd love to go. Next time, can I stow away with you?"

Oh, poor boy, I thought. Does he even realize he's gay?

The two-bell clanged its steely cue: lunch in fifteen minutes.

"You should head to the lodge," I told him.

He nodded but didn't get up.

"I'll be there in a minute," I said. I pushed him off the bench.

IN THE FOLLOWING DAYS, I whizzed from one activity to another, too busy even to jot notes for my novel. I pitched in at the cabin again; I huddled with Colin, ruminating about the camp's future; but most of my hours I spent with Reid and anyone who would join us, rushing to teach the Pathfinder skills before my week was up. We felled a spruce, adzed it into a passably squared-off beam. "Ever heard of spruce gum?" I asked, knifing sap from the bark. "Sticky at first"—I popped the gob of resin into my mouth—"but don't give up, just keep chewing. Trust me!"

I was trying to share all the know-how I could right now, because I planned to return only briefly, for the Fair: an end-of-summer celebration, replete with primitive, hand-cranked carnival rides. If Reid had passed all his tests, I would welcome him then into the kinship.

In my frenzy, I had no time for Ricky, or so I told myself, not admitting what's obvious to me now: I was avoiding him.

When he managed to collar me—late in the afternoon of my last day—he said he wanted to talk. He *needed* to. Alone.

Our previous encounter had left me wondering how much he knew about himself. But maybe he was more self-aware than I'd imagined; maybe my own openness had nudged him toward coming out.

Or maybe—a screw of fear drilled inside my gut—maybe he needed to talk about *me*. Could he have read my secret ink? Had he grasped that teenagers turned me on? I was sure I'd done nothing to show desire for him (desire I felt only very faintly), but maybe, with a kind of gaydar, he could sense the campers I did desire.

I said we could talk for just a minute, but not alone.

His twiggy frame appeared even further whittled by fretting. A frantic sadness seemed to jolt through him.

"But please, Mike," he said. "It's private."

His anguish worked like smelling salts.

"Please," he said again. "You're the only person I can tell."

I can't be the only man in the history of camp counseling who secretly—stupidly—wanted to believe that he alone might save a hurting child. And who, on learning that the child believed this too, succumbed to the rush of heroism.

I led him into the library, a small room in the Lower Lodge. At that hour, it stood empty, its air close with the must of moldy pages. We sat down amid the stacks of boy-adventure novels, near a tattered copy of *The Ashley Book of Knots*. (A good detail, I remember thinking. I should use it.)

Ricky started in on a jittery monologue, talking of how he felt like a stranger in his own family, and also in his small dumb town, where everyone else was white. Camp was somewhat better, but even here, he couldn't be himself.

Lots of people felt that way at his age, I assured him.

But he was different, he said. His bony shoulders started to shake, sending dismal ripples through his T-shirt. At last he said: "I think I'm gay. I'm gay."

Saying this seemed to steady him. Or maybe he found my hand on his back calming—it calmed me too. Nothing but a normal coming out, after all.

I felt awful for having withheld my comfort until now. Panicked about my own secret yearnings being unmasked, I'd iced out the very kid who needed me the most.

He was so brave, I told him. Things were tough right now, I knew, but someday he would flourish. "Being gay can be great," I said. "I wouldn't want to be any other way."

He leaned against me, and I could feel how truly slight he was, as easily wisped away as dandelion fluff.

"Will I see you again?" he asked.

"Sure thing. At the Fair."

He pulled away. "How about before that. Can I write you?"

"Always!" I said. "You can tell me anything you need to."

I gave him my address. We hugged goodbye.

BACK IN BOSTON, I returned to my novel, hoping to sketch the details of camp life: the peaty scent of shade beneath an ancient pine, the blue sound of swollen mountain streams. I would riff on Ricky, too, but wasn't sure just how, because our interaction had been too well resolved. Intense for him, yes—a leap in self-development—but nothing dramatic enough to make it worthy of fiction. Kid comes out as gay: end of story.

It's funny now, and painful, to see how hard I worked to keep myself out of the drama. Concentrating on *his* confession, I could avoid scrutinizing the one I'd failed to make.

In less than a week, a letter came, its only return address "Ricky Camp." The stationery was printed with colorful cartoon sneakers adorned with childish clouds, stars, and hearts. "Dear Mike," Ricky wrote:

> I would love too give you a blowjob and your boy-friend!!!! ☺ please write to me since you are not work-ing here tell me if you would like me to do that if I can come to your house for two weeks would you be my boyfriend?
>
> I love you. I wish you could send me a naked picture of you please please please please I will hide it very well.
>
> I love you.
> Love,
> Ricky

The paper, with its cartoon sneakers, seemed to throb in

my fist. I wanted not to be holding it, but also to keep it out of anyone else's hands.

The whiplash of it: at once so precocious and so naïve, like porn imagined by a second-grader. (Remember, this was '97, before ubiquitous cyberporn; I doubt Ricky had seen the real thing.) At fourteen, how would he think to cross the lines he crossed? The question should've haunted me, but I didn't ask it. What I asked—focusing on myself more than him—was *How could I have missed his desire?*

I had pegged his fascination as simply hero worship: the Pathfinder myth, heightened by my gayness. Never had I suspected he'd make me his sexual fantasy. When I was fourteen, I'd wanted to *be* my counselors, not to *sleep* with them; my crushes were all on other boys. Was that why the thought of Ricky's lust had never struck me?

No, what seems truer now is that I *was* struck by something: not Ricky's lust but *every* boy's, the force of adolescent hormones pulsing through the camp. I'd worked hard to look away, tuning out temptation, and in doing so I had missed the lovesick kid right in front of me.

I told myself I had to handle this quietly, on my own. For one thing, I didn't want to betray Ricky's confidence. Also, I was terrified that people might think I'd led him on. From his point of view, maybe I had. A man guides a boy into a secluded room, rubs his back, pulls him into a hug . . .

But how to reject Ricky's desire without rejecting *him*, without compounding his shame?

"Dear Ricky," I finally typed:

I'm glad you wrote. You're a special person, and I was really happy that we were able to connect at camp. I said that you could talk to me, and I meant it.

But Ricky, you have to understand that things can't be the way you asked in your letter. I met you as a counselor—as a professional staff member at camp—and also I'm twice your age. It's just completely inappropriate to talk about sexual stuff between us. It can't happen. Period.

I feel bad, because I know society is always saying, "Don't talk about sexuality." Well, I'm happy to try to work through issues of sexuality with you, but not sex. Do you understand the difference? I hope that with time you'll grow more comfortable and eventually find peers with whom you can be naturally sexual. But please don't put either of us in an awkward position, okay? If you do, I won't be able to keep being someone to talk to.

Being gay can be about so much—about friendship, about seeing the world with new eyes. Don't make the mistake of thinking it's only about what you do with your body.

I hope you're doing well in the second half of camp. Maybe I'll see you at the Fair?

Take good care,

Mike

I printed an extra copy for my files. A self-protective instinct, but also, it occurs to me now, self-regarding: I must have imagined someday showing off my rectitude, the graciousness with which I'd steered Ricky. (Or did I keep a copy because I *doubted* my rectitude, and wanted a reminder of the right course to take, in case my self-control ever wavered?)

I didn't hear back—a good sign or bad, I couldn't tell.

MAYBE I shouldn't have gone to the Fair. I could easily have made excuses, but what would truly have kept me home—my sheepish, skulking fear—reminded me of being in the closet. Two weeks later, I drove to camp again.

The Fair was a distillation of everything I loved about the place, the whole event—from the rides to the root beer—militantly homemade. Hundreds of family members and alums made the pilgrimage for wacky skits, a square dance, and then a teepee raising, all capped off with a bonfire after dusk.

For much of the trip from Boston, fog fuzzed the road, but just as I was parking, the sun scythed through the mist. At the fairgrounds, herds of campers dashed from booth to booth. The fields smelled of their recent haying, vegetal and wholesome.

I gazed around for Ricky, half expecting him at my hip. Maybe he was working at his cabin's ride, the Aquashoot, a rickety flume that plunged riders down into the lake. I decided not to go looking right away. If I seemed too eager to see him, he might get the wrong idea.

A camper—the freckled boy I'd beaten in slack 'em way back on that first afternoon—saw me and demanded a piggyback ride to nowhere. A different kid then yanked me toward his cabin's concession. ("Try our kabobs! We killed the hens ourselves!") I kept bumping into friends I'd not seen since the scandal broke. We had often joked about our "crunchy-granola nudist camp," but now we smothered each other in unironic hugs.

Eventually someone persuaded me to ride the Ferris wheel, a four-seated, twenty-foot-tall contraption made of wood, spun by boys perched upon a scaffold. As soon as I was belted in, the boys conspired to haze me: turning the wheel so madly that my chair uncontrollably somersaulted. I flipped and flipped, the world a blue blur of Dopplered laughter.

At the end, I staggered off, and there, in my shaky shadow, stood Ricky.

His brown face glowed bashfully, his eyes as smooth as worry beads; he looked like an ideogram for remorse. My own remorse gored me then, for all of my avoidance of him—for being so consumed by my own self-censure that I had dug a deep moat between us.

I had planned a professional greeting—kindly but standoff-ish—but here he was, contrite, clearly jazzed to see me, and I just wanted to crush him with compassion.

When I hugged him, he pinned his face hard against my chest, so I could barely hear him say, "I missed you."

I allowed that I had missed him too.

Staying close, he whispered, "Can we go somewhere . . . private?"

His covert tone snapped me back; my duty was not to con-fuse him. (Why was I such a fetishist for duty? No matter how much peril or discomfort someone put me in, I was intent that they would still see me as upstanding, as if losing a single per-son's love would lose me the world.) "Ricky," I said gently, "can't we both just enjoy the Fair?"

"Fine," he huffed. "Fine, then. Forget it." He sprinted off.

Before I could react—how would it look if I chased him?—Reid appeared with his parents. They both seemed as strait-laced as their matching khaki shorts. "This is Mike," said Reid. "The guy who taught me everything."

His father pumped my hand—"The famous Pathfinder, at last!"—and joked about the thousands in tuition they had blown to have their son *deprived* of food and safety.

"No, but seriously," his mother said, "you're obviously an extraordinary mentor."

Fraudulence crackled through me, as if, under their next ounce of praise, I might fracture. Sure, I'd helped their stellar son. But what about Ricky?

The afternoon was waning; concessions started to close.

Reid's parents excused themselves to buy some hand-dipped candles, and I sat down in a patch of sunlight, breathing in the crowd's kicked-up dust.

After the booths shut, everyone gathered for the teepee raising. A camper in a green felt loincloth beat a rustic drum, while other boys lifted wooden shafts: white kids so self-important about the Native ritual that they achieved accidental humor. One of the kids monkey-climbed to the top and tied the poles. The crowd applauded, and that was when I spied Ricky, across from me. I turned away, pretending not to see.

We all moved across the road, to the mound of lumber scraps whose burning would provide the Fair's climax. The sun had set, and darkness thickened, the wooded hills a spooky charcoal smudge. The oldest boys, in hard hats, oversaw the production. Some wore backpack fire pumps, the kind for fighting brush fires. Others lighted toilet-paper torches soaked in kerosene; the flames trembled against the muddy sky.

A speaker offered Quaker clichés about kindling every single child's "inner light," and then the fire-starters got the nod. They strode up to the heap of lumber, hurled their TP torches, and ran back.

Whump! A fist of flames punched a hole in the darkness. Just then a hand slipped some papers into my pocket, and I turned to see Ricky scampering into the shadows.

There was not enough light for me to read the pages. I stepped up, then stepped again, as close to the fire as I could bear.

Mike would you have sex with me if I was not at camp? I was thinking that if there is a place at camp I would like to talk to you when you are horny. I will let you touch my body at the fair.

I saw your letter and I was mad. I love you I love my
dick is getting big can you please have sex with me.
Love,
Ricky

I looked past the fire, but the blaze had messed with my
vision. All I saw were dull shapes in the distance. Was Ricky
out there, watching? Could he somehow sense the awful stir-
ring within my veins?

Parents and kids were crowded around me, but I couldn't
help myself—I read more. The next page was a disconnected
mishmash: "Mike can I come to your house for a week and
sleep with you please I would tell my mom that I would like
you to help me." "Would you like to see my dick?" In one spot,
in big letters, he'd written, "The Joy of Sex with gay friends,"
but just below that: "I hate myself because I'm gay." Throughout the page were crude stick-figure sketches of guys engaged in
sex. In each, the figures were labeled "me" and "you."

A boy raced past, knocking my elbow; I nearly dropped the
pages. "Quick, stop it!" he called to another boy.

I looked up. A rogue flame climbed a tuft of grass. To my
left, a patch of brush was smoking. What a world, I thought,
so ready with its metaphors, and *ha!* The bonfire erupted.

A mother scooped up her toddler. Campers backed away.
But the pump crew, nozzles gripped like rifles, found the hot
spots, and sprayed and sprayed until the flames were quenched.

I'D LIKE to say I hightailed it to Boston. But one kid took out
a banjo, another a guitar, and I couldn't miss a sing-along with
boys whose attachment to me I was so attached to. When we
quit, way past curfew, all the bunks were spoken for. The only

place for me to sleep was in the Lower Lodge. I lay awake outside the library, thinking of Ricky's sketches.

I'd been hoping that once he saw how out of line his crush was, he'd drop it. But now I sensed how deep ran his trouble. Was something disturbed in Ricky, something more than a puppy love he was too young to process? I was still not thinking of any danger he might be in, only of the danger he could pose to me. If my brush-off rankled him, who could say how he might strike back? Even to be seen with him now could be a risk, if later he claimed I'd done something wrong. Then again, to be with him without having a witness could be worse. The rule against counselors meeting alone with campers was to protect us as much as them.

The camp too: it had to be protected. Colin had fought to bring the place back from disrepute—I knew I needed to tell him, but how?

I got up early and left before breakfast.

BY THE TIME I spoke with Colin, a couple days later, I was in New York for a meeting about a book I was editing: a "state of the gay community" volume, immodestly titled *Gay Men at the Millennium*. I couldn't shake the irony. Here I was, curating the latest in gay discourse, just as I was snagged in the oldest of gay quagmires: the fear of being accused of corrupting a young boy.

Reviewing Ricky's pages to prep for talking to Colin, I'd discovered more writing on the back side of one. Including this: "My Mom had a boyfriend at camp, and she was 13 and he was 29." I could see that initially he'd written fourteen and twenty-eight—precisely our own ages—but crossed them out and changed each by a year. Why, to make his lie slightly less ludicrous?

He'd signed the main letter, "Hate, Ricky the gay." But "hate" was scratched out, replaced by "from."

I'd decided I had to show Colin all our correspondence. We set a time to talk, and then, using my publisher's fax (a crisis, I'd explained; my honor was on the line), I beamed Ricky's letters back to camp.

I took the call in an editorial assistant's cubicle. Colin grilled me, as he needed to do, about my actions with Ricky and any other campers; my answers were honest and exonerating. But he had asked only about actions, not fantasies, and so I volunteered nothing else. The omission felt false—it made my tongue taste rancid—and now I think I should have said more.

As soon as he was satisfied that Ricky, not I, had been to blame, we began to plot our next move. We thought of kicking Ricky out, but what was his crime? Unrequited passion? Plus, the season was nearly over. To send him home, we would have to give his parents a reason, and outing him could be calamitous. What if his parents doubted us and launched an investigation? To save face, what lies might Ricky hatch? Even if we were vindicated, the process would be harrowing; the camp might not survive a second scandal.

Colin suggested the least awful option: he would tell Ricky not to contact me again, and that if he did, the camp would have to tell his parents everything.

As Colin spoke, I stared at the cubicle divider, behind which an editor was carping about a broken contract. I hated that we would wield a threat, especially one depending on Ricky's shame. I still wanted to save him—to free him from that shame—but I had my own species of stigma to contend with. And now, with our imposed distance, I was the person least able to help him.

COLIN'S TALK with Ricky went well. All of us agreed to keep our silence.

Once the crisis ebbed, my imagination started to boil. I saw a novel—a better novel—steaming into shape. The plot was still about abuse but featured *two* key counselors, one accused of molesting a boy, and one (the narrator) who tries to suppress his desire for that same boy. An extra twist: the camper would be precociously seductive and smitten with the counselor who resists him.

It was disconcerting to be buoyant with creativity, knowing that while a fictional boy fluttered free within my thoughts, the actual kid must be miserable. I clung to a notion that now seems too self-serving: inside my imagined world, Ricky had space to roam.

I COULD make up a trigger to explain why, fifteen years after my novel was published, it occurred to me to google Ricky. I could say I saw the news of a dodgy coach or counselor, or that a lanky teenager smiled too long at me. But the truth is there was no one reason Ricky returned to my mind. Which is to say, he'd never really left it.

When the book came out, I had dreaded my camp friends' reactions, worried they would see me in the narrator. But they seemed to take the novel as pure invention, and not at all confession.

The narrator's fate, hewing so close to my own, had felt settled: he would never cross the line with a boy. But I knew nothing of Ricky's fate; I had never heard his side of things. That was the thought—or what I let myself believe it was—that sent me to Google and on the path to writing this account. What if I could report a piece of journalism about his life? He would be in his mid-thirties; the danger was long dispersed. Could I release the real Ricky's voice?

Maybe it seems self-evident that I should have thought harder about the repercussions for him. But my fervor—I could write a fascinating piece!—drowned out my fainter reservations. Then, when I so quickly found the newscast video, I took it as a kind of license: if Ricky had chosen to talk on TV about being gay-bashed, he wouldn't mind letting me profile him. As hard to watch as the video was (his split lip, his unconfirmed claims), its ambiguity amplified my urge to track him down.

Next I found an email address that, although defunct, led me to his profile on a hookup site called SugarDaddyForMe. He'd made the profile in his late twenties: a travel lover, aiming for a health-care career, currently working with underprivileged kids. Calling himself a "sugar baby," he sought a gay "daddy" between the ages of twenty-seven and ninety.

My unexamined reactions: relief, validation. Maybe Ricky had not been unbalanced when he pursued me, but only advanced in knowing his true desires. A daddy-lover, from the very start.

That profile led me to another, on a different site. According to his bio, he valued authenticity, and didn't fret about "things you might've done that you're not proud of." He looked for someone bighearted in a partner.

There were two photos. One, a close-up glamour shot, showed him lying down; his tank top appeared to say HUSTLER. In the other, he stood wide-legged on a poolside deck, aiming a sizzling stare into the lens. He wore a skimpy swimsuit, shockingly white against his skin, his body smooth and sculptural and lean. One hand splayed on his belly, the other pushed the suit down, revealing the shaved-bare patch above his cock.

It's no use trying to squirm away from what I felt: he

looked like someone I would want to fuck. But it was more than Ricky's physique and attitude that turned me on. I'd been aroused—I finally had to admit it to myself—since the moment I'd thought to look him up. I would never have acted on my attraction to someone underage, even if I knew that he, like Ricky, wanted me, but now that he was all grown up, I might have the chance to feel the force of his lust uncuffed: the closest I would ever come to the true forbidden fruit.

Say I got in touch, and he agreed to the profile. And say that after our interview (on his poolside deck?), after I took off my writer's hat . . . Say that then we did all he'd asked for back at camp. I could be Daddy and he could be Boy: safely, now, as role-play.

But what I just said, about taking off my writer's hat? There must be writers who can do that—writers who don't, in every instant, imagine how their life would play on the page. Unfortunately, I'm not one of them. In picturing our reunion, I was already measuring how each possible outcome might affect the written story's ending. The fantasy was dampened.

Many guides to the craft of writing include a common dictum: endings should be "inevitable yet surprising." What if Ricky came on to me, now that he freely could, and again, definitively, I denied him? (*Not that you're not hot,* I'd say. *If you were anyone else . . .*) Readers who craved a healing payoff might expect us to finally touch—but no, we'd find our true healing in this: reaffirming that I should not have touched him. Not then, not ever.

Or what if I did come on to him, but Ricky turned *me* down? Would that ending be more empowering for him?

NONE OF THESE possible endings would matter unless I found him.

Beyond his two dating profiles, the internet trail ran cold. Maybe he'd switched to the mobile apps that aren't as readily searchable (and that I, as a smartphone holdout, didn't have access to). Or maybe he had found his bighearted daddy and stopped looking.

But one of his profiles, I realized, mentioned his parents' jobs. With that information, I soon found his father's obituary. Which led to his mother's Facebook page.

Bingo! I could ask her to pass a letter to Ricky.

Affecting a laid-back tone ("a long-lost friend from summer camp!"), I wrote a draft and almost clicked Send. But then I saw the About button and paused.

I wish I could say I paused for sympathetic reasons: that blindsiding Ricky might reopen his tender scars; that my not having taken advantage of him way back then didn't give me a pass to do so now. In truth, I can't say why I paused. My doubts, if I had them, weren't conscious.

I clicked About, and there, among his mother's details— hometown, high-school alma mater—was her birth year. When I read it, I said out loud, "Really?"

Checking his father's obit again, I confirmed my math: Ricky's mom had been younger than her husband by almost twenty years.

Ricky had said that his mother, at thirteen, a summer camper, had had a boyfriend more than twice her age. Preposterous, I'd assumed. But could his claim actually have been true? Could that man have become Ricky's father? (Ricky's letter suggested an age gap of sixteen years; maybe he'd actually *lowballed* the difference.)

All this time, I'd thought of him as the lying, manipulative one of us. But hadn't his troubles arisen more than anything else from his honesty, his inability to disguise his desires? I was the one who'd not been honest—to him or to Colin, least of all to myself.

And now, as I write this, I wonder what other truths about Ricky I've dismissed. Or not even let myself imagine.

Having endured the camp's scandal, and written about a fictional boy's abuse, how have I not reckoned with the likelihood that Ricky was a victim? (Apparently, I cared only that he was not *my* victim.) His lack of sexual boundaries, his pornographic knowledge: abuse offers a plausible explanation. If his father had truly "dated" his mother when she was thirteen, there was something unsound in that family. Could the father eventually have preyed on Ricky too?

Plausible, yes. Maybe even obvious. Why does it occur to me only now?

My subconscious has labored, I think, not to seek a cause for Ricky's wanting. To ask what might have happened to him to "make him" how he was, would be to judge his desires as damaged or disordered. Which would also call into question my own desires, the flip side of the same taboo coin. The question was—is—too upending.

THE NIGHT I learned of his parents' age gap, I lay in bed, queasy, chasing sleep. Eventually, I opened my computer.

I stared for long minutes at the pic of Ricky poolside, his suit tugged down, the sizzle in his eyes. I still wanted badly to think that he would welcome hearing from me. But mostly I wanted to say I was sorry.

I started googling again, using every research trick I knew. After a particularly inventive tweak of my search terms, I discovered one more breadcrumb: a comment Ricky had posted on a cooking site. It was just a trifling phrase about a pasta casserole. But the more I thought about it, the more its very trivialness compelled me: here was a glimpse of Ricky going about his normal business. Finding a recipe, baking it. *His* business.

Until then, uncannily, everything I'd learned of him had fit neatly into the story I thought I wanted to tell myself, a story about his sexual desires. But that was my obsession, not his. He deserved to live his life unmolested by my preoccupation.

THESE DAYS, when I think of Ricky, I try not to picture the desperate kid at camp, writing "I hate myself because I'm gay." Likewise, I try not to see him in his swimsuit, beckoning his fantasy of a daddy. (I try not to, but sometimes I still do.)

Instead, I place him in a kitchen . . . I'm not sure where. A snug farmhouse, back in the dumpy town he ached to flee? (No, that town is where I fear—where I'm pretty sure—he was harmed.) Okay, then: make it a gritty walk-up in New York. Does he cook for two, sharing with someone who loves or irks him? For all I know, he's cheerfully alone. Or painfully so.

The timer dings. He opens the oven, takes the casserole out—its edges crisp, on the verge of charred—an elevated macaroni and cheese. He spoons some, cools it with his breath, takes a bite (there's the mustard: half a teaspoon that tarts the whole thing up). He composes the comment he plans to type on the cooking site: *I must say, this was mighty good.*

AND ME? What's the scene I haunt?

A summer night, a fire. Errant sparks erupting in a muddy, mixed-up sky. A boy's plea slipped into a pocket.

The flames tease. Can't make out the writing on his pages.

Step up closer, into the heat. Closer. Don't get burned.

Now look out, beyond the fire. Is he there? What are you not seeing?

What I Left Out

IN 2010, I wrote about a trip I'd taken to Nanjing, China, for *The Advocate*. The piece focused on my struggle to find a gay bar in a city I could barely navigate. I end up at a campy club, where one of the local drag performers tails me into the bathroom; we kiss, but when she asks to spend the night together, I make excuses and leave the club alone.

Almost ten years later, I learned that the article had been cited in *Geisha of a Different Kind: Race and Sexuality in Gaysian America*, by C. Winter Han, a sociologist. Delighted, I got a copy and flipped to the part where I was mentioned.

Professor Han was blasting mainstream gay publications for "relegating gay Asian American men to the margins" and for promoting stereotypes that "construct them as being inferior to white men." My *Advocate* article was one of his prime examples. For me, Han wrote, Asian men were clearly outside the "normative definition of sexually desirable, and, thus, [an] 'exotic' experience only to be indulged 12 time zones away."

By now, my delight had imploded into shame combined with defensive brittleness: He was wrong! Wasn't he wrong? I didn't even recognize myself in what he'd written.

I had gone to China with a group of travel writers, all expenses paid by tourist ministries and airlines. Being treated to everything made me nervous; I felt a pressure to mute misgivings, and also to collude in hyping China as fabulously foreign. Travel writing depends, of course, on emphasizing difference. (If everything we found *there* were just the same as *here,* why bother to write about it?) The challenge is to show difference without sensationalizing, without flattening the other to its otherness. A challenge that, Professor Han had pointed out, I'd failed.

I read his critique again, and then the whole book. It pained me to hear the voices of Asian men he interviewed, who talked about the white guys—the domineering "rice queens"—who fetishized them. Said one: "They expect me to be so flattered by the attention of a white man that I will automatically bend over and grab my ankles."

With each account I read, I felt dismay flare like a case of shingles. I forced myself to reread my article, and I was jarred by all the things about the trip I'd buried: the scenes I'd left out, the dicey feelings I'd dodged. Professor Han, I realized, was right about the piece—it was full of Orientalist junk—but not entirely right about the reasons I'd screwed it up. I had been so scared of the truth when I was writing the piece that my true self was missing from its pages.

ONE THING I'd left out was my time in Taipei, where our group had flown before Nanjing.

I'd gone to the infamous public men's room in the Peace Park, where Taiwanese guys cruised for sex, and pissed into the last of a row of urinals. A man slunk out of the shadows and took the spot beside me. He wore a full-length duster, a motorcycle helmet with tinted visor. He began to piss, too, then pointedly raised his visor. From his leathery face, I guessed him in his eighties. I shook myself off and strode away.

But I didn't use that scene, or anything from Taipei, because my view of the city was filtered through doubt and guilt, triggered by Doug, the friend who'd shown me the men's room. Doug, who had emigrated from Boston to Taipei, was the most flagrant rice queen I knew. He was a gentle tech nerd, but his vibe when he obsessed over Asian guys (i.e., always) was that of a fanatical doll collector. His Thai American partner, one of my closest friends, mostly just seemed to laugh it off. Maybe it wasn't my place to object.

In Taipei, Doug's fixation was even more intense. He took me to a bar, where he ogled guys cartoonishly, shooting me conspiratorial glances. I was mortified—by his behavior, and by the way I played along.

What Doug knew—and Professor Han didn't—was that I had slept with plenty of Asian and Asian American men, including several with whom I'd had long-term affairs. Not as many as the white guys I'd been with, but more than those of any other race. Did this make me a rice queen? The possibility rattled me.

I had tried to convince myself I was nothing like Doug. My fetish is for youthful skinniness: wispy waists; hollow, ribby chests. Asian guys who fit that bill, sure, bring 'em on, but others—the pumped-up, the big-boned, the chunky—don't attract me just for being Asian. The line I tried to take, with Doug and with myself, was: *Me, a rice queen? No, I'm a teeny-tiny queen! It's just that lots of Asian men are my type.*

But in that Taipei bar with Doug, I could see the cracks in my façade.

The way Doug preened among those men—the humble computer geek, now a stud—reminded me of a trip to San Francisco, after college. My boyfriend, Chris, and I were visiting his brother John, who took us on a tour of Polk Street, the city's old queer district. Drag queens and hustlers, a dark biker bar. Then John said, "Oh, I have to take you to N'Touch! It was the first gay bar here for Asians."

At N'Touch, the crowd was roughly 80/20, Asian to white. The Asian men were packed into the center of the dance floor, mostly gazing out to the edge, where white guys, including us, hovered. As one man after another on the dance floor locked eyes with me, I felt something new and unnervingly exciting. I'd been out of the closet for only about three years, and although I had finally found a partner in Chris, I had spent high school and college moping over unreturned crushes; I'd concluded I couldn't be attractive. At N'Touch, suddenly I felt worthy of being looked at. Scrutinized by the crowd of seemingly interested Asian men, I was turned on less by any individual than by what I perceived as collective attention. Even as I sensed how fucked-up the whole dynamic was, I could not deny its thrill: perilous unearned power.

Eventually, when I did have affairs with Asian men, I didn't like to think that any of my pleasure might derive from that dubious imbalance. On hookup sites, I never searched according to racial categories or mentioned any preference in my profile. But not infrequently I would end up chatting with an Asian guy who launched into racial-power role-play. *Gimme your hard white daddy cock to fill my Asian pussy!* When this happened, I chatted on as if I hadn't noticed or found a fast excuse to sign off.

All of this was in my mind as I stood next to Doug in Taipei, cringing at his crude comments but also often silently agreeing with his taste.

I wrestled with my feelings about this longtime friend, my mix of scorn and something close to envy. I didn't want to be what he was, but it was hard not to covet his seeming lack of conflict. What he had done—uprooting his whole life to chase a fetish—struck me as a sort of liberation. For him it probably was, but at whose cost?

When I left Taipei, I felt the flickerings of a piece I could write about race and sex, but I snuffed them out. The topic was too charged, especially for my assignment (a fifteen-hundred-word travelogue), and I was too unsettled and confused.

EVEN MORE than the stories I'd omitted about Taipei, the missing episode Professor Han's critique made me reconsider—and made me wish I'd had the guts to write—was what had happened later on, in Shanghai.

It started at Shanghai Studio, a pulsingly fun underground gay nightclub. Literally underground: housed in an old bomb shelter, it was a warren of smoky rooms linked by a labyrinth of tunnels. Cologne clouded the air like communal confidence.

I loved how unlike N'Touch it was. Here, although the crowd's composition was equivalent—roughly three Asian men for every white one—the Asian guys were cocksure, the white guys out of our depth. Few of the dapper Asian men, coiffed as though they'd come straight from the barber, seemed impressed by me or even noticed my presence—ego-bruising but also exhilarating.

In one of the tunnels, I leaned against the wall, letting a stream of men sluice past. I was enjoying my inconspicuousness, or trying to—mulling on how a night of being shunted to the margins could make good fodder for my article—when I detected a pressure against my chest, a pressure both physical and (how is it that we sense this?) metaphysical. Mashed against my breastbone was an upturned heart-shaped face. It belonged to a short Chinese guy—early twenties, I guessed—his slim body all but lost inside a baggy jacket. He looked happily

204 · *What I Left Out*

flustered, both the glee and the bemusement heightened by his slightly crossed brown eyes.

The stream of men oxbowed around him, and he was thrust and thrust against me with tidal inevitability. *What can I do?* his face suggested—even though the bottleneck was his doing.

Being helplessly crushed together increased my sense of kismet. This is what the critics of so-called casual sex must fail to fathom, for there is nothing casual about it. Every time it's happened to me (usually just when I've concluded it never will again), I've been overwhelmed by a sudden fated feeling, which, although baffling, ratifies my sentimental hunch about the universe: that it revolves around the human heart.

In less than an instant, we'd both known that this was what we'd come for: the chance to bring pleasure to each other. We confirmed this with only our eyes, because the music roared, and I speak no Chinese, and he spoke barely any English.

His name was Liang—that was the extent of what I knew when we hailed a cab back to my hotel.

In my room, he pulled out a Chinese–English dictionary. We took turns stabbing at words. Me: *United States. Writer. Travel.* Liang: *Guangzhou. Restaurant. Worker.*

Then we stopped and traded a look: Who needed words when we had flesh?

Fast as we could, we shed our clothes, then lay in bed wondering at each other. Liang couldn't get enough of my big, bony nose, stroking it as if he hoped a genie might pop out. He ran his fingers through my chest hair, then tried to wrap his hands around one of my meaty thighs and laughed at the gap he couldn't close.

Liang's marveling sanctioned me to do the same to him. Without his outsized jacket and his unhip saggy jeans, he was even smaller than I'd imagined. I thumbed the dent of his hairless chest, seized his waist, kissed his concave belly. When I licked, his sighs of pleasure needed no translation.

All our choreography felt predestined. I turned him onto his side and cradled him from behind, making our seemingly mismatched bodies into a brilliant ball and socket. I clutched his knees to his chest, and then, when we'd both finished, we held in place as if the act had fused us.

In the morning, I had to join my group for one last tour. Liang and I exchanged addresses but struggled to say more. We kissed goodbye.

That night—my last in China—following a hunch, I returned to Shanghai Studio. There was Liang, in our same tunnel, smiling. Out of the club we hurried, then back to my hotel, and danced our karmic choreography again.

DOUG EMAILED the next day, asking how things had gone in Shanghai. He would have loved the details, but I withheld them.

Even during my nights with Liang, I had been both living our story and telling it to myself—or, really, to an imagined chorus of skeptics. All that I had reveled in as heartfelt and ecstatic would surely look, from their angle, suspect. White American tourist and younger Chinese native; bigger top and smaller, submissive bottom. *Cliché!* I could hear the chorus shout. Or worse: *Exploitation. Exotification.*

Had I exoticized Liang? Absolutely. But I assumed he'd done the same to me. The spark of our fantasy was mutual foreignness. Also, it had been Liang who'd made the first move. None of this read to me like a tale of exploitation. But every path my story took ended in the same patch of thorns: Liang is Asian, and I am white; like our bodies, our racial privilege was lopsided.

We all like to think we heed our own desires in bed, unaffected by history or culture. But no encounter takes place in a vacuum. Why did what had happened with Liang strike me as predestined? Could it have been coincidence that the roles we readily enacted conformed to deep-set cultural stereotypes? I'd hungered to engulf him, to steer his slender body. I could tell myself that those urges were only physical, but how could I divorce them from preconceptions I've absorbed about racial domination and weakness? And yes, Liang had chosen me, but his desires, like mine, had also been socially conditioned.

A troubling self-critique isn't hard to craft: when I hook up with Asian men with small, skinny bodies, maybe they read to my Western eyes as vulnerable and young, and maybe that makes me view them, no matter how unconsciously, as underdeveloped, as subjects I can master. Postcolonial theory tells me that might well be true. All the same, this is also true: never has any sexual encounter felt that way to me.

BACK IN BOSTON, my *Advocate* deadline looming, I floundered. If my tryst in Shanghai resulted in some insight, I still lacked the guts to grasp it, let alone put it in the pages of a magazine. Even when I dared to think of writing about Liang, I kept smacking up against my ignorance. A Guangzhou restaurant worker . . . but what else did I know? I couldn't say how he viewed white men or anything else. I couldn't quote a single line he'd said.

Instead, I took refuge in my story from Nanjing: the drag queen I had kissed but not slept with. Risqué enough to seem revealing but actually superficial. Kissing a drag queen (who happened to be Asian) was a new experience; by writing about that instead of about Liang and the questions he'd reactivated, I hoped to sidestep the whole rice-queen morass.

It was mostly bullshit. For one thing, I'd done more than just kiss the drag queen. And why had I declined when she asked to spend the night? Not, as my article implied, because she was too "other" for my tastes. I rebuffed her mostly because my hotel forbade local guests.

Hemingway famously said that if a writer knows enough about his subject, "he may omit things that he knows and the reader, if the writer is writing honestly enough, will have a feeling of those things as strongly as though the writer had stated them." But I knew way too little about my subject, and I was far from honest; how could the reader feel what I'd omitted? My article, because of all the racial questions it skirted, ended up only being racist.

In writing and in life, I've too often tried to strip my interracial encounters from their context, panicked by the likelihood that I might cause offense; but it's more offensive to pretend racial context doesn't matter. My article's failures have made me fear omission more than messy truths. Now I aim to better own up to the ways I do feel different from—puzzled by, in awe of—the other. Own up to the thrills of wielding, or abdicating, power. To urges that cause me shame, or should but don't.

I'VE HOPED to give this essay an upbeat ending—something to show that, even though my lapses have been painful, I still hold my bedrock faith in heart-to-heart intimacy, in the face of cultural divides. I don't want to lose sight of the tenderness and grace I shared with Liang.

The scene that I've thought would make the best culmination was in fact our final interaction. We'd woken up after our second spooned-together night. Rushing to pack, I paused at the gift basket—apples, mangoes, dragon fruit—that the hotel manager, eager to curry favor with a travel writer, had brought me. I couldn't take it on the plane, and now the fruit would spoil; maybe I should offer it to Liang? Just as I was going to, I seized up with self-consciousness. What if he interpreted my gesture as patronizing or, worse, thought I hoped to "pay" for our tryst?

Just then, he sat beside me and tipped his head to my shoulder, brushed the back of his wrist along my thigh.

No, I thought, I was projecting my unease onto him. Why should I be so afraid simply to offer something? I jumped up and grabbed the basket and held it out to him. Liang took it, beaming as though he'd won a carnival prize. Minutes later, he would walk out and we would part forever, but now, the basket wedged between us, we kissed.

NICE SCENE, right? That's just how it happened.

And yet, try as I might to fully embrace the memory, I keep straining to hear Liang's reactions. But no, all I have is the last flick of his lips, the lush, almost-cloying scent of fruit. And his eyes, his sweet brown eyes. Slightly crossed. Silent.

Estrangeiro

BY THE TIME I got off at Mercado Modelo, where I had to catch a second bus, to the airport, I'd mostly stopped crying. I rolled my carry-on toward what I hoped was the right stop, heeling it when it snagged on cracked sidewalks. I passed a granny hawking croquettes out of a greasy cart, and then a vendor who clutched a machete, as if guarding his heap of coconuts. They both stared, without compunction. Because of my bag's clatter? My puffy, sleepless eyes?

At the bus stop, commuters also gawked; maybe all they stared at was my foreignness. Usually, here in Salvador, I had dressed like Uílliam: T-shirt, board shorts, flip-flops; no watch, camera, or wallet; in my pocket, never more than ten or twenty *reais*. No one would be fooled into thinking I was Bahian, but I had hoped to show, at least, that I was not a sucker or a prick. This morning, though, headed home, I wore my Timex and crisp Levi's and chunky New Balance sneakers. My pocket bulged with a passport, a wallet full of dollars. I looked like an American tourist—in other words, like myself.

Nervously, I scanned the locals for someone who might help. (I had never caught the bus from here.) I didn't have a smartphone, and neither, I guessed, did any of them. This was 2010, in the northeast of Brazil.

"*Aeroporto?*" I asked a teenager in orange plastic shades. He just shrugged. Next to him, a wizened woman held a threadbare tote bag; she said sorry, she could only direct me to the mall. Had she and the teen, I wondered, never been to the airport? Never jetted above the clouds to somewhere new and wondrous? I'd been wilting already under my heavy daypack, but now I felt the specific sweat of working to hold back tears.

The night before, Uílliam and I had sat astride the seawall, long after the crowd applauded the sunset. He had told me not to be sad: we would always, always find a way to be together. This had been my second return trip to see him; couldn't we plan another very soon? I had wept into his neck, and he had tried to hush me. *Don't cry,* in English, might have come off harsh, but his Portuguese vowels only soothed. "*Não chora,*" he'd said, again and again. "*Não chora.*"

We'd met two years earlier, when I was in Brazil for an artists' residency on an island off the coast of Salvador. Needing a break from my novel-in-progress, I had taken a ferry into the city one Friday night, having booked the cheapest hotel available. I was proud of having made the call in Portuguese, which I was trying to teach myself. My novel featured a Brazilian character, and I was here to dive deep into the culture.

The hotel wasn't bad for sixteen bucks, but I was surprised by the mirrored ceiling, the porn on the toaster-sized TV. I decided to take it as a nudging from the fates. A deep cultural dive, sure—but on this night I would settle (fingers crossed) for sex.

If you'd asked me how this urge related to my home life, I might've claimed it didn't: that was the point. My boyfriend, Scott, and I had been together for thirteen years; recently, we'd bought our first house. Sex was a source of tension for us—a rift about the link between the physical and the emotional—but Salvador, four thousand miles from Boston, made that problem distant. Hooking up with other guys was well within our rules. Tonight, I thought (leaning into the pun), I'd be scot-free.

I'd heard there was a back alley that housed a string of gay bars. After three circuits around the block, I found the guts to enter. The alley was packed: swishing queens, dykes in backward ballcaps, sweaty shirtless gym rats and surfers—Afro-Brazilians, almost all, bumping to a raucous axé anthem. Everyone seemed so unconstrained, all the more so for standing out in the street. My own stiffness felt like a failure of imagination.

I wanted a drink to hide behind, but all I saw were big bottles of beer shared by friends, and how would I buy one? I could find no waiters.

Then a shout in Portuguese: "You alone?"

I turned to find two guys in chairs against the concrete wall. One was chubby, with puggish eyes. The other, shockingly lean, had thick black hair and brown skin so smooth I was sure he'd never shaved. A single dimple flashed in his cheek. "So," he tried again, "you alone?"

His youthful chutzpah made him almost painfully my type. I sat beside him and said, "Not anymore!"

His name was Uílliam, and his pal was Leo. He poured me some beer, then ordered another outsized bottle, dismissing my offer to pay. *The book is on the table* was the only English he knew—a line from a long-ago school lesson—and so we had to make do with my scanty Portuguese, learned from CDs I'd borrowed before the trip.

As Leo sulked (his love for Uílliam leaking from every pore), Uílliam and I vacuumed up facts about each other. Twenty-three, although he could have passed for seventeen, he had moved to the city that year, hoping to go to college and learn law. Hearing that I was thirty-eight and a university teacher, he nodded with apparent satisfaction.

"When I saw you," he said, "I made myself a promise: if he comes by again, I'll say something. Normally, I am not so brave."

"Liar," I said, and goosed his side.

"I'm shy!" he insisted unshyly. "A boy from the interior!" The town where he'd grown up, he said, was ten hours' drive by bus.

His left forearm, smooth as his jaw, sprouted just one hair. I saw him not as a law student but as a cocky, moxie-for-miles newsboy in a classic film.

Uílliam bought another round, and I got up to piss. When I returned, he was standing, asking if I was ready. With Leo scowling, we hurried off, Uílliam bouncing along on his toes, as if overeager to greet the future.

At the hotel, I said I was sorry for its nature, but Uílliam—taking in the mirrored ceiling, the porn, a basket of rubbers and lube for sale—gave my shoulder a flippant punch. "When we grow old together," he said, "we will always remember our first night!" He cackled at his own joke, and I was laughing, too, smitten by his easy confidence.

After sex, we studied each other. "*Pele de mel,*" he murmured, stroking my "honey skin." I stroked his skin, too—a burnished-looking bronze—but I was too nervous to comment. I'd read a piece about Brazilians' racial attitudes, including a list of one hundred and thirty-six variations of skin color. I wasn't sure how to ask him how he identified.

I asked, instead, about his tattoo. Just beside his cock, in a Speedo-shaped patch of unsunned skin: a turquoise dolphin, caught in joyful leap. "What's this color in Portuguese?" I asked. He said, "*Turquesa.*" Undulating his hips, he made the dolphin swim, and then we were laughing again, then kissing. Kissing him was like discovering I could breathe underwater, a blue infinity: I never wanted to surface.

In the morning, I woke up late for a meeting at the residency. Rushing to dress, I managed to say that I was living on Itaparica, an island out in the bay, at a remote artists' colony with sketchy internet. "But here, take this," I said, and wrote down my email.

"Email?" he said. "Seriously?"

Out on the street, he bussed my cheek, then bolted. Had I misread him? For all his charm, was he a "one and done"? I twinged. I was hopeless at shallow sex.

The next day, a staffer told me someone was out front, asking for a Michael: "Local guy. Doesn't even know your last name." What should she do, tell him to buzz off?

"No," I said. "I think I know him."

At the entrance, there was Uílliam, peering through the gate. My body felt like one big muscle, flexing with desire; at the same time, something in me unclenched. "Wow! How did you even find me?" I asked.

Uílliam flashed his single-dimpled grin and told the tale: riding the hourlong ferry to this unfamiliar island, hailing a kombi, then hiking for miles, asking strangers if they knew where "the foreign artists" lived.

The residency didn't allow overnight guests, so we searched for a reasonably priced guesthouse. (I was paying, but he refused to let me get ripped off.) Our room stank of mildew under disinfectant. After we fucked, we were cuddling, watching a harebrained Nicholas Cage caper, when thunder punched the air, and rain poured down the insides of the walls.

"Now," he said, "we will always remember our *second* night!"

I laughed, but his joke, this time, felt a bit less ludicrous. Drunk on hormones and novelty, I could picture a third night with Uílliam, a fourth . . .

Which was why I drew a line. I said I had a boyfriend.

"Of course," he said. "All the guys I like the most are taken." He sounded forlorn but not displeased to have his theory affirmed. He led me in a samba across the rain-drenched floor, stomping like a schoolboy in a puddle.

"HOOKED UP with any of the locals yet?" asked Scott.

We were Skyping, the next night. He sat in the kitchen, at our vintage dinette set, framed by walls we'd painted in a shade called Yellow Brick Road.

"Actually," I said, "I did meet one guy."

Scott was smiling, his strong jaw peppered with ginger stubble. "Details?"

What should I tell him of Uílliam? About his trek to the island, and how he'd grinned to see me again, as if I were the X on a map of hidden treasure?

"Totally up my alley," I said. "Super, super skinny. Tiny ass."

"Hot!" Scott said.

I waited to hear what else he wanted to know.

"Oh, speaking of tiny," he said. "There was a baby rabbit in the front yard yesterday. But now it's gone. I worry it got eaten."

I was only half listening, squeamish at having described Uílliam so reductively. It felt unfaithful—to both him and Scott. But Scott hadn't even asked if I would see Uílliam again. He could not imagine how I'd use someone like Uílliam to patch over the holes in our own love.

Scott was funny, brilliant, perennially impish—the person with whom I always wanted to leave any party, so we could gossip all the way back home. But in matters of sex we clashed, especially since his interest in me had fizzled.

For me, sex and love were strands tied together, the thrill cinching when both ends were pulled. For Scott (so he'd explained, trying to assuage me), they were roads that rarely intersected. Nothing turned him on as much as hooking up with strangers, with whom he felt unleashed. He loved me too much, he said, to do with me the things he did with them.

As a closeted teenager, I had ached with loneliness, scared I'd never find a man to love me. I could not have imagined the lash of this new loneliness, when Scott—the man who did love me—passed me over for strangers. It felt like an unresolvable mathematical riddle: the closer we got, the further away I would push his passion.

"Well, it's getting late," he said. The kitchen glowed behind him. "Really miss you!"

"Miss you too," I said. "I'm homesick."

The word resounded oddly. *Seasick* meant the motion of the sea caused you nausea; *carsick* meant a car made you ill. What did *homesick* say about your home?

Scott blew me a kiss, then leaned into the screen, nearer and nearer, until his face blurred.

THE LIMIT I'd set with Uílliam seemed somehow to free us; we burned through romantic fuel we had no incentive to conserve. At a gallery opening, we scoffed at the vapid art, then scored some coke and skipped out to the street, holding hands. We stayed in another love hotel, this time on purpose. On the beach, at dawn, we stood together pissing, merging our streams into the glinting surf. Even though it was April, he gave me a valentine: *My heart is perfect because you are in it.* He was unafraid to reveal his mushy heart and made this seem not maudlin but courageous.

And yet, the more couplish we got, the more doubts I had.

When we went out, I was acutely conscious of our differences: the almost-forty gringo, pudgy-bellied, sunburned, next to the boyish, dark-skinned Bahian. The city teemed with disparate pairs like us. Brazil, I'd read, was now the world's top destination for sex tourism. Salvador had been the country's colonial capital, the largest slave-trade port in the Americas, and it was impossible not to see vestiges of racist exploitation. Rich white foreigners came in search of Afro-Brazilian culture—the capoeira and Candomblé, the drumming and *dendê* oil—but some also came for "exotic" sex and "primitive" promiscuity. Millions of Bahians lived on only dollars a day, so plenty of locals were willing, for a fee, to go along.

Seeing those gringo–local couples always made me cringe: because I thought we were above them or because I worried we might not be? The night we'd met, Uílliam had bought our beers in the alley bar: not the typical act of a gold digger. (Unless—oh God, how could I be letting myself think this?—unless he had paid for those first rounds as a gambit, all the better to drain me dry later.) Since that night, I had gladly paid for everything, and Uílliam, though he seemed to go along just as gladly, asked for nothing more from me than fun and sex and friendship. But what if I hadn't been paying? Would he still be interested?

Then at a club one night, a man rolled his eyes at us, and Uílliam must have felt my body tense. "Who cares," he shouted over the music, "if some idiot thinks I'm just a rent boy? No one knows the truth of us but *us*." Exultant, he mashed his hips on mine.

Did we see our truth the same? I suspected we both looked for escape: for him, from the limits of his life's opportunities; for me, from the riddle of loving Scott.

I brought him to the residency, where we hung out with a Japanese artist who built "nonfunctional architecture" with light. Telling us we gave off an irresistible glow, she asked to photograph us by the sea. Uílliam wore a Speedo the same blue as the sky, the dorsal fin of his tattooed dolphin peeking above the waist. We lay together on a dock, his head against my stomach, and I imagined someone later (in Japan?) looking at our photos. What would they see? Something sincere, I hoped. Symbiosis.

The artist asked if Uílliam was often attracted to older men. Yes, he said, for as long as he could remember. Early on, disturbed by this, he had seen a shrink, but now he reveled in knowing what he liked. The only problem, he added, giving my wrist a yank, was that he fell for older foreigners—*estrangeiros*—who inevitably went back to their lives.

My wrist burned. Had he meant to yank quite so hard?

Since my mention of Scott, we had not revisited the topic. But then, on our last date—strolling arm in arm along the promenade at Itapuã—Uílliam asked: How old was he? What country was he from? I should have heard the fantasy in his questions: that I befriended young men and ferried them to better lives in America. But what I heard was jealousy, and I was floundering for answers when Uílliam interrupted: "Why do I do this thing? I fall in love with someone, knowing he has to leave, and then he *does,* and I am left alone."

I could have said that I would feel lonely, too, even at home. But, of course, my home was solid: a house I owned, a partner. I said only, "I fell in love too."

At the end of my residency—the weeks had felt like months, a stop-time honeymoon—Uílliam saw me off at the airport. He gave me a pillow to hug, its cover stitched with MON BIJOU, and a stainless-steel promise ring. Oh, how I would miss his mushy heart!

AT THE bus stop, despite my effort, I could not stop crying. I ducked my head, hoping the teen in shades hadn't noticed.

A bus huffed to a halt, and I looked toward its head-sign, hoping for Aeroporto. Plenty of time to make my flight, assuming I caught the bus. But no, this one was bound for the mall. The wizened lady boarded.

I was about to duck my face again, to pat it dry—there was a hankie somewhere in my pack—when I caught someone staring. I turned away, self-conscious of my wet eyes, as though they weren't parts of me but mortifying adornments, like bells tied around a house cat's neck. Then I felt a surge of anger at the rubbernecker. I whirled toward him, glowering, but he just smiled, baring his gums, his guileless bucked teeth.

His grin caught me so off guard, reflexively I grinned back. He nodded, as if to a toddler: *There, there, you see? It's not so bad.*

He looked to be in his early twenties. Six feet something, skinny as a skewer. His face was lighter than Uílliam's, what locals might call *tostada.* His dark hair, cropped at the sides, swooped in front: a cheeky, frosted forelock.

Again I gazed away; bad to cruise so blatantly. *Were* we cruising? Brazilian men often scrambled my gaydar. This guy's fitted slacks, his calculated hair, were fashion choices straight dudes here might flaunt. But something about his posture, the pertness of his hips: he looked like he wanted to be sized up from the rear.

Even if he *was* gay, how could I, only just parted from Uílliam, flirt with him?

I met his eyes, but just then, another bus rolled up. He shrugged sweetly and shuffled toward the door. Now I'd never have the chance to . . . what? What had I wanted?

He mounted the bus, readying bills to pay the *cobrador,* and then, while a girl ahead of him waited for her change, he peeked back, asking a silent question with his eyebrows. I nodded, and he stepped down and strode right up to me.

WHEN I got home from the residency, Scott hugged me, our

bodies slipping into their soothing fit. He treated me to dinner at our favorite sushi place, where, as always, we ate matching pieces simultaneously, to make sure we shared the same delight.

My affair with Uílliam had supercharged my confidence, and I was raring to brandish my new swagger, hopeful I might seem enough like a stranger to turn Scott on. But he, back at the house, wanted only to cuddle.

One night later that week, I awoke to him walking down the stairs. In the morning, his mud-caked sneakers sat in the front closet, stinking of the Fens, where gay men cruised.

I hadn't known how much I would stay in touch with Uílliam, or even how. (Sneak away and call him from a pay phone?) I decided to Skype him from home—and soon, most days, I did. At first, I made sure Scott was out before I called, but then I started lapsing, and there were times, I knew, when he could hear Portuguese behind my office door.

I suppose I wanted him to hear. Maybe I was hoping he would say I had to stop, so I could issue my own ultimatum. Sometimes, after a call, he would pull a face ("Oh," he'd say drolly, "done so soon?"), but he never challenged me directly.

He had long felt guilty for his waning sexual interest, and knew anonymous hookups weren't my thing—which had led him to tolerate a couple of previous affairs. But although he'd gotten along graciously with my "other men," I knew he had worried I would leave him. If he suffered that fear again, hearing me and Uílliam, maybe he felt unworthy to confess it. And although I wanted him to want me to be faithful, I wouldn't pledge my loyalty until he did the same. Thus we spun forward, going nowhere: a car stuck on ice.

And when, after a full year, I decided to visit Uílliam (it had taken me that long to find the money and courage), I didn't quite ask Scott's permission. I made a statement—"I'd like to go to Brazil for a couple weeks"—and Scott didn't openly object.

I flew to Salvador in June 2009.

That spring, Uílliam had been living at his mother's, but they'd been feuding—she was a Christian who disapproved of gayness. Where, then, would we stay? Not to worry, he said; he'd take care of everything. Sounded too good to be true, but I was wary of doubting him or seeming overdelicate, the gringo who required special treatment. Looking back, I also wonder if I embraced his vagueness because I feared knowing the full picture. If I really saw the life he wanted to escape, I would have to face up to the likelihood that I would let him down.

A couple of weeks before my flight, he had called, triumphant, to say he'd finally managed to leave his mother's. Good for him, I thought, but also good for me: the kind of ardent, all-caps gesture I'd been missing at home.

When I got there, I was happy to find that he was thriving. He shared an airy apartment, only a block from the beach, with a guy named Marcos and Dani, a young woman with winningly green braces on her teeth. Uílliam's room was comfy but spare—a bed, a chest of drawers—its only flourish a photo of us, taken at the awful gallery opening. In the picture, I was comically pink from too much sun, which got him calling me *"meu camarãozinho"*—his darling little shrimp. I called him *"meu magrinho,"* my skinny.

Uílliam had started a job as an architect's guy Friday. While he worked, I walked about or sat in a café. I'd never been a coffee drinker but found myself ordering sugary *cafezinhos,* trying on new versions of myself in Portuguese. At five o'clock, Uílliam would bound home, eager to cook for me: rice and beans, collard greens sliced to perfect ribbons. "Is it yummy, Mô?" he'd ask (Mô was short for *Amor*). "I just want my babydoll to be happy." Later, we'd hit his favorite spots: the stall serving the best *acarajé* in Rio Vermelho; the gay bar with the most flamboyant queens. At the weekend, we traveled with

Dani up to Praia do Forte—miles and miles of pure white-sand beaches—to a sanctuary for endangered sea turtles.

Oh, I know how it sounds: middle-aged American wings off to the tropics, finds his bliss with a hot younger native. But I was hoping that being hyperaware of the clichés meant we might manage to subvert them.

One afternoon, I went to Itaparica and didn't get back until past eleven. Uílliam sat in the window, watching for my arrival. First he fed me a plate of mango, and then he said, "We're moving out. Now—before Marcos gets home." He had placed my belongings neatly into my suitcase. His own things were stuffed in grocery bags.

Waiting for a taxi—he didn't say to where—Uílliam unspooled a tangle of explanations. Marcos, after finding a joint in Uílliam's pocket, had pitched a fit, demanding he move out. But why, I asked, had Marcos even been going through his clothes? "Because he's crazy," Uílliam said. "Crazy with jealousy. I told him he can't have me—I'm with *you*." He shrugged with charismatic fatalism.

Close to midnight, we landed at the home of two of his friends, with whom we'd gone clubbing a couple times. They put us in their small spare room: a folding chair, a mattress on the floor. Why didn't I just take us to a hotel? Partly, I suppose, not to flash my relative wealth. But more than that, I wanted to learn from Uílliam. At home, when my life threatened to pull me under, I tried to grasp it all the tighter, but Uílliam, hit by waves of turmoil, surfed. Life can change, he seemed to say. What is life *but* change?

His friend Murilo gave us each a pillow and a hanger. Uílliam took a shirt and a pair of jeans from my suitcase, and hung them, taking up both hangers. Then he took my toiletries and set them on the chair. His was the world in tatters, but he wanted to build a nest for me.

Soon we'd sleep on the grainy mattress, spooning each other, my hand on his tattoo. But first, one more item: the picture of us at the gallery. He kissed it and propped it on his pillow.

"YOU'RE SAD," said the stranger when the bus roared away. He spoke in slowed-down Portuguese.

"Yes," I said. "I am."

"Sad to be leaving, or sad to be going home?"

This was a distinction I hadn't much considered, but suddenly it felt fundamental. "Both," I said. I asked where he was going.

"Work. And now I'm late." He seemed at once apprehensive and easily in-charge. "And you, of course, are going to the airport."

"Right," I said. I made a show of scanning for the bus.

"Tell me, why are we talking?" He poked my chest playfully. "You're about to fly away, so why?"

"I don't know," I answered honestly. Guiltily, I pictured Uílliam's lonely eyes that morning. "Bye, my angel," he'd said. "Come back soon."

The man leaned toward me, not so close that passersby would clock us but near enough for me to smell his passionfruit cologne. He stood a head taller than me but looked like a boy elongated, his face smooth except for stubble just around the mouth. His big teeth—the way his lips barely closed around them—gave him an air of stupefied amusement.

He said his name, stretching it like an odyssey: U-bi-ra-*il*-ton.

My throat—and my balls—tightened with expectancy. A force had taken hold of me, a sense that I could get away with anything. Was this the nervy high that Scott chased? His hookups had always felt like a snub of me, a specific turning away.

But now I got it: not a turning away, a helpless turning toward. More forgivable and all the more alarming.

I wasn't turning from Uílliam now or even thinking much of him. I wasn't thinking anything, I was *feeling*. The urge to lick Ubirailton. The tightness in my pants.

A hiss of brakes. Another bus.

To the airport? No, still not.

My mouth went tinny with dread. Lost in flirting, had I missed my connection?

Ubirailton saw my worry and took me by the shoulder. "It's okay," he said. "I'm with you."

AFTER THE NIGHT of our escape, Uílliam rehashed the story to anyone who would listen: villainous Marcos's tantrum, the taxi as getaway car, and us as heroes in a happily ever after.

Flattered to be his co-star, I went along. But I still couldn't fathom Marcos's rage. Had Uílliam previously led him on, or slept with him, to land a cheap bedroom? I didn't like to think of Uílliam being so transactional, or to admit he might lack the luxury *not* to be.

One morning a few days later, lying on Murilo's meager mattress, Uílliam cradled my chin and said, "You like it here, right?"

"Here?" I asked, glancing around the tiny spare room.

"No," he said. "Here in Brazil. With me."

"Of course," I told him. With him, I felt brand-new but also more like myself.

"If Scott makes you sad," he said, "why do you stay with him?"

He almost never said Scott's name. Why did he want to talk about this now?

"Hard to explain," I answered. For all our troubles, I

always felt lucky next to Scott. Life with him was like driving a turbocharged car, leaving everyone else in the dust. The extra speed meant extra risk—that was the price of admission.

"Why?" asked Uílliam, sharper now. "Why are you still with him?"

In the moment, I thought he was railing at my inertia and pressing home our recent story's lesson: being unsettled is sometimes how you find a happy ending.

"Trust me," I said. "I'm thinking about it. Okay?"

What did I really want, and with who? I wasn't sure. To talk about it honestly would have outstripped my Portuguese, but I was also too afraid to try. Or too selfish.

We decided to go for lunch at the Feira de São Joaquim, the biggest marketplace in Salvador. Riding the bus, Uílliam gazed at the neighborhoods we passed. "No, no," he muttered at a row of sleek condos. Later, as we climbed a hill crowded with concrete houses: "Maybe," he said. "Maybe somewhere here."

Now I reconsidered our conversation. Perhaps he hadn't been thinking about my need to be unsettled but about his own aspiration to settle down: where he would live, after Murilo's; how he would afford it. Maybe he'd been trying to ask: *Can I count on you?*

At São Joaquim, as we got off, two teen boys were boarding the bus. Both had dyed-blond perms and brave queeny smiles. Obviously a couple, and in love. Between them, they clutched what they'd purchased at the market: a quivering, panic-eyed chicken.

"Dinner?" I asked Uílliam.

"Maybe. Probably not. For that, they would just buy some meat."

"Why would they want a live one?"

"For Candomblé. A sacrifice."

I couldn't tell if he was pulling my leg.

Uílliam must have read my face. "What, you don't believe me?"

"No, it's just . . . I hadn't thought of that."

"Of course you hadn't," he said. "But *some* people? To get what they want? Michael, they don't fear a little blood!"

Clasping my neck, he made as if to chomp down on my jugular. Then he laughed and lifted his face. He kissed me.

WHEN I got home, Scott asked almost nothing about my trip, and I didn't ask what he'd done in my absence. I suppose we each considered our reticence to be generous.

If I'd chosen to tell him more, I might've said that he and Uílliam had a lot in common: a boyish, all-in intensity; a careless (in the best sense of the word) romanticism. In odd moments— insomniac, or after a couple of cocktails—I dreamed about introducing them. It was less a fantasy about replacing Scott than one about trying to stay with him. Showing him, through Uílliam, how to bust the wall between love and lovemaking.

According to the boilerplate midlife-crisis plot, I should have been lusting to escape domestic tedium. Actually, though, I'd yearned for life with Scott to be more conventional, and we had trended lately in that direction—especially since, after years of living apart, we had bought our house. But what if we were trapping ourselves within a bitter parable: the couple who sets up house, and works at every detail—hemming curtains, arranging figurines atop the mantel—never seeing the house is built on quicksand.

Uílliam and I were still Skyping daily. He had left Murilo's and moved back in with his mom, who was trying to be more accepting. He was helping to renovate her cramped concrete dwelling, adding on a new room for himself. Whenever he spoke of the renovation, he used the verb *reformar. Reform,*

I heard: it made the work sound vital and decisive, and made me want to undertake my own reformation. I've always been susceptible to false cognates.

IN MAY 2010, celebrating my forty-first birthday, I gave myself a trip to Brazil, to spend a third stretch of weeks with Uílliam.

This time, I rented an apartment. With beige bedding and forgettable furniture, the place was provocatively blank: here, we could imagine ourselves to be whoever we wanted and also imagine anything of each other.

Uílliam had asked his boss for time off. Afternoons, we sat on the beach, splurging on treats from roving vendors: quail eggs, charcoal-grilled cheese, and big Brahma beers, served, as Uílliam liked to say, "*estupidamente gelada,*" stupidly cold. Nights, we danced in smoky clubs or at the steps of an eighteenth-century church, where a bandleader named Gerônimo blasted Yoruba funk. Walking home, we'd trade licks of a tamarind *picolé*; I knew the word meant *popsicle* but thought instead of *piccolo,* to match the ice's fluty, trilling taste. (That was how things felt with Uílliam: synesthetic, songful.) Then we'd fuck for hours, with almost holy franticness, as if in thankful offering.

Even more than partying, what I think we both enjoyed was shopping for our love nest: beans and oil, even toilet paper— the more banal, the more like real life. I had brought some freelance work, manuscripts to edit, and I would sit on the couch, typing on my laptop, while Uílliam tended a pot of rice or mixed bananas into fried *farofa*. At mealtimes, he set the table with touchingly formal rigor, and we would talk.

My Portuguese had improved with the jittery speed of a time-lapse film, but I was nothing even close to fluent. Plus, I struggled with cultural conventions. Uílliam spoke in the hyper-romantic style of telenovelas ("Love of my life! There is no one else!"), but I was never sure what was truth and what was tone. Sometimes, when he could sense me straining to voice my feelings, he paced his index and ring fingers up and down my arm like the legs of a tiny, coquettish dancer; I would add two fingers in a silent *pas de deux*.

That our intimacies unfolded in another language—and no language—heightened my sense that what we shared had nothing to do with life back home; Scott literally couldn't have understood it. This made our affair feel at once more transgressive and, in a way, less far-reaching, as if it didn't count in the same ledger as life with Scott. But how much were we relying on a too-convenient lack of comprehension?

I worried, in particular, about money. Months before, Uílliam had said his mother's renovations had been halted. On Skype, he'd shown the bathroom, with only a tarp for a roof. He didn't want to trouble me, but could I send some cash? Not a problem, I told him, and wired a hundred dollars. Eight or so weeks later, he asked for the same amount again, and thanked me unfussily when I sent it. For him, the calculus seemed simple: I had the money; we were in love; why would I *not* help him? For me, though, the handouts stirred unease. Not about the amount—a hundred bucks every other month. But each gift made it harder to dodge the possibility that he and I were actually what we seemed: a gringo "keeping" his boyfriend-on-the-side.

Every once in a while, a rogue wave of doubt would rise, and I'd be swamped with awful paranoia: What if Uílliam cultivated a whole stable of patrons, and I was only one more suckered gringo? My fear revealed more about me than about him, but, although baseless, it spoke to something real: the challenge of feeling at home in a foreign culture. My uncertainty was only sharpened by the symbolism: I was paying to fix a literal home.

And yet.

Two weeks into my three-week trip, I was felled by a rotten cold, and Uílliam seemed to relish the role of nurse, making me chicken soup and ginger tea. When I moped, he would croon our favorite Brazilian club song ("French kissing is old-fashioned / The in thing now is making out naked") or prance about, parroting a local drag queen's catchphrase, which meant, more or less, "It's the shit." I don't think he got why it tickled me so much—it sounded, to my English-tuned ears, like *eh-ooh-itchy*—he just knew it made me laugh my head off, so he did it.

Maybe my illness was just what we had needed: a test, a glimpse of how we'd navigate adversity. Whenever I thanked him for his care, he smiled and said, "In sickness and in health!"

By my last night, I was better but still feeling vulnerable, as you do after a bout of frailty: your very soul has been skinned, and any breeze of emotion might abrade you. We went out for a final meal of *moqueca* and *carne do sol,* then beers at a rickety beachside bar. Later, we passed the lighthouse, where couples kissed for selfies, then strolled to a dimly lit section of the seawall and sat astride it, holding hands, listening to the black water's hiccups.

I stared across the bay, out toward Itaparica. I could picture Uílliam there, surprising me at the residency gate: his rascally smile and cocksure stance, but just enough fluster in his eyes to betray how much he wanted.

I started softly crying and buried my face in his neck. He let me clutch him, his body so much skinnier than mine but sturdy.

"Shh," he said. "*Não chora*, Michael."

I couldn't stop the tears.

He said we would always, always find a way to be together. "*Não chora*," he repeated. "*Não chora*." Stroking my cheek, my sweaty brow, he asked why I couldn't stop crying.

Sadness at having to leave, of course, but also something more. I had no words to shape it—because of my iffy Portuguese, but more because I hadn't yet fathomed my own feelings. After these weeks together, our bond felt so much tighter. Uílliam had suggested I might come back for New Year's, when we could dress in white and toss flowers into the bay, in honor of the goddess of the sea. Then I could stay for Carnaval; we'd dance our asses off! We had also talked about fighting the long odds and trying to get him a visa to America.

I continued to hold him, his steady, scrawny chest. Our love felt precious, silvered—and so fragile.

Uílliam told me again not to cry, then pulled away. His voice was kind but didn't hide his grievance. "You have your life at home," he said, "but I stay here, alone. *I* should cry, not you. You're the foreigner."

FOREIGNER, *estrangeiro*: that was the word he'd used, and now it wheeled in my head to the bus's rumbling rhythm. I sat with Ubirailton in the rearmost row, his left thigh pressed against my right. He had learned that I'd been waiting at the wrong stop but that if I caught this different bus and then transferred, I could still maybe make my flight. Even though his workplace was miles in another direction, he had said he'd guide me through the route.

We had the last row to ourselves. No one else could see us. Nonetheless, Ubirailton used my pack as a cover when he reached across and grabbed my cock.

I was hard—I had been since we'd pressed our legs together—and when I rubbed my hand along his thigh and then his crotch (his linen slacks were scandalously thin), I discovered that he was hard too.

The bus was muggy, suggestive with body odor. With his free hand, Ubirailton slid our window open. His blond forelock caught the breeze and trembled.

God, he was sexy! His honest eyes and gleaming, eager teeth.

Staring ahead, he stroked me, his hand synced with the bumping of the wheels.

The cognate I had always linked with *estrangeiro* was *stranger*, which made sense: a foreigner is a person you don't know. But now, as the word bumped and bumped around my mind, it rang with a different emphasis. How could I have overlooked its crucial first letter? Not a stranger, but an estranger. Someone who causes estrangement—who alienates, and distances, and splits things apart—sometimes even within his own self.

Suddenly, alarmingly, my hand on Ubirailton's cock felt like someone else's. Only ninety minutes ago, I had wept for leaving Uílliam; momentarily, I would fly home, where Scott awaited; but here I was, splintering my allegiances even further. What was I doing? Who was I becoming? I, who had blamed Scott for chasing the rush of lust.

These days, with more self-compassion than I summoned then, I can see that I was caught between my two relationships, each foot on a different storm-tossed boat; no wonder that when Ubirailton offered a distraction, I seized it. Nothing more than harmless hanky-panky. As it was happening, though, I felt out of control; I went queasy. Was this what I wanted, to fission myself into bits? A bit for Uílliam, a bit for Scott, a bit more for strangers on the street.

My grip must have slackened; I'm sure my face did too. Ubirailton stilled his hand and turned to look at me, his eyes full of what I read as grace.

"You have a boyfriend at home?" he asked.

My long sigh confirmed it.

"But also you like it here," he said. "Away from everything?" Leaving my crotch, his hand found my thumb and gently squeezed. "The question is: Which *you* do you like?"

Now I saw that this was what I'd truly hungered for: the rush not of lust but recognition. Someone who would not push or pull but just hold me.

I could have told him anything, and that was much of the thrill—to be entirely free and unbeholden—but when I answered, I said the truth, a truth so new I didn't know it until the words came forth. I said I had a boyfriend here, too, a loving partner, someone I'd been dating for two years, but I wasn't sure I would see him again.

All at once, the futility of my love for Uílliam hit me. I could come back for New Year's, for Carnaval, for whatever, but wouldn't he and I just endure more goodbyes? Wouldn't each be harder than the last? Even if he got a visa (doubtful, given his poverty), how would I fit him into my life? Finally, I admitted it: I wouldn't.

Being with Uílliam, marvelous as it was, wore me out. Never being able to say exactly what I meant, or knowing if I understood his wishes. I just couldn't sustain it. Didn't want to.

"It's over," I told Ubirailton. "I think it's really over."

Ever since, I've wondered why he tipped me toward this reckoning. Why should someone I didn't know, to whom I owed nothing, spur me finally to hold myself accountable?

Maybe our very lack of ties to each other was the trigger, replicating in miniature my dalliance with Uílliam. With Uílliam, for two years, freedom had served me well: the fantasy of reinventing myself. Recently, though, the freer I'd felt, the greater my sense of fracture. Shouldn't there be a way forward that didn't depend on reinvention—not with Uílliam and not with any random bus-stop hookup? I didn't want to have to leave my home, my own language. I didn't want to be an *estrangeiro*.

UÍLLIAM AND I never officially broke up. For more than a year, we kept Skyping and writing lovey emails; on our anniversary (we marked it from "You alone?" "Not anymore!"), he declared his heart was still with mine. But though at first he pressed about when I might return, I suppose he heard my hedging tone, my excuses. We both started talking about our affair in the past tense.

I missed him, and missed the version of me I'd been with him, but my grief was also liberating: along with all the hopes I shed, I let go of no small load of guilt and ambiguity. He deserved better than a supporting part in my midlife drama; it was a relief to stop exploiting him.

Our correspondence dwindled: birthday cards, valentines. Eventually he took up with a visiting German businessman ("His skin sunburns even worse than yours!"), who brought Uílliam to live with him in Munich. It was a dream fulfilled: a partner who would place him at the center, not off to the side. This was Uílliam's first time flying out of Brazil. Finally, it was he who got to lift off from his life, to see who he would become somewhere new. Finally, he would be the *estrangeiro*.

In Munich, though, the boyfriend turned controlling. He kept Uílliam penniless, wouldn't let him look for work, and made him eat foods he didn't like. Uílliam knew no one else in the country, spoke no German. He had arrived with almost nothing, not even a proper winter coat, and couldn't leave the flat without freezing.

When we talked, he was dismal: "What good is being a foreigner, if this is how I live?"

The surfer of turmoil I had admired: Where was he now, with all his charismatic fatalism? That Uílliam, I realized, was mostly my own invention, a glamorization of all he'd done to keep his head above water. I could never know the pain or dread of what he lacked, or how it felt to yearn and yearn for someone to whisk him off, even at the cost of his homeland, his very heart.

"Can you help?" he asked from Germany. "I just want to go home."

Of course I helped, searching for flights, sending the needed funds. This time, I had no doubts about the money's meaning. I was simply aiding a man I loved.

But there was only so much I could do. At home, Uílliam drifted, sometimes working, sometimes not, moving among various friends' apartments. Later, he got caught up in drugs. Rehab, relapse, repeat. "I will survive," he wrote to me. "I am strong. One day I will be happy."

He no longer answered emails. Years passed. I stopped hearing from him.

I said earlier that he and I were looking for escape, but maybe it's truer to say that we both longed for *arrival*. Wherever he was, I feared he was still searching.

AS FOR ME and Scott, we kept plugging on. Many of our best times came in foreign lands—the Basque Country, Vietnam— being reminded, by forcing ourselves briefly into exile, of how we made each other feel at home. In Arequipa, Peru, shortly before our flight to Boston, I ate shellfish I shouldn't have eaten and came as close as I ever have to dying. After leaving the airport for emergency IV treatment, I insisted rashly that we return and still catch our plane, where, doped with Benadryl, I passed out. Scott told me later that he'd stayed awake the whole way home, watching to make sure I was breathing.

I was lucky to have his love, and yet I wanted more. More than best-companionship, more than coziness. With Uílliam, I had glimpsed the magnitude of that more. I was ready to feel I deserved it.

I had no plans to go looking for someone else, but I suspected a chance might appear. If it did, I promised myself, I would proceed differently. This time, I would level with Scott about my feelings. More important, I would try to level with myself: about what I wanted and how much it should cost me; about the price of being self-estranged. I would look for a happiness that didn't require splitting myself. Not a new me but a whole one. A healed one.

"THIS IS where you change," Ubirailton said. He helped lug my carry-on off the bus.

Waiting on the road's shoulder, we traded bashful smiles, as if to turn back time to when we'd met (only an hour ago!), when all we knew about each other was our own desire. Ubirailton pledged to stay until my connection came.

As it turned out, I would miss my flight. My self-punishing instinct would say: this is your just deserts! For what, though? For *almost* hooking up with Ubirailton? For trying to find out what I really wanted? A kind-eyed airline agent would tell me what to do: pay a hundred-dollar fine, sit for an easy hour, then step onto a different flight home.

For now, though, I was still waiting at the roadside, squinting under the midday sky. Ubirailton pointed to my eyes. "You're going to cry again?" No, I told him. No, it's just the sun.

The right bus finally came. He helped me up the steps. "*Até mais,*" he called as the bus lurched away, a phrase for *See you later* that translates literally as "until more." He stood waving, the image of him shrinking with each yard we gained, looking, at last, like only the distant notion of a lover.

III

A Good Place
(Part 2)

It is not down in any map; true places never are.

—Herman Melville, *Moby-Dick*

Put Your House in Order

IN BUCHAU, we pulled up at the Hotel Pension-Stern, on Schussenrieder Strasse, a modest inn with lemon-yellow stucco walls and green wooden shutters. I couldn't tell if it was quaint or a copy of something quaint.

The owner directed me to park in a side alley, but he clearly doubted our van would fit. It was a hulking rental, designed for a family more prolific than ours. I ordered everyone out and started to inch back, my relatives kibitzing with contradictory tips. What was their worst fear? A slightly scratched rental? But they all seemed inordinately invested in my challenge. Maybe they felt, as I did, the stress of symbolism.

Schussenrieder Strasse was the street where Nana Susi grew up. My sister, booking our rooms, hadn't spotted this serendipity, but I'd recalled the street name from my grandmother's letter about her one and only return to Buchau: when, in 1973, after thirty-some years, she and Papa Eric had braved a visit to Germany. Near the start of the letter—a copy of which I carried in my backpack—Nana Susi recounts a drive full of baffling detours, until she found "the street on which our house used to be, 'our street.'"

In 2015, with GPS, our drive had been smoother. There were six of us: my boyfriend, Scott, and me; my sister, Linda, and her partner; my father and my stepmother, Jane.

But though the ride had been pleasant—tidy towns, festive sunflower fields—I was nervous. Partly just from being unaccustomed to family travel: this was our first trip together (my dad, sister, and me) since a week in Barbados in the '70s. The harder reasons had to do with the hopes I'd invested in what it would mean to stand, at last, in Buchau. Might I finally find there a cure for my place envy?

When I was young, my rootless feeling had been reinforced by my grandparents' reluctance to say anything of Germany, much less to say anything in German. To kindle a sense of Germanness seemed like treason. (Nana Susi had been dismayed when I had once bought an old Volkswagen.) We were Jewish, not German, was the tacit message; we came from a culture, not a place.

Later, though, the more I delved into our family history, the more I'd felt I *was* German, or should have the chance to be. But I knew little more of the country than dachshunds and *gesundheit*. The Nazis had stripped my grandparents of German citizenship, and I felt stripped too—of a possibility of belonging.

In my late thirties, I learned about Germany's "right of return" for descendants of Jews who fled the Nazis. When I told Dad and Aunt Judy I might apply for citizenship, they both seemed indifferent, if not puzzled. Surely I didn't plan to move to Germany?

No. And although citizenship would confer useful benefits—I could live anywhere in the EU—my reasons were moral more than material. I brought the requisite documents to the German consulate. Weeks later, as if it were the most mundane of errands, not the reclamation of a fundamental identity, they said I could come back, weekdays between nine and noon, to pick up a citizenship certificate.

My German passport sometimes seemed a mere conversation

piece (odd to see my eyes listed as *grün*); other times, it was a righteous fuck-you to the Nazis. Still, my sense of Germanness remained theoretical.

That is, until I'd started driving the route to Buchau: the town where Nana Susi was from, and her parents, and their parents, as far back as anyone could trace.

Our itinerary would take us later to cities where Papa Eric had lived, but I don't think my grandfather *belonged* to those locations; like me, he'd grown up in places his family wasn't from. But Buchau was what I had always envied: a true home turf. "Everyone is related" is a small-town cliché, but Nana Susi's family tree—reaching back into the 1600s—featured common surnames on both sides. Her own parents were second cousins, once removed.

From what I'd learned on the internet, Buchau seemed bucolic: a town of four thousand, renowned for its mud and mineral spas, its moorlands popular with birders. Residents speak a broad rustic dialect called Schwäbisch.

Of course, for its Jewish citizens, all of that was shattered. Of the 270 Jews in Buchau when Hitler rose to power (ten percent of the population then), only four returned at war's end. More than a hundred had fled Germany; some, including my great-grandmother, had died while still in town, including at least three by suicide. A hundred and thirteen were sent to Hitler's camps.

Here was the source of my nerves: I feared the grief of reckoning with all that we had lost, but I was also harboring a contradicting fear—that I might *not* feel that grief, or anything, in Buchau. What if, even here, I felt less connected than I longed to?

ON THE DRIVE, my dad had stayed unusually quiet. Was he nervous too?

In the realm of political science, he is boldly probing—his

CV lists fifty countries he's traveled to for research—but in matters more personal, he has been more blinkered; his travel list
never included Buchau. Recently, though—in his mid-seventies,
retired from college teaching—he had taken a self-reflective
turn. A shiver of mortality, maybe, spurred by a bout of cancer, and sharpened by Chaninah's recent death. He'd begun to
contemplate the forces that had shaped his parents, and him.
In his typical fashion, he started doing research, then joined the
board of an archive of German-Jewish culture. And now this:
our family-roots trip.

Planning the trip together had tightened our relationship.
Still, with all that had stayed unspoken between us, an under-
tow of tension was inevitable. He was clearly thankful for the
family history I'd amassed, and yet sometimes I also sensed that
he begrudged that knowledge—or resented how my knowledge
pointed up his own unawareness.

One thing I knew he did know: his mother's letter from
1973. He had been its recipient then, and we'd discussed it in
prepping for our trip.

Steering our too-wide van on the narrow roads to Buchau—
the British-voiced GPS bungling names like Krauchenwieser
Strasse—I had wondered aloud if we could use the letter like a
map for our exploring: "Starting with the cemetery, of course."
The letter's climax is Nana Susi's visit to the Jewish cemetery, to
see, for the first time, the gravestone of her mother, whose death
she'd mourned from four thousand miles away. For months, I'd
been picturing it: our homecoming to a place we'd never been.

"But other things too," I'd said. "The Staudachers—think
we could track them down?"

Nana Susi writes that when she got to town, she stopped her
car almost unconsciously in front of a house she'd known as the
Staudachers'. Karl Staudacher was the brother of one of her old
schoolmates, and she had heard that during the Nazi period he'd

stayed "decent." She rang the bell, and Karl, "unchanged though much older," opened the door. He summoned his wife, who, sixty years earlier, had used to play at Nana Susi's home. "She showed me a toy chest of drawers," Nana Susi says, "which I remember from my childhood, and which my mother brought to her when things began to fall apart. . . . Now her granddaughter plays with it, and it still looks like new. It really stabbed me to see this old toy of ours, so well and lovingly preserved."

"Mrs. Staudacher would be dead, of course," I called over my shoulder. "But the granddaughter—let's say she was six or seven then? She'd be less than fifty now. My age."

"Think their house is still their house?" my sister asked excitedly.

As a novelist, I'm always on the prowl for props and images, tangible ways to manifest a theme. "Imagine if she still has that chest of drawers!" I said.

I looked into the rearview to catch my father's eye, but if he reacted, I missed it.

"And the church," I said. "The church is still there, surely."

Jane, my stepmother, said, "What about a church?"

"Another thing from her letter," I explained. "A beautiful Catholic church across from her house. She and the sexton's daughter, as little kids, snuck inside and doused themselves with holy water. Later, she found out her parents had been searching for her. She told them she was playing in church—and got the biggest spanking of her life."

"A pilgrimage is definitely in order," said Jane, who laughed.

My father drowned her out: "That's not in my mother's letter. She says it on her tape."

"Mentions it on the tape," I said, "but she also wrote about it."

"No," he said.

Glancing back, I saw him cross his arms above his gut. "Or wait," I said, "maybe you're right. Maybe it's in those other notes."

"What other notes?"

"You know, her memoir? Where she talks about making her sister pay to rub her nose. And then . . . then that stuff about her marriage?" Reading that part again recently (*my husband hit me for no reason; he was incapable of loving*), I'd been just as shocked as the first time.

"I don't know what you're talking about." My father's voice was sharp.

This was not the first time he'd implied I kept him in the dark. Two months back, I'd digitized the tapes of my grandparents' memories, figuring we should listen to them again before our trip. My dad, after I'd sent the files, contended he'd never heard the tapes before. My hackles rose at his apathy, then just as quickly fell: the tapes had sat inside my closet, not far from Ilse's letter—all those details I'd kept to myself about my uncle Peter's life and death.

In fifty meters, turn left onto Schussenrieder Strasse. The GPS's singsong was discordantly melodic.

I turned onto Nana Susi's street—"our" street—a moment I'd been planning to celebrate, but my dad had spoiled it with his sulking. Then, at the hotel, after I managed to park (I angled wrong, pulled back up, made it on my second try), he stalked in silence toward the lobby.

Jane, whose honest brokering makes her the family diplomat, pulled me aside and asked to borrow Nana Susi's notes. She would make Dad read them, then give them back tomorrow.

WE WEREN'T DUE to meet up with our guide until the morning, so Scott and I chose to walk about. Instead of heading downtown, toward the official sites, we strolled in the opposite direction.

Schussenrieder Strasse was one of Buchau's main streets, crowded by old buildings with steep clay-tiled roofs. Then, after half a mile, it was flanked by farmers' stubbled fields. The air changed—fast as if a storm front had passed—sharpened with the odor of manure.

I've always loved that smell, candid and alive, but now it soaked me with a wave of bewildering emotion. I'd never thought of Nana Susi as knowing the country life, never pictured her setting foot on a farm, but if, in 2015, Buchau was still this close to rural, of course she'd have known the funk of farmyard animals. Then it struck me: when she was a girl, cars were in their infancy; most of the traffic here was drawn by horses.

Scott said, "What is it? Something wrong?"

I hadn't been aware I'd stopped walking.

I wanted to explain, but would he get it? He was one of those folks I envied for having come from somewhere: he'd grown up in Kansas, in a town of five hundred, spending time with his grandparents on a farm with no running water. But he had burned to leave all that behind.

"The smell," I told him. "This is what my grandmother might've smelled."

"Oh," he said sympathetically. "Lots of things here will make you miss her."

I tried saying that no, it didn't make me miss her, it made me think of all the things about her I'd missed out on. She'd been so determined to erase her past's sadness that all of her past, even its sweet and lovely parts, got lost. "Being here, I should feel much closer to her," I said. "So far, I only feel more distance."

BACK AT the hotel, the owner introduced himself as Dieter. With his tonsure and his sweater vest, he gave off the pent-up avidity of a stamp collector hoping you might ask to see his albums. What were we Americans, he asked, doing here in Buchau?

Looking for our roots, I said. "My grandmother grew up on this street."

"Really?" said Dieter. "What's the family name?"

"Moos," I said, and explained that Franz Moos, my great-grandfather, had owned the town's knitwear factory.

"Moos? Oh, my goodness. Wait a minute." With mousy intensity, he scurried into his office, then reemerged and handed me something akin to a banknote.

The paper was a washed-out pink, six inches by four. *Zwanzig Millionen Mark,* it read, the Z in *Zwanzig* bold against an ornate floral background. Below that, the words *Buchau* and *Trikotfabriken Hermann Moos.* I had no idea what I was holding.

"Look," said Dieter, pointing to a signature on the currency. "This is your great-grandfather, Franz Moos."

I recognized the handwriting from his Red Cross cable to Nana Susi, among her box of papers, signed "*Vater.*" On that form, he had also signed his full name; I had studied the page again, only days before, making a copy to give to the museum in Buchau. ("Thank God I'm healthy," he had cabled, two weeks before being forced onto the train to Theresienstadt.) That page, along with copies of other documents, sat now in a folder at the bottom of my pack, next to Nana Susi's "Dear Children" letter.

Dieter asked, "You know about 1923? The hyperinflation, when the German mark fell to a trillionth of its value?"

Nana Susi mentions the inflation in her letter, saying she worked that year in the Moos factory office. She had once described to me, in a rare moment of reminiscence, the image of a Buchau neighbor pushing a wheelbarrow full of worthless cash.

"The people suffered," Dieter went on. "Their savings up

in smoke. The Moos factory employed almost a quarter of this whole town. What did the Mooses do? Printed their own money! This," he said, tapping the banknote, "is twenty million 'Moos marks.'"

"Whoa," said Scott, elbowing me. "Your family's totally famous."

I laughed him off but couldn't deny a sizzle of satisfaction.

"We remember your great-grandfather Franz," Dieter said. "He kept people fed when they had nothing." Dieter beamed an oversimple smile.

"That's so nice to hear," I said. "That makes me so happy."

Why, then, was my satisfaction already starting to crumble? Might it have to do with what Dieter had failed to say? He had evidently cultivated a thoughtful sense of history; didn't he know—he must—what had happened later to Franz Moos? How the Moos factory was forcibly "Aryanized," and Franz was reduced to beggar status?

Dieter must also know about the town synagogue: finished in 1839, famed for its rare bell tower (one of only two on a German synagogue). The temple had been burned down in the Kristallnacht pogroms by a group of Brownshirts from a neighboring town. Had Dieter, the history buff, heard what happened next? Buchau's leaders, deeming the ruined synagogue an eyesore, required the Jews themselves to pay for its removal. ("Used bricks for sale" read a local paper's ad; much of the rubble ended up as fill for soggy roads.) The Jews were then forced to relinquish the plot of land, as well as the insurance payout (ninety thousand Reichsmarks), owed to them for the loss of the building. On the plot, the mayor planned to build a new town hall—the Nazi Party needed office space—for which the Jews had to pay an additional sixteen thousand marks.

Franz was one of the synagogue officers coerced into signing away their holdings. I had seen his name on the perverse "donation agreement." If Dieter knew these facts, he gave no indication; in his telling, my family's place in town was one of honor.

But Dieter's lack of qualms wasn't what eroded my satisfaction. In fact, I'm chagrined to say, I paid little mind to his story's sugarcoating until I sat down to write this scene.

When Dieter had explained the meaning of the Moos mark, I had swollen up with self-worth. (Smugness—was that what people felt who knew their roots? Descendants of the Pilgrims, say, who jaunt through New England towns named Bradford or Brewster and smile, thinking, *Us! That's us!*) I decided I should acquire my very own Moos mark. Buy one on eBay, maybe? Would Dieter give me his? Such a relic deserved to be restored to our family, for me to cherish and then pass down to—

(now began the crumble)

—to whom? Who was there to pass anything down to?

I don't want children, and mostly never have. When, every now and then, their absence does distress me, the angst is largely intellectual: the guilt of being a genetic dead end. My grandparents fought so hard to flee, to keep us going; after all that, who do I leave behind?

My sister is also childless, and so is Aunt Judy's daughter, Devorah. The only one of us four grandchildren who chose to procreate is my cousin Andy, whose Orthodox kids I don't know and likely never will. All of which leads to the flip side of the wistfulness I felt on first seeing my grandparents' papers: instead of a nostalgic twinge for a past I wasn't part of, I yearn sentimentally for a future I'll never live.

None of these thoughts were new as I stood in front of Dieter, turning the old Moos mark in my hands. Why, then, did they catch me so off guard?

I had hoped that being in Buchau would soothe my pangs of disconnection, but so far, the trip had only further frayed my doubts. The skirmish with my dad, the distance from Nana Susi, and now, too, this vexing by the Moos mark: it all had me questioning the purpose of our visit—and, by extension, of my fixation on the past. What was the point? Who was it all for?

OUR GUIDE, Charlotte, said we'd start at the cemetery. She had met us in the hotel lobby after breakfast, along with her colleague Elmar, who would translate.

When Dad and I had first started mulling a trip to Buchau, it was clear we'd need to enlist Charlotte, whose name came up with every Google search. A Buchau city councilor and self-taught historian, she's spent decades documenting the town's Jewish past, and founded Juden in Buchau, a small museum and archive. Honored by the German government for lifting "the veil of oblivion," she guides visitors, like us, who hope to reconnect with their origins.

Emailing with her to make arrangements, I had pictured a pasty bookworm, but the woman who herded us now out of the hotel was as hale as a phys-ed teacher. Sixtyish, with short gray hair swept back from her brow, she wore a sleek, no-nonsense blue duster.

On this raw October day, the sky was blurred by fittingly mournful rain. As we walked to the cemetery—I was up front with Charlotte, my family trailed behind—I asked, via Elmar, how she'd become an expert on Buchau's Jews.

When she was small, she said, she walked this route to school every morning: past the walled cemetery, which no one ever spoke about or entered. She knew the Jews were buried there, but what was a Jew exactly? If Buchau had had so many once—enough to fill a graveyard—why were there no longer any here? Grownups told her, "The war is over. Leave it."

She trained in sales, got married early, and settled into

family life, bothered all the while by this blanking out of the past. Later, in her thirties, working as a tour guide, she would be asked by Jewish visitors about their long-lost forebears, and finally she put her curiosity to use. She photographed the cemetery's eight hundred–plus gravestones and catalogued all of their inscriptions. Next, she studied civil records and Jewish-related monographs, then wrote her own texts on Buchau's Jews.

The publications (she'd shown us copies) told a rich history, from the earliest record of a Jew, in 1382; to the first minyan, in 1570; to the flourishing of Jewish factories after the emancipation of 1828. The Jewish community, though small—eight hundred, at its peak—had had an outsized impact. Among its notables were Rudolf Moos, who founded Salamander, the biggest shoe business in Germany, and the parents of two Nobel Prize winners: Joseph Erlanger and Albert Einstein.

Turning onto Friedhofstrasse—Cemetery Street—Charlotte spoke of learning that when she'd been a schoolgirl, not *all* the Jews, in fact, had been gone. One was left: Siegbert Einstein, who, after surviving the camps, returned to his Christian wife in Buchau. But he had died, Charlotte said—the last Jew buried here—when she herself was only twelve years old.

Siegbert Einstein, I knew, was a cousin of Albert's, and both were cousins of Nana Susi's parents. In my pack, I carried a postcard sent to this cousin Siegbert by Franz Moos, from Theresienstadt. I asked Elmar to tell Charlotte this; she seemed delighted.

Only recently had I wondered how the card—addressed to Siegbert in Buchau—had ended up in Nana Susi's papers. Maybe Siegbert had forwarded it, knowing she would crave news of her father. Or maybe it was given to her only decades later, when she returned. By that point, Siegbert was dead, but Nana Susi's letter describes a visit with his widow, Elsa. As a Protestant of Swiss origin, Elsa could have sought safety in

Switzerland during the war but refused to leave Germany, and "by this heroism, she saved her husband's life."

We had reached the graveyard and waited for the group to catch up. The wrought-iron gate was bracketed by pillars with bold inscriptions: German on the left, Hebrew on the right. I knew each language just enough to note the correspondence between *Haus* and the Hebrew root בית (bayit).

I asked Elmar—a bald man with a savvy-sidekick air—to translate.

"It's from the Bible," he said. "'Put your house in order, for you are going to die.'"

Instinctively, I glanced to my dad, twenty yards behind. In his rain-stained slicker and baggy chinos, he shambled alone on feet numbed by diabetic neuropathy, looking like he fought a personal headwind.

Earlier, he'd been late for breakfast, with the useful side effect that we'd been seated separately and hadn't had to talk. My stepmother had come down first and given back my grandmother's memoir, assuring me that Dad had gone through it. Now, as he wobbled resolutely toward the graveyard—white hair wisping out from an ill-fitting ballcap—I envisioned him reading the parts about his parents' marriage, and I suffered a spasm of compassion. He had always revered his parents and never, I was guessing, doubted their love for each other.

Charlotte unlocked the gate and ushered us inside. Past the entrance were toppled stones that looked more like Greek ruins than graves: remnants of the synagogue, recovered only recently from a nearby farmer's land. Charlotte noted their place of honor with preservational pride, but I was stuck in brooding about the farmer. Preservation? To him, surely it felt like confiscation. Did history and its ownership have to be zero-sum?

"The graves go back to 1675," Charlotte said. "Let me take you first to one that's newer."

She led us through the grounds, a hundred hues of green, shaded by trees so ivy-swollen that they resembled Dr. Seuss inventions. We passed pale-gray graves and moss-shrouded reddish ones—our name, Moos, means *moss* in German—until Charlotte halted at a shiny black stone.

"These, as you know," she said, "are Susi Moos's parents."

Nana Susi had photographed this grave in 1973. Then, the stone had borne only her mother Ida's name, but now Franz's had also been inscribed, along with where he'd died: Theresienstadt. Nana Susi, after her visit, must have had this added, even though her father was not here. (His corpse had most likely been incinerated at the camp, the ashes dumped into the Eger River.) I'd often thought of my grandmother as meek, if not defeated, but here was a glimpse of her granite-tough resolve: insisting that the Nazis' crime be literally set in stone.

Just for Nana Susi to have come back to Buchau: How much granite-toughness had that taken? The place's very air must have smothered her with heartache—or rage, or a poisonous amalgam. Only with the help of Karl Staudacher's wife, her playmate from sixty years before, had she managed to navigate the town. Nana Susi had asked to steer clear of the family factory. She did visit her girlhood home on Schussenrieder Strasse—it had been turned into a hotel—but couldn't bring herself to go inside. "It is there that my mother died," she writes, "and it is from there that my father was deported after suffering much abuse and humiliation."

The sole place in Buchau where she says she "felt at home, where I knew I had come home," was the cemetery. The Staudachers had led her and Papa Eric there. It was the day of her mother's Yahrzeit, her death's anniversary: the fifteenth of the Hebrew month of Elul. Nana Susi must have planned their trip around that date.

Standing now precisely on the spot where she had stood, I closed my eyes, envisioning the moment. The same autumnal breeze (she'd come in mid-September), the same mulchy consoling smell of soil; the ivied trees and tilting, huddled graves. For her, though, everything here was measured against her memory, against a time when she could never have dreamed of *not* belonging. Did she recite the Kaddish? Did she weep?

Her letter doesn't say. And if the visit grieved her, as of course it must have, it also spurred surprising optimism. "You can't imagine," she writes, "how many Mooses, Einsteins, Dreifusses, and Neuburgers are buried there, many if not all somehow related." In such a place, surrounded by centuries of family, she felt herself as "a bridge from the past to the future"—a future for which her hopes were vested, she says, "in you, my beloved children and grandchildren, and through you I am looking forward toward life. Not to forget the past, but learning from it, honoring it."

"A good place"—*ein guter Ort*—was a common German-Jewish euphemism for *cemetery*. The cemetery in Buchau was "indeed 'a good place,'" writes Nana Susi, "and it was a good place for me to go to."

Opening my eyes, I saw my dad approach his grandparents' headstone, a smooth whitish pebble in his palm. He reached out and, in the Jewish tradition, set it on the grave.

Sometimes it takes a vivid moment to make you see the obvious. I had been so focused on trying to place myself vis-à-vis my grandparents, that I had failed fully to consider that my father had never even gotten to meet his grandparents. Never heard their voices or felt their arms around him, never had the privilege of chafing against their silence. My dad—professorial, authoritative, aloof—was also, like me, a searching grandson.

Charlotte now took us to the graves of other forebears. A

scavenger hunt of sorts, searching among the stones, scanning the weathered Gothic German letters. Showing us the chipped grave of Jakob Maier Einstein, Charlotte said he was Nana Susi's "*ur-ur-ur-Grossvater,*" a term Elmar didn't need to translate. Which made him—she pointed at me—my "*ur-ur-ur-ur-ur-Grossvater.*"

I thought of the word *urtext*: the original, the source. If any spot in the world would be my *ur*-place, it was here—the very ground beneath my feet now—but I was still unsure how to feel.

Standing among my ancestors was different from how I'd pictured it, profound but not exactly personal. There was the warp effect provoked at any burial ground, a sense of the past as both nearby and utterly out of reach. I was grateful for those whose lives had made my own possible, but did I feel *more* among them—more than I've felt at other ancient sites? What did it mean to claim as "mine" these long-extinguished strangers?

My dad placed a pebble on another forebear's grave, and my thoughts—just as when I'd held the old Moos mark—got snagged. One day, not too long from now, I would put a stone upon his grave. Later, after I was gone, who would visit him? And who, who on earth, would visit me?

People think of cemeteries as having to do with death, but death, in a sense, is merely the stuff cemeteries are made of; what they're really about is inheritance: bloodlines and marriages and begetting. For me—gay, unmarried, unwilling to beget—such places embody an irresolvable puzzle. I'd been so intent on belonging to these kin; would they ever have felt the same of me?

That was when I saw the matching gravestones.

Like queens from a giant chess set, the stout columns (my arms would've failed to reach around them) were topped by stately star-ringed crowns. Identical in construction—pink sandstone with carved ivy winding beneath the crowns, chains boldly chiseled around the bottoms—they were clearly meant to be a pair. Their bases stood but half a foot apart.

Moses H. Moos read the left-hand stone's inscription, above his birth and death dates and a hard-to-make-out poem.

"Uncle of your great-grandfather Franz," Charlotte said.

I calculated: my great-great-great-uncle.

I turned right, to read his wife's name on the matching stone—she would be my great-great-great-aunt—but what I saw was the name of a man: Rudolf.

Moses and Rudolf. Brothers? But no, Rudolf's last name was not Moos but Mändle. Why would brothers have different surnames?

There were no graves of wives or children to shed further light. Checking the dates, I computed that Rudolf had died at twenty-three, and Moses at only seventeen: young enough to still be bachelors. But why would they be buried so close together?

I called Scott over. "What am I missing? Two young guys, died in the same year, 1862."

"Not just the same year," he said. "March 14 and 16. Only two days apart!"

"Cousins?" I said. (Weren't the Jews in Buchau all cousins?) Cousins but also small-town neighbors, confidants, best friends—as brotherlike, perhaps, as Andy and I had been, before he froze me out.

Charlotte heard me and flipped through her list of our family connections. "No," she said, pointing to Rudolf. "He is not related." She offered me an enigmatic shrug.

I studied the pink columns again, their mossed bases on the verge of touching. On each tombstone was chiseled an acrostic epitaph, riffing on the letters of the dead man's first name. The first line of Moses's poem began with the word *Mutter,* the next line began with *Ohne,* the third with *Seinem,* and so on. (Other graves here had similar acrostics.)

I asked Elmar what they said. He stood a long time, chin in hand, looking taken aback. "The words are formal," he said. "An old, emotional style. I don't know if I can quite explain."

I couldn't read his tone: Reticence? Confusion? "Can't you say at least the gist?" I asked.

Elmar considered the graves again. Then, aiming his voice squarely at the stones, as if apologizing to the dead for indiscretion, he said, "Friendship. Both the poems talk about friendship." He looked at me and Scott, taking us in together. "I guess these boys were maybe . . . very close?"

I COULD tell you what we did later that day, and also during the rest of our roots trip—

I could describe asking Charlotte to help us find the Staudachers, eager as I was to meet the girl, now middle-aged, to whom Nana Susi's chest of drawers had been bequeathed. Even though the family had lived in town for decades and Karl Staudacher had once been deputy mayor, Charlotte couldn't track them down.

We visited the Catholic church where Nana Susi had sinned, rife with gilded baroque melodrama. Passing a font, I dipped my pinkie into the holy water, hoping that she, somewhere, somehow, glimpsed my little joke.

That night we did what she, on returning, couldn't bear to: went into her girlhood home, now a hotel and tavern called Poseidon. The Greek-immigrant couple who ran it made me think of my grandparents starting life again in a new land. We conveyed to the couple what the building meant to us, and they sweetly offered us a bottle of Greek wine.

Then there were our days in Freiburg, Wiesbaden, Hamburg, and, finally, Berlin. There, we found my grandparents' last address in Germany, the place where the Nazis had wrecked

Papa Eric's sukkah. On the site now sat a boxy apartment complex; the building they had lived in was long gone.

—I could tell you all of that and more, in full detail, but the truth is, although the whole trip was compelling, nothing else hit me with the force of those two gravestones. Whether we were contemplating Holocaust memorials or gorging on Black Forest cake next to the Black Forest, I returned to the mystery of Moses Moos and Rudolf Mändle. Although I'm not often prone to inklings of predestiny, I was sure that finding those men's stones had been my fate.

BACK AT HOME, I looked for answers. I typed the men's epitaphs into Google Translate, but, due to the poems' style, what came out was sludge. I turned to JewishGen.org, the "Family Tree of the Jewish People," and, with some difficulty, found my uncle Moses (one of at least seven Moses Mooses born in Buchau), but the only data was his birth year. I could locate no mention at all of Rudolf Mändle, even though I did find a listing for his parents, whose names I had jotted down in the graveyard. Leonhard and Louise Mändle were shown, for some reason, as having had four children, all daughters.

The Mändle tree, however, revealed this: Charlotte had erred in telling me that Rudolf was unrelated. In fact, he and Moses had shared a set of great-grandparents. Cousins, after all.

Searching further, I landed on a site called Find a Grave, which documents burial information. Rudolf's listing confirmed some facts and also brought news: "Unmarried. Died of typhoid fever."

Next, I clicked on Moses. "Unmarried. Drowned in a swimming accident."

Swimming accident? Really?

Just two days after the death of his very close friend—beside whom he would be buried under a matching stone—Moses has the rotten luck to drown?

I couldn't help playing out a story. What if it was no accident? What if Moses, brokenhearted, flung himself into the Federsee, the boggy lake that hugs the north of Buchau?

MY VERSION had the ring of truth, but it was pure conjecture.

I wrote to the anonymous stranger who'd posted on Find a Grave, asking where they'd found their information. They told me that the Nazis, obsessed with tracing Jewish blood, had microfilmed local communities' records—with the effect, ironically, of preserving Jewish history. The Baden-Württemberg State Archives, they said, were now online.

Amazingly, with a few clicks, I was viewing the page of the Buchau death register on which the deaths of Rudolf and Moses were recorded—their entries, like their tombstones, abutting. The old cursive was florid, the loops and tails of certain letters swooping histrionically, as if to match the book's tragic subject. The records were divided into columns: Name, Parents, Spouse, Religion. Also: Place and Time of Death, and Place and Time of Burial. The date of Moses's death—two days after Rudolf's—was, perhaps more meaningfully, the very day of Rudolf's burial. Moses had died at eleven o'clock that night.

Swimming at 11:00 p.m., in the middle of March, when the temperature is typically in the forties?

A thrill crackled up my neck, as my conjecture shifted into epigenetic certainty: my uncle and his cousin had been lovers. Or, at least, Moses had loved Rudolf.

I pictured him at the gravesite, fighting not to cry. Family members sprinkle dirt into the fresh-dug hole, and Moses adds his own handful, wincing at its thud. Later, at the Mändles' for the shiva, he stays stoic. But then, after nightfall, alone in his room at home, he can't stop thinking about life without Rudolf: life without *living,* is how it feels. The poor kid is only seventeen! Silently, he slinks from the house, past his sleeping parents. Then he runs and runs, northward toward the water, until he hits the inky lake's edge.

I could see it all so clearly—more clearly than I could read the register's antique longhand. Each man's cause of death was a single lengthy word. For Rudolf's, I'd expected *Typhus* or *Typhus-Fieber,* which Google said were German terms for typhoid. But although the word possibly did end with *fieber,* it didn't start with a capital *T,* and there were no descenders that could be a *y* or *p.*

Moses's cause of death was even more confounding. I had looked up "swimming accident" and "drowning" and their variants, but the word simply could not be *Schwimmunfall* or *Ertrinken*—not given the two curving strokes below its ending, plainly those of *z*'s and/or *g*'s.

I wrote back to Find a Grave, flagging these discrepancies. Also, I asked: What was their interest in Buchau? Could we be kin?

The source revealed herself as a British medical doctor (no stranger, then, to death and illness) whose grandmother had been a German-Jewish refugee. The grandmother would never discuss her past, the doctor said, and so she herself had gone digging. Finding she had a knack for deciphering German cursive, she had transcribed hundreds of archival-record entries— a way to help fellow roots-seekers.

So, then: not kin, but kindred spirits.

I told her, without precisely confessing my own stakes, that I was keen to confirm my relatives' causes of death.

She re-checked the archive and stood by her judgment that Rudolf had died of typhoid. The scribble I had failed to parse said *Schleimfieber,* a dated term for any fever involving the excess secretion of mucus. In most cases, that illness was typhoid.

As for Moses's cause of death: looking again at the register, she believed the stated cause was *Stirnentzündung*—the word's second half was quite clear—which meant Moses had died, the night of Rudolf's burial, of "forehead inflammation," i.e., a sinus infection.

I was perplexed. If "inflammation" was clear, how would she have come up with "drowned in a swimming accident"? Years had passed, she said, and she could not remember, but now she'd go back and change the record. Cheerfully, she added, "Thanks for highlighting!"

No, don't change it, I longed to shout. *I want it to be true!*

It seems ghoulish, to say the least, to have wished for evidence of someone's suicide, but I wasn't thinking of the trauma. I was focused on finally finding a queer predecessor (the search I'd once centered on Uncle Peter), and gaining, if I could find him, a comfort straight folks take for granted: the sense that merely being myself didn't dislocate me from my whole family lineage.

My new friend offered a last suggestion. I should look for a "family register" of marriages and milestones; maybe that's where she'd gotten "swimming accident." Using the same State Archives, I found the Buchau registers and clicked through to Moses's parents' page. There he was, fourth of twelve children, but nothing about a drowning or anything else dramatic.

Of course not, I realized—even if my theory held true. *After his male lover's death, a teen boy kills himself*: not a fact to ink into the civil registry. A scandal, never to be discussed.

But no. What about the headstones? They were the opposite of trying to hush things up.

After a death, Jews commonly wait a full year to place a headstone. Twelve long months of mourning, then, for Rudolf's and Moses's families, time to ponder the tributes they would erect. The parents must have consulted about the two boys' bond, in order to plan look-alike graves, and also discussed it with the stonecutter. They'd have had a hand in the poems to be inscribed—poems that, if Elmar was right, glorified their dead sons' connection.

The poems. I needed to read the poems.

AS I SEARCHED for a translator of German funeral verse, I immersed myself in contextual information. I boned up on *Liebestod,* the German Romantic "love-death" trope—lovers who die of despair over the death of their beloved—dramatized most famously in Richard Wagner's *Tristan und Isolde.* The opera, whose lovers are joined in "the long night of death," had been composed but not yet premiered when Rudolf and Moses died. Maybe love-death floated in the cultural air they breathed?

I read debates among historians about nineteenth-century homosocial "romantic friendships." Were they ever consummated? Every study I read was inconclusive.

I learned that in the history of homosexuality, Germany in the 1860s holds a primal place. In 1862—the year Rudolf and Moses died—a man named Karl Heinrich Ulrichs started to write pamphlets defending sexual love between men. Five years later, he would address the Congress of German Jurists to argue against anti-sodomy laws: perhaps the world's first gay activism. Two years after that, another German writer would coin the term "homosexuality."

But these advances were taking place at Germany's cutting edge. Moses and Rudolf were small-town boys, citizens of an insular Jewish merchant clan. To them and to their parents, the name Ulrichs would have meant nothing.

To understand their rural culture, I read a book called *Portraits of Our Past: Jews of the German Countryside,* by Emily C. Rose. (Her ancestors, like mine, came from Baden-Württemberg.) A section on burial practices offered useful details, such as that headstones were carved by Christian cutters, who, for any Hebrew words, copied texts supplied by Jewish teachers. But Rudolf's and Moses's poems of "friendship" were carved in German; the cutter would have understood them. As for why the boys were interred beside each other, Rose noted that graves in Jewish village cemeteries were customarily placed in order of death—instead of, say, being grouped by family. But this left unsolved the boys' nearly identical graves, with poems that apparently clinched their link. The book made no mention of homosexuality.

It did, however, mention Buchau. The author's great-great-aunt, an immigrant to Chicago, had married a man from Buchau. Included in the text was a letter he'd sent his mother: Willhelmine Moos, née Mändle.

Looking her up, I learned—another crackle up my neck—she was my cousin Rudolf Mändle's aunt.

THAT SIGN of fate was followed by another:

I had contacted the archive on whose board my father sat, and the archivist unearthed a trove of Buchau-related files. The most promising pertained to Rudolf's parents, Louise and Leonhard. A note about the contents of Box 1, Folder 14, made me almost teeter with expectation: "Speech given at the grave of the unmarried merchant Rudolf Mändle."

With all that had been lost—to the Nazis, and just to time—what a wondrous, boggling stroke of luck!

The archivist sent me a scan of the handwritten eulogy, the

very pages someone had held in front of Rudolf's casket. The penmanship was bold and slashing, somehow holy-looking. The speech had been composed by a man known as Lehrer Löwenthal. Teacher Löwenthal.

EVENTUALLY I FOUND a translator skilled at old-style cursive and sent him the trove of documents. Awaiting his response, I wondered at my obsession. We all know that queer people, or people with queer desires, have lived in every time and culture. Two lovestruck boys in a German-Jewish backwater, even if I found foolproof evidence of their gayness, wouldn't be dispositive of anything—not historically, and not personally, either. Did I think that if I could say, "See? I told you so," my family would treat me any differently?

Truth was, by this point, they all fully embraced me. Except Andy—and he would not be swayed by some tale of old tombstones.

Why, then, all this fuss? What did I have to prove?

I thought about Chaninah, whose story I had avoided, and of the trip to visit her I'd failed and failed to make. Maybe my compulsion to follow Moses's story, and to "complete" the pilgrimage to Buchau, was a kind of overcompensation. *This* was a journey I would not—I did not—evade.

Maybe so. But that could not be all.

If it were, I'd be facing up to the appalling facts: one young cousin under the dirt, another dead that night. Nothing remotely romantic about that.

WHEN THE TRANSLATIONS arrived, I went woozy with hope and apprehension, like someone at the threshold of a fortuneteller's den, even though the fates to be revealed were past not future—and not mine. Superstitious, I read the files in what I guessed was the reverse order of their importance.

Most of the Buchau documents were fairly immaterial: anecdotes of small-town life, Schwäbisch jokes whose punch lines perished in translation. Plenty of Mooses were cited, but not my uncle Moses.

The Mändle cache was more compelling. I learned that Rudolf's father, Leonhard, was one of Buchau's richest Jews, a seller of silk and ribbon products. But he and Louise, as parents, were no strangers to tragedy, even before Rudolf's early death. He had been their seventh child, and all three boys preceding him had died in infancy. After Rudolf, Louise gave birth to five more offspring, four of whom also died young. In other words, when Rudolf died, he'd been one of five surviving children out of twelve, the only son out of seven to have lived.

As if it wasn't woe enough to lose their last son, Rudolf's death was followed within a year by Leonhard's—leaving Louise a single mother of four. When she, too, eventually died, her epitaph memorialized this awful double blow:

Many were the sorrows and trials in your life,
O, you endured it all, resigned to the Lord,
And when your husband and your son departed,
In God you found solace . . .

Her epitaph was the only allusion I found to Rudolf's fate. Except, of course, his eulogy—which, at last, I let myself read.

"MY DEAR MOURNERS!" begins Teacher Löwenthal. "When death severs the most precious bonds, when night and darkness spread around us and cloak the heart and spirit in sadness, to

whom shall we turn . . . if not to You, the Most Good?" He
goes on in that vein, beseeching God to "breathe life back into
[the mourners'] shattered souls," so that "those who have come
here weeping to deposit the last of seven sons, such a costly
collateral, may leave this place strengthened and upright."

Countless times I had tried to conjure this occasion—tried
to conjure Moses there, watching Rudolf's burial—and now I
had a soundtrack for the scene.

I also knew more details now, from Emily Rose's book,
of how village funerals unfolded. Rudolf's body, after being
cleansed by the Sacred Society, would have been robed in a
burial shroud and lifted into a plain pine box. Into the coffin
was also placed a bag of earth from Palestine: the next best
thing to a Holy Land interment. Rudolf's friends and family
would have stood at the coffin's foot and asked forgiveness for
any ways they'd wronged him. Six men then hefted the box
and marched it to the graveyard, where the cantor chanted and
tore the shirts of loved ones. Then it was time for the eulogy.

"A good and honest man in the prime of his youth" was
Rudolf, according to Teacher Löwenthal. "A son, brother, and
friend."

I could imagine Moses there, hearing the man say "friend"
and wondering how that puny single syllable (*Freund* in German) could measure all that Rudolf had been to him and he
to Rudolf. Waiting, then, for the teacher to say his name—his
own name, Moses—and recognize his role in Rudolf's life.

The eulogist said nothing of the sort. He was now recounting that Rudolf, after excelling in local schools, had been sent
to Stuttgart at fourteen, to study in a fine academy. There, the
boy was admired for "his good soul and his good mind." After
two years, he'd returned to train in the silk-and-ribbon business. As a traveling salesman, he had "fulfilled perfectly" his

family's expectations, and, says Teacher Löwenthal, "became the joy of his parents, siblings, and other relatives."

Rudolf's father planned to retire, and Rudolf had been meant to take charge. "However," says the eulogist, "this was not to be the will of the Heavenly Father. Five weeks ago, having returned unexpectedly from a business trip and feeling unwell, he entered his parents' home in tears, with a heavy heart, anticipating a fatal conclusion to his illness. He laid himself down in sickness and . . . gave up the ghost last Friday night at midnight."

Did Moses, hearing this, recall that sickbed scene? Or did anguish deafen him to the words? Rudolf had been the joy of "other relatives"—so said Löwenthal. Was that the most acknowledgment Moses could now expect? Yes, he was a relative—Rudolf's second cousin—but was he not also much, much more?

Oh, how selfish, he might have thought, *Rudolf will poke such fun at me*—but then the stab of recognition: Rudolf would never tease him, not for this or anything else. Rudolf would never. Never again. Gone.

Löwenthal ends his speech with advice to the grieving parents. "Look to the high priest Aaron," he says, who, when his two sons died, accepted the Lord's will "in silent resignation." Look to King David, too, he adds, referring to 2 Samuel, chapter 12, in which, after David's beloved son has been struck down, the king bids his servants to bring food. The servants are puzzled: "While the child was alive, you fasted and wept, but now that the child is dead, you get up and eat!" To which David responds: "Now that he is dead, why should I fast? Can I bring him back again? I will go to him, but he will not return to me."

As Löwenthal concluded with a quote from the Book of Job, Moses's ears must still have echoed with David's words: *Can I bring him back again? I will go to him.*

It must have seemed a message from on high.

WHY WAS I so quick to see Moses as I did: sidelined in his longing, incurably bereft? Why was I so sure *that* was the story?

Projecting that torment onto Moses came to me instinctively; at his age, what had I done but pine? Always gazing out from within a cage of shame at boys who hovered ever out of reach, certain that my yearnings must be hidden.

But now, as I write this, I can see that I was holding on to a bygone narrative. I was no longer the lonely teen who'd needed to invent a gay uncle. In middle age, I was thrilled to be queer; my family loved me; Andy's rejection was only a dull old scar. Maybe I was addled by my search for answers in Buchau because the questions behind that search had mostly gone moot.

Often, people who freeze to death experience something called "paradoxical undressing." Blood rushes out from their core to their extremities, and victims, though they're freezing, have a feeling of "hot flash," take off all their clothes, and die naked. My burning to romanticize the trauma of two young men, my overheated investment in their story: Could this have been the last flash of my old self-conception, before I let that stale sadness die?

It makes me wonder if I'd been thinking of "roots" in the wrong direction, if rootedness was not something conferred on you by the past but a feeling you had to find within your present self—and which, once you found it, you could then stretch back to antecedents.

TURNING AT LAST to the epitaphs, I began by trying to read aloud the German versions. Despite not understanding them,

I marveled at their form: acrostic *and* composed in coupled rhyme. Their well-made structures pointed up the obvious: this was writing built to last, aimed at future visitors to the graveyard. Like me.

Finally, with a catch of breath, I opened the translations. First, Rudolf's poem:

Ripe not for the coffin, but ripe for heaven,
I am cloaked in peace, far from earthly strife,
The Earth covers me now, separated from my parents,
Though joys are extinguished here below,
Friendship will lead me into Eden's realm,
Guiding me softly and sweetly to bliss.

Next, Moses's poem, which I read while picturing his headstone, tight to Rudolf's:

I left my mother and father in the Spring,
Without having enjoyed life, I fell early upon the funeral
    bier.
With childlike submission I have followed His call into
    heaven.
United with my friend in death, united with him also in
    life,
We now slumber peacefully together until the sun shines
    upon our reunion.

Elmar was right: the poems were about the young men's closeness, suggesting something more intense than friendship. I was at once unsurprised and utterly thunderstruck.

Rudolf's poem is coded but direct. "Friendship," it says, will lead him "sweetly to bliss." Which bliss, though—that of Eden, or that of Moses's company? The poet seems to imply that the latter creates the former, that Rudolf's version of paradise *is* Moses.

Moses's poem is even more blatant. "United with my friend in death, united with him also in life": the first phrase is religious license; the second reports a fact. Although their union's nature isn't specified (of course not, on a headstone, in 1862), the verse sounds astonishingly spousal: "We now slumber peacefully together . . ."

Together. As coupled as their mossy matching graves.

I wrote in thanks to the translator, to whom I'd said little about the context of the poems, not wanting to put a thumb on the scale. Now that his work had seemed to ratify my theory, I divulged my motives, and he wrote back with a possible revision:

"Perhaps the line 'With childlike submission I have followed His call into heaven' is intentionally ambiguous. I originally interpreted it as a purely religious statement, but the word *His* (*Seinem*) is actually the first word in the acrostic and doesn't necessarily refer to God, nor does it have to be capitalized. If we take the alternative meaning of *ergeben* as *devotion/loyalty,* the sentence could read: 'With childlike loyalty I have followed his [Rudolf's] call into heaven.'"

Yes, I thought. Yes, that fit! It all fit so well: an echo of the eulogist's Bible quote. *Can I bring him back again? I will go to him.*

The translator, unprompted, shared his similar thoughts: "That Moses died on the same day as Rudolf's funeral strikes me as very odd—suicide? Do we assume that Moses was at the funeral?"

When I explained the trouble I'd had in verifying Moses's cause of death, the translator asked to see the death-register page. His opinion was unequivocal: in old German, *St* and *N* were often misconstrued; Moses's death was not from

Stirnentzündung, as claimed by my Find a Grave friend, but rather *Nierenentzündung.* Kidney inflammation, or nephritis.

Now the translator had to reconsider. With Moses dying of kidney failure, it was doubtful he would have attended Rudolf's funeral, seven hours before. But he reassured me: "I still think there is something more to the headstones."

SURPRISINGLY? I was no longer as needy for reassurance.

My narrative had been muddied, yes—renal failure didn't fit my high-romantic plot—but the discrepancy hardly threw me off. The epitaphs, with their spousal passion, had been a confirmation, one that left me feeling sure of the story. This was a sureness that wouldn't be upset by further facts, because I could see it wasn't really about my forebears. The story I was finally sure of was my own: a story about the telling of stories.

I might never procreate, but that did not make me a dead end. My role in keeping alive our lineage was to narrate it: to gather what facts I could and make sense of the gaps, leaving behind a different sort of posterity.

For years, I had grasped at our history for validation, clutching tight to every tiny scrap, but the power was really in my own hands.

Hands, grasping and letting go: I thought about my father's hands, in the graveyard, dropping the pebble onto his grandparents' headstone, but also in another moment not long after that, a scene I still struggled to make sense of.

AFTER WE LEFT the cemetery, Charlotte led our family to the small museum she runs. Hung on the walls were relics of the ravaged synagogue and artifacts of Jewish daily life. Kiddush cups, a wedding veil. A Moos mark.

We gathered around a table. Charlotte presented an album with photos of my great-grandparents. Now was the time for the documents I'd brought. I pulled out the folder and spread them on the table: Franz's Red Cross letters; a codicil to his will, scribbled after the deportations had started; and his final known message, the card he'd sent to cousin Siegbert Einstein.

Charlotte studied the papers: testaments to so much loss but now, to her, treasures.

A writer from the local daily newspaper had come, to chronicle our family's return. Odd that just by visiting, we were making news, but if we could help some Germans face up to their history, I was game—as would be my father, I was sure. He was usually keen to play professor.

The writer sifted the documents with evident fascination. Maybe because I was the one who'd brought them, she turned to me. How did it feel to be here? What were my impressions?

I was only just beginning to tussle with those questions, but I suspected she wanted pithy quotes. "We grew up with a feeling," I said, "of not coming from anywhere. It's amazing to finally feel we have a family history." Before this visit, all we'd known of Buchau, I explained, was a letter from my grandmother about her one trip back.

The writer's eyes widened. "Maybe you have this letter with you now? Could I quote it?"

I had an extra copy; I'd brought it for Charlotte. Just as I was starting to tell the writer, "Sure, of course," my dad barked, "No! It's personal."

He half stood from his chair and loomed over the table. "And what are these?" he said, pointing to the papers. "These are new. You've never shown them to me."

"Dad," I said. "Please. What are you doing?"

Before the trip, my sister had suggested we bring gifts for Charlotte. Linda proposed to gather some small New Englandy items—maple syrup, a book about Cape Cod—and I said I could copy a selection of family papers. "Wonderful ideas," my dad had emailed back.

But now he was lunging, snatching up the pages.

"What are you doing?" I said again. "I brought these for Charlotte."

I tried to wrest the papers away, but he only pulled tighter. His hands shook—with fury? fear?—hands that once seemed massive to me but that now, if I fought, couldn't fend me off.

"This is crazy!" I yelled. "They're only copies of copies."

The others looked away or down, anywhere but at us. The journalist hid her notebook in her lap.

"Dad," I said, "everything here was copied from a box that's at your house."

This time, when he tugged the papers tighter, I let go.

FOR A LONG TIME, his outburst baffled me. What was he so furiously holding onto?

Then, after my monthslong obsession with Moses and Rudolf, I began to see that Dad and I were not so different. With family history in short supply, we'd each groped about for a piece to call our own. Not until this trip to his mother's hometown, his first chance to meet even the ghosts of his grandparents, had he been able to stand and say: *Mine! Hands off, that's mine.* He had made his ruckus about the papers, I now thought, not to change the outcome but simply to assert his own claim.

Wasn't that what Chaninah had done, setting down her "Lifetime of Addresses"?

AFTER SEEING ELSA, the widow of Siegbert Einstein ("so

simple and good," "not far from death, yet without fear"), Nana Susi got into her rental car and drove away, never again to return to her birthplace. She and Papa Eric then sped to Bad Ragaz, a Swiss resort, relieved to be out of Germany.

The next day, with memories fresh, she composed her letter. "Now Buchau is part of my memory again," it concludes,

> . . . my history, and that of my family. The cemetery and the people I saw made it come alive again.
>
> Buchau as it is now has nothing to do with me, and I have nothing to do with it. The presence of a very prosperous self-satisfied nation cannot make me forget the humiliation and destruction done to my folks and my people. Therefore, the air becomes oppressive.
>
> Yet, I am grateful to have been able to make this trip.
>
> Love,
> Mom

For me, since I'd never known Buchau in its better days and didn't have to witness its destruction, the town didn't feel oppressive—in fact, almost the opposite. Charlotte's hospitality—her life of reparation—let me see beyond the grief, to grace. And the graveyard, despite all the sorrows it embodied, became a place of potential, even comfort.

Still, I doubt I'll ever travel back there.

THE GRAVE I'd like to visit is that of my uncle Peter. No such place exists, though—not in the physical world. Yes, they've built memorials at the site of Bergen-Belsen (the camp itself was burned at war's end), but the pits where tens of thousands of bodies were heaped in piles are nothing now but grass-covered berms.

IN THE MUSEUM, after my father's squall, no one spoke. Then my stepmother, flexing her diplomacy as usual, suggested that we break for lunch—to give Charlotte time to xerox the papers. That way, Charlotte could have a copy for her archive, and my dad could also keep a set.

In that moment, I was still too flustered to detect the metaphor, but now I admire its fittingness: anyone who wants a copy can have one. My dad and I can equally feel we have a place in this history, and so, in her own way, can Charlotte. No one's possession needs to negate anyone else's; belonging is an infinite inheritance.

What of my cousin Andy? Does he, too, think of Buchau's history as his own? If he does: Good! Welcome home.

The journalist, hesitantly, altered her request: Could she refer to Nana Susi's letter in her article, if she promised not to quote from it? I braced for another storm from my father. With my eyes, I tried to send a message of placation: *Your call, Dad. Either way is fine.* I'm not sure he saw me, but his face unhardened. He held out the papers—crumpled from our tug-of-war—and let the stranger take them.

Acknowledgments

EARLIER VERSIONS of some essays appeared in the following publications: "Face the Music" in *Ploughshares*; "Used-Car Salesman" in *The Rumpus*; "You Don't See the Other Person Looking Back" in *Tin House* and *Out*; "Loss of Orientation" in *The Advocate* and *Wonderlands* (Raphael Kadushin, ed.); and "Unmolested" in *True Story*.

Thanks to the Instituto Sacatar for a residency that supported the completion of this book.

And thanks to Scott, for all the miles and years.

About the Author

MICHAEL LOWENTHAL is the author of a story collection, *Sex with Strangers*, and four novels: *The Same Embrace*, *Avoidance*, *Charity Girl* (a *New York Times Book Review* "Editors' Choice" and a *Washington Post* "Top Fiction of 2007" pick), and *The Paternity Test* (an Indie Next selection and a Lambda Literary Award finalist). His shorter work has appeared in *Tin House*, *Ploughshares*, *The New York Times Magazine*, *Guernica*, *The Southern Review*, and many anthologies. The recipient of fellowships from the MacDowell Colony, the Bread Loaf Writers' Conference, and the Mass Cultural Council, he has taught creative writing at Boston College and Hampshire College, and as the Picador Guest Professor for Literature at Leipzig University in Germany. For more than twenty years he was a faculty member in the low-residency MFA program at Lesley University. He lives in Boston and Pittsburgh.

MACHETE

Joy Castro and Rachel Cochran, Series Editors

This series showcases fresh stories, innovative forms, and books that break new aesthetic ground in nonfiction—memoir, personal and lyric essay, literary journalism, cultural meditations, short shorts, hybrid essays, graphic pieces, and more—from authors whose writing has historically been marginalized, ignored, and passed over. The series is explicitly interested in not only ethnic and racial diversity, but also gender and sexual diversity, neurodiversity, physical diversity, religious diversity, cultural diversity, and diversity in all of its manifestations. The machete enables path-clearing; it hacks new trails and carves out new directions. The Machete series celebrates and shepherds unique new voices into publication, providing a platform for writers whose work intervenes in dangerous ways.